The Daily Telegraph

CASTLES & ANCIENT MONUMENTS

OF IRELAND

The Daily Telegraph

CASTLES
& ANCIENT
MONUMENTS
OF IRELAND

BY DAMIEN NOONAN

AURUM PRESS

To Olivia, with more love

Illustrations

Frontispiece: *Aughnanure Castle, Co Galway*

This page: *Kilcooley Abbey, Co Kilkenny*

Next page: *Lough Corrib, Co Galway*

Base maps supplied by Perrott Cartographics, Machynlleth, Wales

First published 2001 by Aurum Press Ltd,
25 Bedford Avenue, London WC1B 3AT

Printed and bound in Italy by Printer Trento srl

10   9   8   7   6   5   4   3   2   1

2005   2004   2003   2002   2001

Foreword
Welcome to this book

Ireland is a country of tremendous scenic contrasts, with spiky mountains soaring next to crashing seas, and great rivers cutting across the flat central plains. One of the most enjoyable things about exploring the country's heritage is that by going in search of the scattered stones of an ancient burial place or the rugged remnant of a medieval tower, you find yourself in the midst of some of the most beautiful scenery in western Europe.

It is said that there were more castles in Ireland than in the whole of England, Scotland and Wales put together. Since the Normans came to the country so late, however, they did not build so many of the spectacular keeps that you'll find in England and Wales – though the castles at Trim and Carrickfergus can be ranked amongst the finest Norman fortresses. Instead, most of Ireland's castles are defended residences of

a type known as tower houses, and the source of their appeal is their exuberant variety. Some are huge and imposing, while others are tiny and humble. Some are crumbling away, forgotten in a field; others have been restored to something like their original glory.

Castles apart, the most striking monuments in Ireland are the many reminders of the long history of the Christian church here. The round towers which marked out the early monasteries, the modest churches that developed in early medieval times, and the great abbeys of later, wealthier periods are all memorable. Perhaps most of all, the remarkably well-preserved ruins of the Franciscan friaries built in the 1400s are worth seeking out.

The jewels in Ireland's crown, however, are far older. Nowhere else in Europe is there anything that quite matches the Irish passage graves of the neolithic era – spectacular megalithic monuments decorated with the swirling spirals and jagged lines of a unique form of prehistoric art.

Contents

Key map to the regions of Ireland

Each chapter covers one of the tourist regions of Ireland as defined by the Irish government. Northern Ireland is, of course, part of the UK and is covered in a separate chapter.

Northern Ireland
Fermanagh, Tyrone, Londonderry, Antrim, Armagh and Down

North West
Donegal, Sligo, Leitrim, Monaghan and Cavan

West
Galway, Mayo and Roscommon

Midlands East
Wicklow, Kildare, Laois, north Offaly, Westmeath, Longford, Meath and Louth

Dublin
City and County

Shannon
Limerick, north Kerry, north Tipperary, Clare and south Offaly

South West
Cork and south Kerry

South East
Wexford, Waterford, south Tipperary, Kilkenny and Carlow

About this book

Practical information

Ownership and access

Far and away the majority of sites are in the care of the state: these are managed by Dúchas in the Republic of Ireland and by the Environment and Heritage Service in Northern Ireland. Sites in the care of the state are likely to be well signposted, tend to have more convenient opening hours, and are usually good value for money.

Incidentally, places listed in the book as state properties are not necessarily owned by the state or on state land. In many cases, they are simply in state care.

Sites owned by local councils also tend to give excellent value for money and be open at convenient times, as do those run by a charitable organisation, such as a local archeological trust. The National Trust operates a number of historic properties in Northern Ireland; these are very well run, but tend not to be open in winter.

Privately owned sites can be a lot more expensive to visit, are often open only in the summer months, and are sometimes not so well presented.

Prices

Prices are changed quite frequently, so any attempt to state them exactly would simply mean that this book was quickly out of date. Instead, we have employed a simple system of pound signs (£) to indicate roughly how cheap or expensive a place is to visit.

£ – Very cheap (a pound or less)
££ – Good value
£££ – Rather expensive
££££ – Very expensive

Sites rated as ££££ are few and far between, but they are ones where the price is high enough to make you think twice about going.

Membership

Free entry to all sites operated by Dúchas in the Republic of Ireland can be gained by purchasing a Dúchas Heritage Card, which is very reasonably priced and lasts for a year. It's well worth getting one if you are likely to go to six or seven Dúchas sites.

Membership of the National Trust entitles you to free entry to their properties in England and Wales as well as Northern Ireland, and there is a reciprocal arrangement with the Scottish National Trust whereby members get free entry to National Trust properties.

Opening hours

Unfortunately, it's not practical to give the full opening hours for each property; they change so often that the book would be out of date before it was even printed, and some places have quite complicated dates and times of opening. Instead, we've simplified it by using a brief phrase to sum up the access arrangements. Be warned, though, that if you want to be *absolutely certain* that a property is open on the day and at the time you are visiting, you should telephone in advance to confirm the hours.

It is generally the case that any site or property that has opening hours will be open roughly during standard business hours, from 9am to 5pm, or 10am to 6pm. Sites are often open longer in summer, but tend to close at 4pm in the winter months. In this book, I have assumed that 'usual hours' applies wherever it is not stated and I have simply given details of the times of year during which a property is open.

Opening hours are described in this book using the following phrases:

'Open access at any reasonable time' – Indicates that a monument stands in a field or similar open setting, so you can see it whenever you like, provided that you do not disturb anyone who lives nearby.

'Open access *at reasonable times only*' – The distinction shows that there are houses very close to the monument and people are particularly likely to be disturbed if you visit at a strange time.

'Usual hours' – Means that a property is open roughly during usual shop hours, including weekends. State-owned properties are usually open from 10am to 6pm (or later) for seven days a week in summer.

'Summer only', 'Closed Mondays' *etc* – Many properties have good opening hours in the summer months but are closed in winter, and I have tried to indicate this by adding short notes such as these.

Broadly speaking, most sites are open from the beginning of May to the end of September, but there are many variations: some places are open at Easter, for example, or at weekends in October.

'Limited hours' – Not open every day of the week (perhaps just at weekends) or only open in the afternoon, for example. Again, I have tried to give an idea of the limitations.

Directions

Generally, I would hope that a road atlas and this book should get you there. In the Republic of Ireland I have used the road atlas produced by the Ordnance Survey of Ireland, but it is not without errors.

In any situation where signposts can't be relied on, I have tried to give accurate directions from personal experience.

If you do come across a situation where you find these directions difficult to follow, I would be very grateful if you could let me know by writing care of the publisher.

Please note
I have done everything I can to ensure that the details given are correct at the time of going to press, but I'm afraid that we cannot accept responsibility for any loss or inconvenience caused by errors. Access to private land in particular can change. It is not to be assumed that rights of way or rights of access exist.

Introduction, part one

Ireland's archeology

Above: Tomb No 7 at Carrowmore Megalithic Cemetery, Co Sligo. This odd arrangement of stones is the remnant of an unusual type of neolithic chambered tomb, and is probably one of the oldest monuments in Ireland.

THE FIRST PEOPLE TO COME TO IRELAND were the hunter-gatherers of the mesolithic era (middle stone age), who arrived after the last ice age ended and the glacial ice had melted, more than 10,000 years ago. Their presence after 8000BC is indicated by their distinctive flint tools, some made from tiny, razor-sharp flakes of flint known as 'microliths', and by the seashells and other food refuse left in heaps called 'middens', which they left at places where they exploited the natural resources.

Traces of these mesolithic people are scarce, and museums like the National Museum in Dublin are the only place to get much of a sense of them, though there are shell middens on the Sligo coast at Ballysadare Bay.

The people of the neolithic (new stone age) era also used tools made of flint but what makes them so different is that they were the first farmers, settling down after 4000BC to grow corn and keep cows, goats and sheep. Their fields and houses have been found buried under peat at Céide Fields in Co Mayo, but their most striking contribution to archeology is the *passage grave*, in which a stone-built passage leads to a chamber deep inside a mound of earth. The most famous passage grave is Newgrange.

The bronze age, which lasted from roughly 2000BC to 500BC, was a time of great interest in all metals, especially gold and silver, as well as the tin and copper used to make bronze. It was a time of increasing social organisation, and its characteristic monument is the *stone circle*.

The iron age in Ireland was the time when Celtic culture arrived from Europe. With no Roman interference, it continued into what is known as the Early Christian (or Early Historic) period, considered to have started about 500AD.

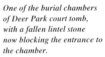

Court tombs

This unusual type of neolithic chambered tomb is unique to Ireland and is often said to be the oldest of the monuments found here, with the earliest examples dating to 3500BC (though many authorities say that some passage graves are even older). Court tombs are large monuments with plenty of intriguing features, so they are enjoyable ones to visit. There are more in the north and west, but they occur all over Ireland.

The distinctive feature of a court tomb is an open, courtyard-like area in front of the tomb, usually defined by large upright slabs of stone set in an oval shape. The chambered tomb itself – which usually has several compartments, one behind the other – is reached through a doorway leading off this courtyard. The chambers, which are not very high, would presumably have been roofed over with capstones, but these are generally missing.

Some court tombs are surrounded by large, straight-sided cairns of heaped-up stones, and it is presumed that most of them would originally have had a similar cairn or mound.

The court is big enough for ceremonies of some kind to have taken place there, but what exactly the function of this design was will only ever be guesswork. Some court tombs have just a semi-circular area in front of the tomb defined by uprights (rather than an enclosed court), and these are reminiscent of the forecourts of neolithic long cairns found in Scotland and England.

One of the burial chambers of Deer Park court tomb, with a fallen lintel stone now blocking the entrance to the chamber.

The larger and more dramatic court tombs can have several chambers – as at Deer Park in Co Sligo, where there are two chambers at one end of the court and one at the other – while smaller examples are sometimes found in pairs, back to back.

Typical items found during excavation are almost identical to those found in passage graves, and include cremated human remains, stone tools and ornaments, and pottery.

The ones to see…

Creevykeel court tomb, Deer Park court tomb, *Co Sligo* (*page 142*)

Left: the larger chamber at Deer Park court tomb is on the right of the picture, with the court beyond. On the far side of the court there are two smaller chambers, with a lintel stone over the entrance to each chamber.

Passage graves

There is no question that the passage graves of Ireland are the country's most dramatic and fascinating monuments. A visit to the four major passage grave cemeteries, which lie in a band across the middle of the country from Brú na Boinne, near Drogheda, in the east to Carrowmore, near Sligo, in the west, would make an excellent aim for a holiday for anyone interested in archeology, whether you live in Ireland or are visiting the country.

The passage grave is one of the earliest forms of neolithic monument. Similar tombs are found in northern Scotland (a fine example being Maes Howe on Orkney) and in North Wales (though they are rare here, the only notable example being Bryn Celli Ddu on Anglesey), but the most closely comparable tombs are found in Brittany, northern France.

The passage grave is so called because it consists of a passage, its walls made from upright slabs of stone and roofed over with similar slabs, leading to a chamber built in similar fashion. The chamber often has a corbelled roof, made from much smaller stones in a technique similar to drystone walling; the roof curves gently inwards until a single large capstone can be placed on top.

The passage and chamber are always covered with a mound of earth or a cairn of stones, and in most cases the mound or cairn is defined by more upright slabs of stone, set so as to form a kerb around the perimeter of the mound.

The chamber is generally cruciform: that is, made up of three compartments, one on either side of the passage and one at the end. Where any evidence is found of burials, they are nearly always cremated; often remains of many individuals are heaped up together.

One of the most unusual features of some Irish passage graves is a huge, shallow stone bowl placed in one of the chambers, in which human remains were deposited. Bowls like this were found at Newgrange, Knowth, and in one of the tombs at Loughcrew; the one at Knowth has patterns carved on the outside.

The cremation burials are nearly always accompanied by grave goods: ornaments of stone and bone, pottery of a distinctive type, stone tools, and animal bones.

The two most remarkable features of the passage graves, however, are the so-called 'astronomical alignments' that the passages of some tombs exhibit, and the extraordinary 'passage grave art' which is carved into the stones of some of the tombs.

Similar decoration is not found anywhere else in the British Isles – though there is a fabulous tomb on the island of Gavrinis off the coast of Brittany, the passage of which is decorated with huge, swirling spirals.

There are superb designs on some of the tombs at Loughcrew, and both outside and inside the most famous tomb of the lot, Newgrange; but the greatest range of different designs is at Knowth, where the huge slabs that form the kerb of the monument are all decorated – and usually on the side facing the mound as well as on the outside.

The most famous alignment is at Newgrange, where the rising sun shines down the passage for a few days on either side of the midwinter solstice, the shortest day of the year: but the large tomb known as Cairn L at Loughcrew is aligned with sunrise at the equinoxes in spring and autumn, while the remarkable Knowth has a passage on either side, facing both sunrise and sunset at the equinoxes.

The ones to see...

Far left: The extraordinary entrance to the passage grave of Newgrange. The slab across the entrance is decorated with flowing spiral designs, while above the entrance is the 'light box' which enables the sun to shine right along the passage only at midwinter sunrise.

Above: Cairn L at Loughcrew is a classic example of a passage grave, with a number of smaller satellite tombs grouped all around it. Its interior is decorated with all manner of 'passage grave art' designs, and its passage is aligned with sunrise on the morning of the spring and autumn equinoxes, when the day is as long as the night.

Left: One of the smaller tombs near to Cairn L at Loughcrew, all of which have had their covering mounds of stone robbed away. Simple spiral designs decorate the stones that make up the tomb's cruciform chamber.

Portal dolmens

Perhaps it's the contrast between the huge, heavy stones and the delicate, precarious way they are balanced that gives these distinctive monuments their appeal, but certainly photographs of them are perennial favourites on postcards and the covers of tourist brochures.

Portal dolmens are another variety of neolithic tomb, though they are thought to be from later in the period – from about 3000BC to about 2000BC. They occur all over Ireland, mostly near the coast, but many of the best examples are in the south east. Perhaps there is some sort of seagoing connection across the Irish Sea, since in Britain monuments of this kind are found more or less exclusively in west Wales, Devon, and Cornwall.

The typical portal dolmen has an arrangement of two upright slabs of stone set parallel to each other, like gateposts. These are sometimes referred to as the 'portal stones'. The gap between them is blocked by a third stone set sideways, like a gate, and sometimes called the 'gate stone'. If seen from above, the whole arrangement would look like a capital letter 'H'. On top of this rests a capstone, often of imposing size and weight, and frequently tilted so that it looms dramatically over the front of the monument. There's usually a chamber of some kind behind the portal.

The evidence suggests that portal dolmens were probably not covered by mounds, though they often seem to have been surrounded by a low, cairn-like 'platform' of stones. Traces of a kerb of slightly larger stones around the edge of this cairn are apparent at a number of sites.

Because the monuments were not covered, it is rare for evidence of burials to be found during excavation. There is one in Wales which was incorporated into the mound of a later chambered long barrow, and here evidence of cremation was found, which would fit in with practices at passage graves in Ireland.

The ones to see...

Poulnabrone portal dolmen, *The Burren, Co Clare (page 114)*

Browneshill portal dolmen, *Co Carlow,* Knockeen portal dolmen, *Co Waterford,* and Kilmogue portal dolmen, *Co Kilkenny (pages 72–3)*

Poulnabrone dolmen is not really typical of this sort of monument, but its sculptural quality and scenic setting make it the most satisfying portal dolmen to visit.

Wedge tombs

Another type of chambered tomb, but this time much later in date. Wedge tombs are from the early bronze age, not long after 2000BC. They get their name from the fact that they are wider at one end than at the other in plan (when seen from above), but some also look wedge-like from the side, because the capstone covering the chamber slopes down towards one end.

Wedge tombs are found all over Ireland (though most are found in the south-west) and they come in all sorts of shapes and sizes. There's a small variety, fairly common in Kerry, that consists of just two uprights set not quite parallel to each other, with a capstone on top. However, the largest examples can be complex and impressive monuments. Probably the best of the lot is Labbacallee wedge tomb, near Fermoy in Co Cork, where a truly huge slab of stone is used as a capstone and covers not one but two large burial chambers.

It is thought that all wedge tombs would have been covered over with mounds of earth or stone. At Labbacallee, you can see the remains of a horseshoe-shaped arrangement of kerbstones that would have supported the mound. Finds at Labbacallee included uncremated human remains, pottery fragments and stone tools.

The one to see…

Labbacallee wedge tomb, *Co Cork (page 87)*

The 'Fulacht Fiadh'

The remains of bronze age houses, which were usually round huts, are few and far between, but by contrast these communal cooking places are relatively common. They're generally not much to look at, but the idea is interesting.

The visible sign of a Fulacht Fiadh is a crescent-shaped mound, which on investigation turns out to be composed of fire-blackened, shattered stones. Excavation reveals a trough near a ready water source. Water was boiled in the trough using stones heated in a fire, and meat was cooked in the boiling water.

The remnant of one of the smaller and simpler varieties of wedge tomb, this exposed burial chamber stands in a field on the Beara peninsula.

Left: Labbacallee wedge tomb is the most impressive tomb of this type in Ireland, with a massive capstone covering two large chambers.

Stone circles

Exactly why stone circles were built and how they were used is not known, and indeed their air of mystery is one of the things that gives these monuments such enduring appeal. There are no particularly large stone circles in Ireland, but there is an intriguing variety of different types. Oddly, the most impressive ones are not really stone circles at all.

The most numerous of the Irish stone circles are the small circles found in the south-west, which are known as the Cork-Kerry type. These come in two main varieties: very small arrangements of just five stones, and slightly larger circles that, similarly, always consist of an odd number of stones. There are also many short alignments of stones – a row of three is pretty typical – found in the same region and associated with the circles.

Cork-Kerry circles, the most famous of which is Drombeg stone circle in Co Cork, often have an entrance marked by two taller stones on one side of the circle, and sometimes have a recumbent stone (one lying on its side, rather than set on its end) opposite the entrance. This combination gives the monuments an obvious axis, and a line drawn through the middle of the circle crossing both the entrance and the recumbent stone sometimes shows an aligment in a particular direction. At Drombeg, for instance, the monument seems to be aligned on the setting sun at midwinter.

Excavation at Cork-Kerry stone circles has sometimes found burials, as at Drombeg, where a pot in the middle of the circle contained a cremation, or at Kenmare, where there is a simple megalithic grave of a type known as a 'boulder burial' in the middle of the monument. Dating evidence suggests that these circles were in use during the later bronze age, from about 1000BC to 700BC. It has also been suggested that these circles are found in areas where copper, tin and other metals could have

been mined. A concentration of Cork-Kerry circles is found on the Beara peninsula in Kerry.

Another area where there are lots of small circles is Ulster. Here, the stone circles are nearly always made up of tiny stones, often less than 0.5m (1ft 6ins) in height, and they are associated with stone rows and small cairns, as at the impressive site of Beaghmore, near Cookstown in Co Tyrone, Northern Ireland. Limited dating evidence suggests that the circles at Beaghmore were also in use during the late bronze age, between 1500BC and 700BC.

In the south-east and the west of Ireland, stone circles are few and far between. There is a handful of circles near Cong in Co Mayo and at the feet of the mountains of Co Wicklow, however, and in both areas there are examples of a slightly different kind of stone circle too, properly referred to as an embanked enclosure. This consists of a circular area defined by a bank of earth in a ring around it, with upright stones set into the bank, either just on the inside or on both sides. On one side is an entrance.

The largest 'stone circle' in Ireland, Grange stone circle, near Lough Gur in Co Limerick, is actually one of these embanked enclosures. What the purpose of these monuments was is not known, and it can only be assumed that the enclosure was the venue for meetings or ceremonies of some kind.

Two more stone circles deserve attention. One is Beltany stone circle in Donegal, the most rewarding Irish circle to visit, which seems to have been built as part of a now-ruined passage grave. There are no other examples in Ireland of circles being built to accompany passage graves, but there is a group of cairns ringed by circles at Clava, near Inverness in Scotland. Up here in the north of Ireland, some kind of Scottish influence is clearly possible. The other notable example is the huge circle built around the passage tomb of Newgrange. This was the largest circle in Ireland, and the few massive stones that remain are impressive.

The ones to see...

Above: Beltany stone circle in Donegal may have been built around a passage grave that has now disappeared.

Near right: The group of tiny stone circles, stone rows and cairns at Beaghmore in Northern Ireland includes this unusual circle in the middle of which lots of stones are set upright.

Far right: Grange stone circle at Lough Gur consists of an embanked enclosure with upright stones set into the inner face of the bank.

Drombeg stone circle, with its 'recumbent stone' on the left.

Stone forts

These fascinating monuments are very difficult to date, partly because the sort of evidence that might define when a fort was built seldom turns up during excavations, but mainly because they remained in use right into medieval times, often with alterations to the buildings inside. So the picture can be confused. It's safe to say, however, that some of the earliest must belong to the later iron age, after about 100BC. Similarly impressive stone structures elsewhere in the British Isles, such as the brochs and duns of Scotland, were built and used throughout the time of the Roman occupation of Britain, from about 60AD to 400AD – but again, they were often re-used right up to the 1200s.

Stone forts take two main forms: round ones, such as Staigue in Co Kerry and Grianán of Aileach in Co Donegal; and promontory forts, where a stone rampart cuts off a promontory overlooking the sea, and no further defences are needed on the seaward side. Some of the most impressive variants on the latter design are those found on the Aran islands in Galway Bay, where the spectacular Dun Angus is just the biggest and best-known of several fine forts.

Common features at these stone forts are an entrance passage roofed over with large slabs, occasionally defended by guard chambers; small corbel-roofed chambers in the thickness of the wall, usually high enough to stand up in, which were presumably just used for storage; and steps running up the inner face of the wall to allow defenders easy access to the top.

The ones to see...

Staigue stone fort, *Co Kerry* (*page 89*)

Grianán of Aileach, *Co Donegal* (*page 144*)

Dun Beag promontory fort, *Co Kerry* (*page 92*)

Staigue in Co Kerry is one of the two finest round stone forts in Ireland.

Left: The criss-cross flights of steps inside the stone fort of Staigue were presumably designed so that defenders could get to the top of the wall as quickly as possible. It's rather a cunning design.

20

Raths and cashels

The rath, also known as a ringfort, is the commonest kind of iron age residence in Ireland. It consists of a small, usually more or less circular enclosure defined by a bank with a ditch outside it. There would have been a wooden palisade around the bank, and in the middle of the enclosure there would have been several round wooden huts – some for storage, and some for living in. Raths are very common, the same idea having remained in use into the early Christian period (500 to 1100AD), but they are usually not much to look at.

The cashel (also sometimes called a caher) is simply a stone-built variant on the rath, consisting of a wide but usually not very high stone wall encircling an enclosure of similar size.

Souterrains are found associated with both raths and cashels, though a well-built cashel is more likely to have a well-built souterrain.

Identical cashels were also used to defend monastic sites in the early Christian period.

The one to see…

Two cashels at Mooghaun, *Co Clare (page 111)*

Souterrains

These slightly mysterious underground passages are only found at habitation sites such as cashels or forts. They are usually very well built, with drystone walls, flagstone floors, and roofs made of large, flat slabs of stone. They are sometimes high enough to stand upright in. Often the passages curve round and have branches or chambers off the side.

At one time, it was thought that souterrains had a defensive function as a place to hide during an attack, but it is now generally accepted that they are for the storage of food. Clearly it might be advantageous to store meat or dairy products in a cool place like an underground passage, but it is also possible that grain was stored here, under conditions that would prevent it from sprouting. This purely functional role does not mean that there was not also some element of ritual associated with underground gods who cared for the food.

Equally, many Irish souterrains seem to lead under the ramparts or up to the entrance of a fort, and it seems likely that they also functioned as a secret entrance which could be exploited to surprise enemies attacking the fort.

Below: Rathgall stone fort in Co Wicklow is certainly not a typical cashel, and its date of construction is very uncertain, but the inner enclosure seen here is a very similar type of stone rampart encircling a small round enclosure.

Crannogs

These fascinating residences are basically houses built on artificial islands. The idea is similar to the promontory fort or cliff-castle, in that the water provides a natural defence on all sides of the crannog except where it is reached by a wooden causeway, but the advantage of the lakeside setting of a crannog is that ready resources of food would be available – and not just the fish of the lake, but all the produce of the fertile land around it.

A crannog was built by first driving piles into the silt of the lake bottom, and then heaping up brushwood on top. This might be covered over with a layer of mud and stones. On the artificial island that resulted, a fairly large platform could now be built, with a palisade around the edge of it. There would be enough room to build several round wooden huts in the crannog, and a causeway of stones or a wooden walkway raised on piles would be built to connect it to the lake shore.

In Scotland, crannogs were in use from the bronze age onwards, but in Ireland they seem to be a product of the iron age. The people who built them would no doubt have been very

familiar with boats, but all the evidence from excavations suggests that they were also farmers, and their animals would have been driven on to the crannog at night.

Unfortunately, crannogs are really not much to look at. There are, however, reconstructions of iron age crannogs that you can visit at the Craggaunowen Project in Co Clare and at the Irish National Heritage Park in Co Wexford, to name but two.

Real crannogs are not much to look at: in this view of Lough Gur, Co Limerick, the crannog is the clump of trees by the shore of the lake on the left of the picture.

Below: This reconstruction is of a bronze age crannog on Loch Tay in Scotland.

Early churches

Travelling in Ireland, it is not at all uncommon to come across a small ruined church, the stump of a round tower (or perhaps a complete one) or a carved high cross, abandoned long ago but standing in a graveyard which is still in use. The monasteries to which these buildings belonged often owe their origins to the 500s and 600s, and it is surprising how frequently the names of their founders are recorded.

In their original form, the early monasteries were simple places, with wooden buildings surrounded by an enclosure wall or cashel. Some idea of this early simplicity can be seen at the excavated site at Reask in Dingle.

The earliest churches can be recognised by features such as *antae*, where the side walls project a short way beyond the end walls, a design that is thought to derive from wooden churches and to make the roof simpler to build. Also typical are 'whale tail' stone fixtures at the point of the gables, to which barge boards would have been attached; and flat-topped doors, with massive lintel stones, the sides of which are often splayed outwards.

Some early churches have interesting stone roofs, a style they share with the boat-shaped oratories such as the one at Gallarus on the Dingle peninsula. These oratories were once thought to have been from the 700s, but it is now thought that, despite their archaic design, the simple fact that they are built in stone suggests that they may be no older than the other early stone churches.

Not long after 1000AD, the simple, box-like design of churches was swopped for a nave-and-chancel design, with a small room tacked on at the east end (the chancel) joined to the nave by an often elaborate arch (the chancel arch). Many existing simple churches were converted by the addition of a chancel.

Finally, the building of Cormac's Chapel at Cashel ushered in the Irish Romanesque style, and many of the churches of the 1100s show superbly ornamented doorways and arches.

The ones to see...

Reask early monastic site, Gallarus oratory and Kilmalkedar church, *Dingle peninsula, Co Kerry (pages 93 & 94)*

St Kevin's Church, Glendalough, *Co Wicklow (page 156)*

Cormac MacCarthy's Chapel at Cashel, *Co Tipperary (page 60)*

Killeshin church romanesque doorway, *Co Laois (page 163)*

Below: The early monastic site at Reask consists of a stone-walled enclosure inside which there are the remains of a chapel and several beehive huts, as well as a number of carved stone slabs.

Opposite page: The splendid round tower at Glendalough had its conical top rebuilt in Victorian times, but using the original stones.

High crosses

Surprisingly, the main reason high crosses are called 'high' is simply that many of them are very tall. The art of carving stone crosses seems to have flourished during two particular periods – the 800s and the 1100s – although why this should be so is not clear, and dates for the crosses are never very certain. They are rarely given an inscription that helps date them.

Perhaps unsurprisingly, some of the finest examples are associated with the greatest of the monasteries: there are particularly good crosses at Clonmacnoise and Cashel. However, there are also good crosses at places where the monastery that produced them is barely visible, as at Castledermot, in Co Kildare, or has vanished altogether, as at Ahenny.

It is thought that the crosses would originally have been painted in bright colours. The scenes carved on them include all sorts of episodes from the bible, but the simplest have just a crucifixion and pleasing abstract decoration.

The ones to see...

Clonmacnoise, *Co Offaly* (*page 154*)

Moone high cross, *Co Kildare* (*page 158*)

Round towers

The standard explanation given for round towers is that they were refuges in times of trouble. When a monastery was raided by the Vikings (or just as likely by a neighbouring king) the important monks could leg it up the ladder to the door high above the ground, taking all the books, jewelled crosses and other valuables with them for safe keeping, then simply pull up the ladder and wait for the threat to go away.

No doubt this tactic worked – though it is a certainty that from time to time it didn't, since there are records of the entire libraries of some monasteries going up in smoke inside a tower. But it hardly seems a sufficient reason for the development of these unique structures, so it appears likely that they had a day-to-day function too, as belfrys from which monks could have been called to prayer – similar in a way to the minarets of the East.

Inside, a round tower would have from five to eight wooden floors, with a trapdoor in each and a ladder leading to the next one up. At the present time, the only round tower you can climb up is the one at St Canice's Cathedral in Kilkenny, which has modern ladders and floors. It's an experience not to be missed.

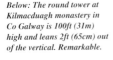

Below: The round tower at Kilmacduagh monastery in Co Galway is 100ft (31m) high and leans 2ft (65cm) out of the vertical. Remarkable.

Introduction, part two: the history of Ireland

Celtic Ireland

ONCE UPON A TIME it was assumed that every great cultural change in the archeological record was the result of new people arriving in an area. Folk-movement, invasion, call it what you will – the idea was that only new people could introduce new technology and new habits. So when someone started using weapons made of bronze, or burying their important dead under earthen round barrows, these people were no doubt bronze-using, barrow-building invaders from the continent.

Nowadays, however, the view of prehistory that prevails is very different. Cultural exchange is considered far more important than warfare, and trade between distant areas is seen as a more likely way for ideas to spread than by entire populations upping sticks and moving.

In this context, the idea of a people called the Celts arriving and settling in Ireland and thereby ushering in the start of a new era known as the iron age is seen as old-fashioned and even a bit silly. Rather, it was Celtic culture that spread to Ireland – the ideas, tastes, designs and habits that already dominated central and western Europe.

Here that culture flourished, and here it was fortunate enough to escape the Romanisation that spread across Europe in the first century AD and survive into the 500s and beyond.

ONE OF THE OUTSTANDING FEATURES of Irish Celticism is that it speaks a different language from the rest of Europe; and the difference tells an interesting story. The variety of the Celtic language spoken in Ireland is known as Goidelic or Q-Celtic, and is thought to be an earlier form of the language. The kind spoken by people elsewhere in Western Europe, such as the Welsh and the Bretons, is known as Brythonic or P-Celtic, and it is thought to have developed in a number of ways at a time when Goidelic stayed the same.

One possible reason for this difference is that the earlier form of the language spread to Ireland at a time when this form was spoken all across Europe, and that the Irish then became isolated, and did not pick up on changes that happened to the language elsewhere. Oddly enough, this theory is backed up by archeological evidence.

It is clear that in neolithic times, Ireland was part of a greater community on what is known as the 'Atlantic facade' of western Europe: similar passage graves to those that occur in Ireland are also found in Spain, north-west France, Wales and Scotland. Equally, there is plenty of evidence that similar cultural links were kept up in the bronze age, when the seaways were the best roads and the metal-rich areas along the south coast of Ireland were linked by trade with the west coast of Europe.

However, from about 600BC the evidence of Irish connections with Europe more or less completely evaporates. Until almost 100BC, there is scarcely any sign of European ideas or European goods in Ireland. At the same time, it appears from analysis of pollen found in archeological digs that forests were regenerating over large parts of the country, which suggests a drastic decline in population. For about 500 years, it appears that Ireland was an isolated backwater of Europe.

Surprisingly, then, evidence of how the Celtic people of Ireland lived during the iron age is fairly scarce, and this situation is not helped by the fact that many of the iron age structures are difficult to date, nor by the way that patterns of settlement remained very much the same into the historic period.

However, it is clear that Celtic life in Ireland was not greatly different from that in Brittany, Wales and Cornwall. The main dwelling-places were defended farmsteads with a number of huts – some for living in, some for storage – protected by a bank and a ditch. Small, round versions of this kind of enclosure, known as raths, are common in Ireland, just as they are in Wales and Cornwall.

A frequent feature of these small defended villages or farmsteads is the underground passage known as a souterrain. Again, these are common in Brittany and Cornwall.

Another type of defended community was the cliff-castle, or promontory fort, where ramparts were built to defend a promontory from the landward side, allowing the natural defences of the cliffs to do the rest of the work. Cliff-castles occur all around the Irish coast, particularly in the south and west, and again they demonstrate a connection with the Celtic

people elsewhere on the western coasts of Europe, but again not much is known about when they were built.

One link with Brittany that is not found in either Wales or Cornwall is the small, rounded stone pillar known as a *stela*. Several have been found, the most famous being the Turoe Stone, elaborately carved with decoration in the flowing La Tène style, which still stands in Co Galway. Similar *stelae* occur all over Brittany: some tall, some small, a few carved with patterns, but always with the same deliberate rounded shape. The lack of them in Britain may mean that wooden pillars served a similar function.

BY FAR THE MOST DRAMATIC monuments of Celtic Ireland, then, are the four great ritual centres of Tara, Emain Macha (at Navan in Northern Ireland), Cruachain (in Roscommon) and Dún Ailinne (Co Kildare). At these sites, the remarkable story told by archeological exploration can be blended with the glimpses of Celtic splendour offered by surviving fragments of mythology to create a colourful picture of Irish society in the iron age.

The best-known of the four sites, from the archeological point of view, is Emain Macha.

The oval-shaped hilltop enclosure was found to have contained a series of wooden buildings in the remains of which prestige goods dating from 700BC to 100BC were found. In 94BC – the date comes from tree-rings – a huge oak was felled and set up as the centre post of a round building some 40m (130ft) across, consisting of several concentric rings of posts. It may have had a roof. This building was then filled up with stones, piled up in a cairn as much as 2.5m (8ft) high, and whatever bits of it stuck out were burned. What this was all about is anyone's guess, but it must have taken some doing.

Excavations at Dún Ailinne and Tara also show that a series of circular wooden buildings was constructed in the middle of a large, oval hilltop enclosure. At Dún Ailinne, the final phase involved two concentric palisades enclosing an area 37m (120ft) across, with a building in the middle, 5m in diameter, surrounded by a setting of large posts. Some burning took place near the posts, then the whole lot was dismantled. After that, it seems that the site was given over to periodic feasting.

What this was all about will never be known, but it certainly suggests that the truth of Celtic Ireland was just as interesting as the mythology.

One of the four great Celtic ritual sites, which seem to have gone through some major change in use not long after 100BC, Tara is now little more than a bewildering series of earthworks, the true interest of which can only be appreciated by paying close attention to the archeology.

First steps in history and the arrival of Christianity, 400 to 795

Early Christian Ireland

THE ROMANS NEVER CAME to Ireland, though the great general Agricola, who completed the conquest of most of Britain, is said to have stood on the west coast of Scotland, looked out speculatively at the nearby Irish coast, and declared that he could take the whole island with just a single legion.

Rome did, however, trade with Ireland, as is evident from Roman goods that have been found in excavations of Irish settlements of the time – mostly jewellery – and there was a major trading base on the promontory of Drumanagh, just north of Dublin.

'History' simply means events that are written down and recorded. Without the presence of Roman soldiers, clerks and historians to write about the nature of the country and the events that took place here, Ireland managed to stay out of the spotlight of history until the arrival of educated monks from Europe brought both Christianity and writing. The period from about the middle of the 400s is known either as the early Christian period, or as the early historic period.

If the Romans never invaded Ireland, however, the Irish certainly invaded the Roman Empire. Not only did Irish raiders join the Picts, Saxons and any other 'barbarian' worth his salt in devastating the periphery of Roman Britain in the years leading up to the final withdrawal of Roman soldiers from the island in about 400AD, but also settlers from Ireland

Below: the monastery founded by Columba on the Scottish island of Iona became the most influential in the Celtic church. It was really only eclipsed following its frequent devastation by Viking raiders after 802.

travelled eastwards across the sea in the years after the collapse and helped themselves to new territories in Wales, Devon and, most successfully of all, Scotland.

The name Scot actually means Irishman, and derives from the people from Dál Riata in the north of Ireland who settled in Argyll in the west of Scotland in the late 400s. By the time that Columba made a mission to Iona in 593, the Dalriadan kings were already making headway against the Picts to the east, and by the mid-800s a Scot named Kenneth Mac Alpin had become heir to the Pictish throne, which descended through the female side, and unified the Picts and Scots as their king.

The effect of contact with Britain was felt at home in Ireland, too. There is some evidence that the wealth generated by raids provided the resources for campaigns of expansion by tribes in several areas of Ireland. For example, the Eógonacht, who took the kingship of Munster from the Érainn, may well have been colonists returning from Britain.

THE ARRIVAL OF CHRISTIANITY was a much more significant import in the long run than the portable wealth of Britain, though according to the stories, at least, it arrived in the same way: on board a pirate ship, following a raid on the coast of Devon.

Saint Patrick, who is credited with bringing Christianity to Ireland, is said to have been the son of wealthy parents in Devon. While still a boy he was carried off as a slave by Irish pirates and taken away to Connacht in the north-west. He eventually escaped and slowly made his way home, only to return to Ireland in later years as a grown-up monk on a mission to save the Irish people.

In fact, of course, the arrival of Christianity in Ireland was a long process and involved much more manpower than just a single saint. The first date in Irish history is 431, when a monk called Palladius who was probably a deacon at Auxerre was sent as a bishop to 'the Irish who believe in Christ' (the phrase is thought to refer to orthodox Irish Christians, as opposed to followers of the Pelagian heresy). Round about 433, it was said that Pope Celestine had managed to make the Irish Christian, but in

reality the process would have been a very gradual one, involving the persuasion of many a local king and the building of dozens of tiny local parish churches. It is said that the last pagan king of Tara was Diarmit Mac Cerbaill, who ruled in the mid-500s.

The Celtic church gradually developed its own distinct character, based on close relationships with the rich and powerful men in society (who were often close relatives of the leading figures in the church) and not too intolerant of the old pagan ways, and yet with a strong monastic element. This monasticism was influenced greatly by Britain, in particular by Ninian and St David, and led to the founding of a host of monasteries in the 500s and 600s by such notable figures as Columba (founder of the monastery on the Scottish island of Iona), Ciarán of Clonmacnoise and Brendan of Clonfert.

The biggest monasteries attracted patronage from wealthy men and grew into centres of learning, arts, crafts and trade. These were the cities of the age, and some – such as Kildare – were also the seats of the provincial kings.

The great centres of ecclesiastical power were at Armagh (which made the most of its associations with St Patrick) and Iona, which founded monasteries at Durrow, Derry and Kells. The ninth abbot of Iona, Adomnán, was one of the greatest figures of his age, with influence over the rulers of Northumbria as well as Ireland. In 697, on the centenary of the death of Columba, he held a synod of bishops, abbots and kings at Birr at which he gave out his Law of the Innocents, which said that women and children must not be involved in battle and women must be protected from violence.

THERE WERE BETWEEN 80 and 100 kings of various ranks in Ireland in the 700s, some of them little more than local lords, others overkings of whole provinces. The most powerful were the Uí Néill dynasty, who ruled in the midlands and the north and had the advantage of having Armagh in their territory. They took on the mantle of Kings of Tara for themselves, which seems to have had great historical resonance.

Their principal rivals were the Eóganacht of Munster, based at Cashel and Glanworth. Their king, Cathal Mac Finguine, who died in 742, defeated the Uí Néill and was considered by the people of Munster to be high king of Ireland. They were later eclipsed by the Dál Cais, one of whose kings made that dream a reality.

The hillfort of Dunadd in Argyll, Scotland, is where the Irish settlers of Dalriada, who became known as the Scots, set up their early capital in the late 400s. Eventually, Scottish kings descended from these Irish settlers managed to take over from the Picts.

Norse raiders settle and become townspeople and traders, 795 to 950

The Vikings in Ireland

THE RAIDERS FROM THE SEA first appeared in the waters off the Irish coast in the late 700s. These were bands of young men borne in ships across the North Sea from Norway, led by lords and kings, spending their summer months in search of a harvest of riches to carry off home. Their most obvious targets were monasteries, which not only possessed their own treasures, but also were like small towns, acting as centres for crafts and trade.

In attacking these targets, however, it has to be said that the Vikings were certainly not alone. It was already common for disputatious kings to raid the monasteries of neighbouring territories; indeed, the heads of these wealthy establishments were often relatives of the ruling families, men of worldly wealth and power, and were quite willing to take up arms and defend themselves.

The first recorded Viking raids on Ireland took place in the far north in 795, two years after the first attacks in England, when a monastery on Rathlin Island off the Antrim coast was burned. The influential monastery founded by Columba on the Scottish island of Iona was also attacked in the same year. In 798 another island monastery, off the coast not far from Dublin, was attacked and burned, and many other raids were made on the Irish coast. In 806 Iona was raided for a third time, and 68 members of the community were killed, prompting the establishment of a new Columban community at Kells in Co Meath, more than 20 miles inland, where the famous Book of Kells was created in later years.

The raids on Ireland continued on the same sporadic, hit-and-run pattern for the next 40 years. By 823, Viking ships had sailed all the way round the Irish coast; in the following year a monastery off the Kerry coast, in the extreme south-west, was attacked. From time to time, the Irish caught up with the raiders and defeated them in battle, but for the most part they were gone as quickly as they had appeared.

In 836, however, the pattern suddenly changed. Large bands of Viking warriors arrived and began to pursue extensive campaigns inland, just as they had been doing in England and France. The first major raids were on the lands of the southern Ui Neill and in Connacht, with extensive destruction and

many people killed or taken captive. In 837 large fleets of Viking ships terrorised the land near the rivers Boyne and Liffey, and a major defeat was inflicted on the southern Ui Neill. Ships travelled up the Shannon and the Erne, as well as the Boyne and Liffey; and in 839 a fleet entered Lough Neagh, plundering the country all around and launching a major campaign against Louth and the major centre of the Irish church at Armagh. It was not only the jewels on the silver crosses and altar-pieces that had value to the raiders: important men like bishops and scholars could be held captive and ransomed, while lesser mortals might be hauled off and sold as slaves.

THE INTENSITY OF THE ATTACKS was now increasing, and for the first time bands of Vikings stayed in Ireland for the winter: first on Lough Neagh in 840–41, and then in Dublin, where they had already set up a defended camp, in 841–42. In the next couple of years, it seemed perfectly possible that the Norsemen would bring Ireland to its knees. The longships were unopposed on the Shannon, the country's major inland waterway, and from the river they raided the important monasteries at Clonmacnoise, Birr and Clonfert. In 845 no less a figure than Forannán, abbot of Armagh, was captured while in Munster and was taken off to the Shannon estuary.

The heads of the monasteries took to the field of battle and joined the kings in putting up a fierce resistance. In the next couple of years some significant successes were achieved, and although further fleets arrived in 849 and 851, it seemed that the main threat was now drying up. In the next two decades, the Vikings concentrated their efforts in England, and for a while Ireland could feel safe.

The men from the north didn't all just pack up and leave, however. Besides a major settlement at Dublin, there were also Viking communities at Wexford, Waterford, Youghal and Cork on the southern and south-east coasts, and even some way inland, up the River Barrow, at St Mullins in what is now Co Carlow.

Sometimes these communities lived in an uneasy peace with their neighbours; some even joined in alliances with local kings against their native Irish enemies. In other places, however,

they were not tolerated: in 866 a king of the northern Uí Néill named Áed Finnliath wiped out all the Viking bases on the north coast.

THE RETURN OF THE RAIDERS came in 914, when the arrival of a large fleet of ships at Waterford signalled the beginning of a second phase of Viking attacks in Ireland. More joined them in the following year, and they started a campaign of raids throughout Munster and Leinster.

In 917 the entire might of the Uí Néill, now united under overking Niall Glúndub, marched south into Munster to face the Vikings, but they made no real impact; and the men of Leinster, whom Niall had stirred into action, suffered a heavy defeat. In 919, in a decisive battle near Dublin, Niall was killed and many of the finest Uí Néill warriors died with him.

This left the Vikings of Dublin in a very strong position, which they were able to maintain for the next couple of decades; but they did not attempt to expand their territory. Instead, they devoted all their efforts to developing an English power base in the great Viking city of York, and establishing control over the other major Viking towns of Ireland, Limerick and Waterford. By about 950, the era of Viking raids was more or less over, and

instead the Ostmen, as they called themselves, began to make their own crucial contribution to the development of Irish society.

Whereas the Vikings in Scotland mostly settled in the country to become farmers, ending up more or less indistinguishable from the native population, those in Ireland set up towns and became traders. Their experience as merchants, as well as their skill as builders and sailors of ships, helped them become a wealthy and influential part of the Irish population. Vikings introduced the first money to Ireland and they acted as its link to the rest of Europe.

The major ports were all towns of the Ostmen, and the two largest – Dublin and Waterford – were to remain the most important urban centres in the country. It was no coincidence that when King Henry II came to Ireland in 1172, he arrived at Waterford and then made his way directly to Dublin.

Traces of the Vikings are few and far between today, but Waterford's medieval town walls run on the same course as the Ostmen's original town defences, and excavations under the Norman castle at Limerick have revealed the houses of the original Ostmen city there, which was attacked and destroyed by the Irish high king Brian Boru in the 970s.

The ancient monastery of Clonmacnoise was an easy target for Viking raids, since it stands on the banks of the River Shannon, and must have made for rich pickings. It was raided six times between 834 and 1012.

The struggle for the high kingship and changes in the church, 960 to 1166

Before the Normans…

Above: Grianán of Aileach stone fort, Co Donegal, was the royal seat from the 400s to the 1100s of a branch of the O'Neill kings, who were one of the major dynasties of early Christian Ireland and continued to be a major force right into medieval times. The fort is said to have finally been destroyed by Muirchertach O'Brien, King of Munster, in 1101.

HOWEVER EFFECTIVE THEY WERE at trading overseas and setting up towns on the coast, the Vikings were never much more than just another group of armed men taking part in the continuous struggle for power – sometimes on a purely local scale, sometimes on a much broader one – that went on between the rulers and peoples of the various regions of Ireland.

In later times it would be the Norman-descended Earls of Desmond, Ormond and Kildare who competed for influence; but in the two centuries before the Normans arrived, the major players were whichever of the regional dynasties could come to the fore in each of the provinces of Ulster, Connacht, Munster and Leinster. The prize was the right to be considered High King of Ireland – by your own people, at least. The earliest of the high kings of this period, and one of the greatest of all, was Brian Boru, who in 976 succeeded as king of the Dál Cais.

From roughly the mid-600s, the Eóganacht had ruled Munster, the south-western province of Ireland, from their base at Cashel. In the early 900s, however, their dominance was overthrown by the Dál Cais of north Munster, whose territory was positioned so as to give them a stranglehold on the River Shannon, which the arrival of the Vikings had made into an even more important thoroughfare.

One of Brian Boru's first acts when he succeeded his assassinated brother as king of the Dál Cais in 976 was to take revenge on his brother's murderers. Among them was Ímar, king of the Viking town of Limerick; Brian destroyed the town and pursued the Ostman king and his sons to Scattery Island, where they took refuge in the the monastery. There, he killed them in defiance of their traditional right to sanctuary. Within the space of three years, he had taken control of, first, the area around

32

Limerick, and then the rest of Munster. Next, allying himself with the Ostmen of Waterford, whose fleets he would need, he pushed east into Leinster and north into Connacht, where he came into conflict with the dynasty that had dominated Ireland, the Uí Néill (O'Neills).

IN THE PAST, THE UI NÉILL had been a loose aggregate of different branches all competing with each other for dominance in the north west and the north midlands. Between 940 and 960, however, a series of power-struggles had taken place to determine who would emerge as the leader of a united Uí Néill kingdom. Ruthlessness was the decisive quality that earned victory for Domnal ua Néill, overking of the Uí Néill from 956 to 980: he was from the northern branch, and imposed his will on the southern Uí Néill by setting up a permanent garrison in their Meath homelands.

The man who succeeded him, however, was from the southern Uí Néill, and would be the last of the old-style Uí Néill kings of Tara. King Mael Sechnaill II now made strenuous attempts to stop Brian Boru's expansion, but in 997 he was finally forced to accept that this would not be possible, and the two kings met at Clonfert in Galway, where St Brendan was buried, to divide Ireland between them.

One of Brian's gains was the right to rule Leinster and Dublin, and this he now set about making a reality. Towards the end of 999 the men of Leinster and Dublin rose against him, but he defeated their forces in battle and took the King of Leinster prisoner. That winter, Brian devastated the city of Dublin, eventually obliging its Ostman king, Sitric Silkenbeard, to surrender to him. Thereafter, the Dubliners were important allies as Brian steadily worked to bring the whole of Ireland under his sway. In 1005 he visited Armagh, formally recognised it as the foremost ecclesiastical community in Ireland, donated an offering of 20 ounces of gold, and had himself described in the annals as Emperor of Ireland. By 1011, this title was more or less a reality: Brian Boru had not only broken the dominance of the Uí Néill, but had also become the first actual High King of Ireland.

Perhaps inevitably, however, Brian's reign over all Ireland did not last for long. In 1012 there was already growing disquiet among the men of Leinster, and the Dubliners were never easy with his rule. In the early autumn of 1013, Brian sent his son on a campaign against Leinster which devastated lands as far north as Glendalough in the Wicklow mountains. Then Brian joined his son at Kilmainham, just outside Dublin, and from September to Christmas they attempted to blockade the city. The reaction of the Ostmen was to send to the Isle of Man and the Western Isles of Scotland for support, and they raised a large Viking army.

The combined force of Leinstermen and Vikings fought a bloody battle against Brian at Clontarf, near Dublin, on Good Friday 1014. Although his side finally won, Brian was killed. The battle lived long in legend, with the defeated

Below: The Rock of Cashel was where Brian Boru was crowned as King of Munster. He went on to be recognised as the high king of Ireland.

Ostmen as well as the victorious Irish, and has been credited with being the final, decisive Irish victory over the Vikings – but in fact its significance was rather different. It was proof that no king, however great, would find it easy to turn the kingship of the whole of Ireland into a concrete reality.

THE POWER VACUUM created by Brian Boru's death was filled immediately (and inevitably) by Mael Sechnaill II of the Uí Néill, who claimed to be high king up until his death in 1022. However, in reality, the political situation in Ireland was never again likely to make it possible for one king to rule the whole island.

Instead, there was a gradual process by which more power became concentrated in the hands of the dominant kings in each region, but none of those kings found it easy to impose himself on other parts of Ireland. Struggles continued to ebb and flow across the country in the 11th century, but they were too numerous to go into in detail, and were never conclusive.

Between 1086 and 1114, however, most of Ireland was dominated by Muirchertach O'Brien, King of Munster, who played on an international stage, having dealings with the Anglo-Normans and the King of Norway. Perhaps his most famous act was giving the ancient royal capital of Cashel to the church in 1101, as the seat for an archbishop – a generous gesture, certainly, but also one which deprived his Munster rivals of their ancient royal seat.

Muirchertach O'Brien was always held in check, however, by Domnall Mac Lochlainn, king of the Uí Néill, and he was finally brought down by the most forceful ruler of the period, Turlough O'Connor, King of Connacht from 1106 to 1156.

Turlough O'Connor was astute enough to fortify his native Connacht in modern style by building a ring of fortresses, sometimes referred to as 'castles' in the annals of the time, and building bridges over the Shannon at strategic points, as well as keeping a large army and navy at the ready. Between 1115 and 1131 he destroyed the power of Munster, and then he too tried to make himself King of Ireland.

Following Turlough's death in 1156, the balance of power swung away from his successor Rory O'Connor, and instead the Uí Néill became dominant once again, this time in the person of Muirchertach Mac Lochlainn. He quickly realised that the best way to dominate Ireland would be to gain control over the city of Dublin, and in 1166 he joined forces with the King of Leinster, Dermot MacMurrough, in an unsuccessful attempt to take Dublin.

The consequences were disastrous not just for the Uí Néill king, who was overthrown, but also for Dermot MacMurrough, who was ousted by the men of Dublin with the help of the O'Connors. MacMurrough fled over the sea to England, where he appealed to the king for help and thereby set in motion a train of events that would prove to be fatal for the aspirations of all the Irish kings. Of which, more later.

DESPITE THE CONSTANT WARFARE between the rival royal dynasties – the O'Briens of Munster, the O'Connors of Connacht, the Uí Néill – and all the distractions it brought with it, the 11th and 12th centuries were a time when Ireland grew closer to Europe, and nowhere was this more evident than in the affairs of the church.

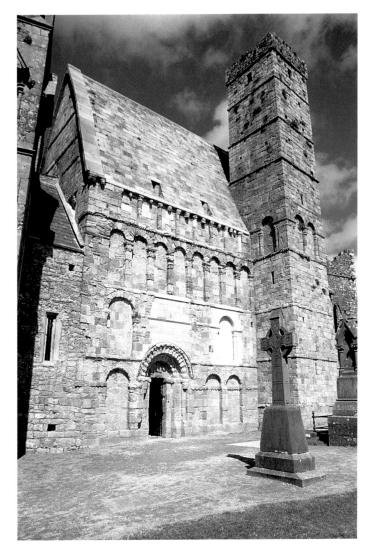

Below: Cormac's Chapel at Cashel was the inspiration for the Irish Romanesque style of architecture in which so many small churches were built all across Ireland throughout the 1100s. It is concrete (well, stone) evidence of the way contact with Europe was changing native Irish ideas long before the Normans arrived.

Irish kings were by no means strangers to Europe, or to the influence of the Roman church. Brian Boru's son Donnchad died while on a pilgrimage to Rome in 1064, and the Viking king of Dublin, Sitric, journeyed to the holy city as early as 1028. However, ecclesiastical links with England were of more importance than direct contact with Rome.

Also in 1028, and under Sitric's patronage, the first ever bishop of Dublin was consecrated, and the ceremony took place at Canterbury in England. Links between the Ostmen in south-east Ireland and the English kingdom of Mercia were strong, especially through the port of Bristol, and through this connection Canterbury kept up its influence over Dublin. Potential future bishops of Dublin were sent to Canterbury for their training as monks, and each new bishop was consecrated at Canterbury. In 1096 the first bishop of Waterford was consecrated, and again it was Archbishop Anselm of Canterbury who performed the ceremony.

Not all the Irish churches were happy to go along with the gradual acceptance of the dominance of Canterbury, however. In 1121, as a new bishop of Dublin, Gregory, readied himself for consecration, there was talk of a jealous rivalry with Armagh. In 1152 the same

Gregory became the first Archbishop of Dublin, making the Irish church directly responsible to the Pope and ending Canterbury's influence.

In church architecture, the Irish Romanesque style that grew so popular in the 1100s also shows how European ideas were spreading throughout the country long before the arrival of the Anglo-Normans. The earliest example of the style is thought to be Cormac MacCarthy's Chapel at Cashel, built between 1127 and 1134, but the influence of the style is everywhere. The smallest and oldest ruined churches you come across in Ireland are built in this simple but attractively ornamented style, and most of them date from the mid-1100s.

The other significant arrival from Europe, which again predates the Normans, is the springing up of a series of abbeys. By far the most important proved to be the Cistercian abbey at Old Mellifont, not far to the north of Dublin, established in 1142 thanks to the influence of an Irish monk of the old school called Malachy, who had travelled widely in Europe. He had set up at least 20 Augustinian monasteries by the time of his death in 1148, by which time Mellifont had also produced daughter houses at Boyle, Bective, Baltinglass, Monasteranenagh and Suir.

Though it doesn't look it, because it was given a defensive aspect in the 1400s, Bective Abbey is one of the earliest monastic foundations in Ireland, established as an offshoot of Mellifont Abbey in the years before the Normans came to Ireland.

Henry II tries to control the ambitions of his barons, 1169 to 1175

Anglo-Norman arrival

Above: The Anglo-Normans who first arrived in Ireland built motte-and-bailey castles to secure their territories, just as the Normans had on first arriving in England a hundred years before. The mound was topped with a wooden tower. This example is at Kilfinnane in Co Limerick

THE NORMAN INVASION of England in 1066 had been sudden and decisive, turning on the events of a single day. At the Battle of Hastings, Duke William of Normandy's men not only triumphed over King Harold, but also in the process killed many of the lords who owned the estates of England. This made it easy for the Normans to replace the English as landowners; and they then imposed their own ideas about the rights and duties attached to the ownership of land.

It was a century later before the Normans came to Ireland, and the circumstances of their arrival were very different. This was not a carefully planned full-scale invasion, but an expedition by a mere handful of Anglo-Norman (or, since they were mostly from South Wales, perhaps they should be called Cambro-Norman) barons who went on the pretext of helping an

Irish nobleman regain his rightful place, but who in truth were motivated mainly by the chance to gain lands and income if their adventure was a success.

In Bristol the exiled King of Leinster, Dermot MacMurrough, was befriended by Robert Fitz Harding, who may have been instrumental in securing the written permission of King Henry II for 'any person from within our wide domains' to lend assistance on a campaign to restore Dermot. There was a good response from the barons of South Wales, and Dermot ended up making an agreement with Earl Richard Fitz Gilbert of Strigoil, who would be known to posterity as Strongbow. Their arrangement was simple: in return for helping restore Dermot to his rightful place, Earl Richard would marry Dermot's daughter, Eva, and become heir to all his lands. With the chance of carving out for themselves a patch of any land belonging to Dermot's rivals, there were plenty of volunteers to go along and help.

A small group led by the Flemish Lord of Roche went to Leinster with Dermot in 1167, but the first band of armed adventurers arrived in May 1169, when Robert fitz Stephen landed near the mouth of Bannow Bay with 300 men. They met up with Dermot and attacked the town of Wexford, which soon surrendered.

Before long, Rory O'Connor acknowledged Dermot's control of southern Leinster. The forces available to Dermot were weakened when Maurice of Prendergast took his men to serve as mercenaries for the king of Ossory, but then were bolstered by the arrival of Maurice fitz Gerald with a further 140 men. They undertook a brief campaign in the area around Dublin.

In 1170, however, the main influx of troops from England and Wales began. An advance party of ten knights and 70 archers led by Raymond le Gros landed at Baginbun, where they built earthwork fortifications. They were attacked by a far larger force from Waterford, but managed to fight them off after stampeding a herd of cattle towards the attackers. In August, Earl Richard himself finally arrived, at the head of an army of as many as 2,000 men.

Before long, this massive army had taken the walled Viking city of Waterford, where the marriage of Earl Richard and Eva took place. They then turned their attentions to Dublin, which they captured and made their base.

In April 1171 Dermot died, and Earl Richard was left as the principal claimant to Leinster. He fended off an attack on Dublin by Asgall, former king of the city, and then an assault by Rory O'Connor. Finally, he and his men were ready to begin a campaign of expansion into Meath. At that point, however, another factor suddenly came into play.

IRELAND WAS A PRIZE that had tempted the Norman kings of England in the past. Indeed, in 1155 Henry II had gone so far as to send an envoy to Pope Adrian IV (who conveniently was English) seeking the right to be recognised as ruler of Ireland. The Pope, who was considered to have dominion over all the islands of the sea, granted the right to rule Ireland to the English king and his heirs, and sent a gold ring set with a large emerald as a token of his permission. Perhaps that's why Ireland is known as the Emerald Isle.

Henry had not previously felt the need to actually impose his rule on Ireland, but now he began to be alarmed at the way Strongbow was carving out his own personal kingdom there.

Belatedly, he made it clear that the venture no longer had royal support. Earl Richard took this uncomfortable position very seriously: first he sent Raymond le Gros with reassurances, and then he travelled to Gloucester to meet the king in person, offering to hold Leinster only as a fief with royal consent.

Throughout 1171 preparations were made all across England, gathering materials and men for a full-scale expedition to Ireland. A sum of £1,900 was raised by special taxation to pay for the campaign. In October 1171 Henry landed at Waterford with an army so large that there was no question of any opposition. There he granted Leinster to Earl Richard, in return for fealty and the service of 100 knights, though the king kept the port towns of Dublin, Waterford and Wexford for himself.

King Henry's march to Dublin then turned into a triumphal progress rather than a military campaign, with all the Anglo-Norman and Irish lords turning up to pledge their loyalty to the king, offer hostages, and agree to whatever terms he decided to impose. Irish kings from Cork, Desmond, Thomond, Bréifne, Oriel and Ulidia all submitted to Henry, as did the MacMurroughs, who had lost their lands in Leinster to Earl Richard.

In Dublin, Henry granted the city by charter to the men of Bristol, giving it all the same rights that the port of Bristol already possessed. This was good news for Dubliners, whose futures looked considerably brighter as a result. He also established garrisons in the ports of Cork and Limerick. The king's most significant decision, however, was to put an end to any hopes that Strongbow had of expansion into Meath by setting up Hugh de Lacy with a lordship there.

With plenty of business requiring his attention elsewhere, Henry left Ireland in April 1172, and both Strongbow and de Lacy turned their attentions to imposing their newly granted lordships on their Irish subjects. Not until 1175 did they have their lands under control. In the same year, Henry came to an arrangement with Rory O'Connor, still effectively high king of all the non-Norman parts of Ireland: O'Connor accepted Henry as his overlord, and in return Henry acknowledged O'Connor's right to lay down the law in all the territory he controlled. For the Anglo-Norman lords, however, Henry's intervention had determined that English law would now apply.

Inevitably, things soon got complicated, with the expansionist aspirations of the Anglo-Norman barons and the unwillingness of the Irish to accept their presence acting as the

Cong Abbey, Co Mayo, was founded by the last high king of Ireland, Rory O'Connor, who retired there in 1183.

Affreca, daughter of the King of Man, which gave him strong links with the Viking-descended lords of the Western Isles of Scotland, and he proved a valuable ally for Aedh O'Neill, the strongest of the Irish leaders in the north.

In the meantime, the political situation in the rest of Ireland was slowly changing. King Henry had decided that it would be a good idea to give his youngest son, Prince John, a challenging role to keep him occupied, and in May 1177 he officially transferred all his rights in Ireland to the prince.

At the same time, Henry decided it would be a good idea to grant away the O'Brien lands in Desmond and Thomond to English noblemen, with the idea of keeping both sides usefully occupied. Desmond (which comprised large parts of Cork, Kerry and Limerick) was given to Robert fitz Stephen and Miles Cogan, heroes of Strongbow's victories in the south-east, while Thomond (the land west of the Shannon from Limerick) was granted to Philip de Braose. Unfortunately for them, the English lords could make no headway at all against the Irishmen who already possessed the territories.

In 1183 Rory O'Connor, the last high king of Ireland, retired to the abbey he had founded at Cong in Co Mayo, and King Henry took the cue to ask the Pope to have Prince John crowned as King of Ireland. For a while, there was a possibility that there would be two Plantagenet kingdoms in the British Isles, but the idea was presumably not encouraged by the Pope, and slowly died out again.

By this time, relations with the native Irish lords were becoming fairly strained. It was widely felt that by granting away the kingdoms of Meath, Cork and Limerick the king had broken the terms of his original agreement with Rory O'Connor. The treatment that the former ruling family of Meath received at the hands of de Lacy was perhaps no worse than they might have expected from an Irish conqueror, but it was still not easy to swallow. To emphasise the fall of their O'Melaghlin dynasty, de Lacy kept their royal seat of Dun na Sciath in his own hands, and the family was pushed out to the small barony of Clonlanon on the western fringes of the territory. Other small dynasties from around the edges of Meath survived, but all the families from central Meath disappeared.

Not all Irish lords were pushed out: in Leinster, Earl Richard's brother-in-law Donal continued to occupy the royal residence at Liamhain. He was treated as an Anglo-Norman baron, and his descendants were known by the family name of FitzDermot. This is is the only known instance of such respectful treatment, however.

main catalysts for the events which followed. The first difficulties occurred in the west, where the O'Brien descendant of the kings of Munster succeeded in destroying Limerick, so that its garrison could not be put in place.

In 1176 Strongbow died, leaving heirs who were not yet of age. The king sent over William fitz Audelin from England, to control Leinster while the Earl's son was still a minor, and one of the people William brought with him was a knight from Somerset called John de Courcy, whom the chronicler Gerald of Wales praised highly, both for his gentle character and for his skills as a commander.

Within a few months of arriving in Dublin, de Courcy had gathered together a group of 22 knights and 300 soldiers all of whom were discontented with the opportunities available to them in Ireland, and had led them off on an ambitious expedition to conquer Ulidia, on the north-east coast, in what is now County Down in Northern Ireland.

By January 1177, de Courcy had managed to take the principal stronghold of the Ulidian ruler Rory Mac Dunlevy at Downpatrick, and had a stranglehold on Ulidia. He was clearly having a tough time holding on to his conquests, however, since before long he was constructing a series of castles: at Carlingford, Dundrum, Carrickfergus and Coleraine. Eventually he also turned his attention to the small neighbouring kingdom of Argialla (or Oriel), but he was not as successful there.

The trouble John de Courcy had was that he did not have the clear permission of the king in pursuing his campaign in the north, and eventually his adventure would be brought to a sudden conclusion. However, for 27 years he prospered, maintaining what in effect was his own personal kingdom in Ulster. He married

Opposite page: the great stone keep at Trim Castle was built not long after 1176 by Hugh de Lacy, who was given the kingdom of Meath by King Henry II in 1172. The king's aim was to stop Strongbow from expanding his territories in Ireland.

Further Anglo-Norman growth and the native Irish response, 1185 to 1260

King John and expansion

PRINCE JOHN OF IRELAND was sent to Ireland by his father in 1185, and he did not make an auspicious start. It is said that Irish courtiers who came to meet him at Waterford had their amusing beards tugged by John's (no doubt clean-shaven) companions. Following this flagrant act of disrespect, none of the provincial kings sent any submissions to John.

However peculiar his attitude, though, John was a good administrator, and he efficiently put in place a framework of royal government. He also continued his father's policy of limited Anglo-Norman expansion in the west, granting parts of the O'Brien kingdom in the fertile farming country around what is now Tipperary to Theobald Walter, Philip of Worcester and William de Burgh. He also appointed Walter as the first hereditary Butler of Ireland: both the Butler and de Burgh dynasties would become major players in medieval Ireland.

Hugh de Lacy, Lord of Meath, was assassinated by an Irish subject in 1186, and for a long time Meath joined Leinster in being administered by 'men who spent all their time in pursuit of wealth', as Gerald of Wales put it. In 1194, however, Hugh's son Walter finally came of age, and in the same year, William Marshal arrived from England to marry Strongbow's daughter, Isabelle de Clare, and take up the lordship of Leinster.

The economic development of Leinster and Meath was now greatly boosted by the full-time presence of their lords. At the same time, the coastal plain to the north of Drogheda, by now known as Louth or Uriel, was also extensively settled. Tenants were set up with farms; towns were established at which farm produce could be marketed. Inevitably the greater lords had the best choice of land, and so it is no surprise to find that the towns they set up were more likely to thrive and survive into modern times: Kilkenny, Trim and New Ross are all good examples of towns established in this period.

In 1199 John's brother Richard I died and John succeeded him as King of England. By the early 1200s, he had grown uncomfortable with the still-expanding power of John de Courcy in the north, and in 1204 he sent William de Lacy of Meath's younger brother Hugh (known as Hugh de Lacy the younger) on an expedition against de Courcy. Hugh's mission was a great success: he besieged and captured all the castles of Ulster, defeated de Courcy, and threw him into prison. The following year, the king made Hugh palatine earl of Ulster, possessing all the lands that de Courcy had held on the day he was captured.

In 1209, however, an event occurred that almost overturned the fortunes of all the great Anglo-Norman lords. King John's former favourite William de Braose quarrelled with the king and then fled to Ireland, where he was sheltered by William Marshal and the de Lacys, against the orders of the king's justiciar, who was the representative of royal law in Ireland.

In 1210 King John came to Ireland in person at the head of a large army. William Marshal managed to make peace with the king more or less without consequence, but the lordship of Meath and the earldom of Ulster were both declared forfeit to the crown, along with the honour of Limerick, which in name at least was in the possession of de Braose.

Right: Boyle Abbey, in the modern Co Roscommon, was built by the Cistercians in native Irish territory in the early 1200s, at a time when there were relatively peaceful relations with the newcomers. This happy situation did not last for long, however…

THESE OCCASIONAL TURBULENT EPISODES APART, life was quiet in the early 1200s, thanks in no small part to the fact that many of the Irish kings who had by now become used to the *status quo* enjoyed long and settled reigns.

Cathal Croibhdhearg O'Connor ruled Connacht until 1224; Aodh Méith O'Neill was king in Tír Eoghain in the north until 1230; Donough Cairbreach O'Brien ruled Thomond, or north Munster, until 1242; while in south Munster, or Desmond, Dermot MacCarthy was succeeded in 1229 by his brother Cormac Fionn, who ruled until 1247. All these kings paid rent or tribute for their lands to the English king, and only went to war to defend themselves.

One result of this was that there was a period of relative prosperity, in which the setting up and building of abbeys flourished – and not just amongst the Normans, where there was a strong tradition of founding abbeys, but also in the Irish territories, as at Boyle in Roscommon, where the beautiful church of the Cistercian abbey was started in about 1180, sacked by William de Burgh in 1202 and finally completed by about 1220.

However, after King John's death, the kingdom of England was put in the hands of a regent, since the new king Henry III was still just a boy. This regent just happened to be Hubert de Burgh, brother of William de Burgh. In 1226, following the death of its king, the whole kingdom of Connacht was declared forfeit to the crown, on the grounds that the Irish kings did not have the right to name their own heirs. Instead, Connacht was granted to William's son, Richard de Burgh.

This was the cue for a swift Anglo-Norman expansion into Connacht, followed by a long struggle to consolidate the gains. The dust settled in 1235 with Richard de Burgh holding most of Connacht. Meanwhile, the son of former king Cathal Croibhdhearg O'Connor, whose name was Feidhlim, became a tenant-in-chief of the English king in a small territory around Athlone, paying a rent of £400 a year, though he still called himself King of Connacht.

The other great expansionists of the period were the Fitzgeralds. One branch of the family, based at Shanid in Limerick (where there is still a castle, though it's in poor condition), acquired lands in Waterford and north Kerry, and thereby laid the foundations of the Desmond earldom which would become so powerful in later years. More important, though, was Maurice Fitzgerald, baron of Offaly, who served as royal justiciar between 1232 and 1245. He used his time in office to encourage the territorial ambition of his fellow nobles, and he

himself acquired most of what is now Sligo, as well as lands in Mayo and Galway, before claiming the kingdom of Fermanagh, building a castle at Belleek in 1252. On his death in 1257, however, both his castle at Belleek and his town at Sligo were destroyed by Godfrey O'Donnell, king of Tír Conaill.

By this time, a brief but spectacular period of Irish resistance was taking shape. In 1258 Aodh O'Connor, son of the dispossessed king Feidhlim of Connacht, got together with a number of other discontented kings at Belleek to declare Brian O'Neill of Tír Eoghain as high king of Ireland. In 1260 their armies were beaten at Downpatrick by local Anglo-Norman colonists, and Brian's head was lopped off and sent to King Henry II in London. It was the last time an Irishman tried to make himself high king.

The tower-like keep of Athenry Castle is typical of the sort of defensive structure built by the Anglo-Normans following the invasion of Connacht in the 1230s.

Economic troubles and the collapse of the large lordships, 1260 to 1399

Gaelic resurgence

THE REIGN OF KING EDWARD I was a time of great centralisation and control elsewhere in his kingdom, as the king's extended campaigns to subdue Wales and Scotland show. But Edward's attitude to Ireland, for which he was first given responsibility as a prince in 1254, was different: essentially, he looked on it as a source of revenue for his campaigns elsewhere, but he was willing to leave it to its own devices.

At the same time, a consequence of the upheavals of the 1250s and 1260s was that most of the native Irish rulers now held their lands not as direct subjects of the king, but as tenants of the Anglo-Norman lords. Far from being a source of even greater strife, this acted as something of a leveller, with English lords entering into a variety of complex relationships with their Irish counterparts, through marriages, alliances and agreements of all sorts.

For example, Walter de Burgh gave the hand of his cousin Eleanor de Nangle in marriage to the O'Neill king of Tír Eoghain, cementing their family bonds; while Thomas de Clare is said to have become the blood-brother of the O'Brien king of Thomond, though this did not stop him from having the O'Brien king executed in 1277. Additionally, a tradition of godparenting led to a rash of Norman names like Henry, Ralph and Thomas among Irish nobles.

Even without resort to arms, there were still frequent changes in who possessed which lands. In 1296, bringing to an end a long feud between

Below: Ballymote Castle in Co Sligo was constructed by the 'Red Earl' of Ulster, Richard de Burgh, in 1300, after he became ruler of the whole of Connacht. It was later taken over by the Irish following a collapse in the fortunes of the de Burghs.

the FitzGeralds and the de Burghs, the former family gave lands in Sligo to Richard de Burgh, the 'Red Earl' of Ulster, in exchange for lands further south. This meant that de Burgh was now lord of the whole of Ulster and Connacht.

The western parts of the country were now increasingly defended by castles – for example, de Burgh started work on a castle at Ballymote in 1300, not long after acquiring Sligo – and provided with towns, but there was a big difference between this region and the richer lands of the south-east. Essentially, the human resources were not available to settle, farm and bring the English way of life to the west. Instead, the traditional way of life went on with very little alteration, and this way of life was actively hostile to towns and markets. The town of Athenry never expanded to fill the huge set of town walls which had been built to protect it.

Edward's campaigns drained money from the exchequer, and this continued under Edward II. This left nothing to spend on good administration, and as a result the barons were increasingly left to sort the law out for themselves. The resulting feuds and private wars devastated farmland and disrupted trade. In addition, by the time of Edward II's death in 1327, almost half the colonised land was held by absentees, who left their castles to go derelict and their land exposed to encroachment.

A major shake-up followed when Ireland was invaded by the Scots in 1315. Robert the Bruce, victorious over the English at the Battle of Bannockburn in 1314, had the idea of halting English expansionism by opening up a second 'Celtic' front, and so he sent over his son, Edward Bruce, at the head of a small army.

Landing at Larne, Co Antrim in May 1315, Edward declared himself King of Ireland and received the assistance of some of the most rebellious of the northern kings. This almost immediately ensured the failure of his mission, since none of the Anglo-Norman colonists was at all likely to have any sympathy with such obvious troublemakers. Edward then went ahead with a campaign that took him all over Ireland, until he was killed at Faughart, Co Louth in October 1318.

The only real effects of this bizarre rebellion were to devastate large quantities of agricultural land at a time when the whole of north Europe

was already gripped by famine, and to stir up all sorts of trouble for the major Anglo-Norman landholders. The Red Earl lost control of Ulster after being defeated by Bruce in 1315, and his troubles were magnified when the Irish of Connacht revolted against him; they were only brought back under control after a savage battle at Athenry in 1316, in which five Irish kings were killed.

There were more lasting effects for Irish rulers elsewhere in the country. After lending his support to Richard de Clare in stopping the southward progress of Edward Bruce in 1317, Muirchertach O'Brien found that de Clare was attempting to encroach on his territory. In a pitched battle at Dysert O'Dea in May 1318, de Clare was killed; and after his heir died in 1321 leaving no children, the de Clare lands were divided up amongst a number of absentees, leaving the O'Briens of Thomond to rule their own little corner of the world with no outside interference for many years to come. Their huge tower house at Bunratty in Co Clare, where they set themselves up in about 1500, is well worth visiting.

Many other Irish rulers found similar opportunities to re-establish themselves, and by the late 1300s the elaborate verse of the bardic

poets enjoyed a revival, as patrons sought to legitimise their claims. Meanwhile, many of the major Anglo-Norman earldoms suffered a period of upheaval that left them severely weakened. When the de Burgh heiress married Edmund Mortimer, the consequence was that the earldom of Ulster, the lordship of Connacht and the liberty of Trim in Meath all came into the possession of a single absentee owner, and eventually they all passed to the crown. The result was that Ulster, like Thomond, was now left pretty much to its own devices.

Many of the lands that had been devastated by Edward Bruce did not recover for decades. For the remainder of the century, the barons who met at the Irish parliament made constant appeals to the king, complaining of decaying defences and incompetent administration in the lands of the absentees.

A series of major expeditions was launched by both Edward III and Richard II with the idea of providing an army to impose the rule of law, and an authoritative figurehead to symbolise it. Eventually, Richard made two trips in person: one in 1394–5, at the head of an army of up to 10,000 men, and another in 1399. Each time, however, the situation simply slid again as soon as the expedition ended.

Timoleague Friary is typical of what didn't happen in the 1300s. It was built in the 1240s and was remodelled in the 1400s, when there was an explosion in the founding of Franciscan friaries – but in the 1300s scarcely any building work of note took place anywhere in Ireland.

A quiet recovery occurs with little interference from England, 1400 to 1513

An era of prosperity

IF THE 1300s HAD BEEN a time of economic decline and widespread upheaval, the following century saw something of a revival. Very little building took place at all in the 1300s, but in the 1400s little tower houses sprang up all over the country – even in the towns. These were symbolic not just of the need for landowners and merchants to defend what they owned in a time where the law was a very personal matter, but also of a generally stable political situation, and a fair degree of economic recovery.

Besides the tower houses, Ireland can also boast also another substantial architectural legacy of this period, in the form of the Franciscan friaries that popped up all over the western parts of the country in the first half of the century. Again, there must have been plenty of money around to contribute to the foundation and construction of these large and elegant establishments. The friaries occur exclusively in Irish lands primarily because the English church already had a monopoly on the territories held by the Anglo-Norman lords, and its administrators were not prepared to tolerate any challenge to the pastoral work of their parish clergy: the Observantine Franciscans were a hands-on lot who believed in playing their part in the community.

The resurgent Irish chieftains in the north enjoyed a period of wide-eyed optimism in which anything seemed possible. In 1403 a dispute over succession amongst the various branches of the O'Neills allowed Niall Garbh O'Donnell, lord of Tír Conaill, to become the dominant force in the north, and he persuaded the men of Ulster to band together against their absentee overlords. They made a series of devastating raids on Louth and Meath, and by 1423 they had forced Louth to pay a kind of protection money known as 'black rent'.

Similarly, the Irish lord of Offaly, whose daughter Niall Garbh married, waged a similar campaign against the colonists on the southern borders of Meath. In 1466 the son of this same lord of Offaly succeeded in capturing the Earl of Desmond, then one of the most powerful men in Ireland; and subsequently, the O'Brien lord of Thomond invaded Desmond and managed to extract a promise of perpetual black rent from the city of Limerick.

None of these small triumphs ever started to overflow into a widespread Irish dominance, however, partly because the Irish were never able to drop all their rivalries with one another, but mostly because the Anglo-Normans had the better land and greater resources.

One result of the Irish raids was that the area under royal administration shrank to just the counties of Louth, Meath, Dublin and Kildare. These areas were now separated from the rest of the country by building a vast earthen rampart fortified by a fence. The boundary became known as The Pale (meaning 'the fence') – as, by association, did the land inside it.

THE MAIN AND MOST LASTING change to occur in the 1400s, however, was that the greatest lords of the Anglo-Norman territories were able to make their influence even more widespread. The Earls of Desmond had been able to bring tenants in Munster under their influence; the 'White Earl' of Ormond had managed to add the royal county of Kilkenny to his own lands in Tipperary; and the Fitzgerald earls of Kildare were exerting an influence over the Irish chiefs who had lands in Meath.

The way these three earls were able to wield even more influence was by taking control of the royal system of administration and turning it to their own ends. Between 1420 and 1444, the Earl of Ormond built up his own faction among government officials and tried to pack the Anglo-Irish parliament with his own men. Then the Ormond fortunes fell for a while, after his sons took the losing side in the Wars of the Roses, and the Fitzgeralds of Desmond and Kildare enjoyed the ascendancy for a while. But after the Earl of Desmond was executed in 1468 during an attempt by Edward IV to regain control of his Irish earls, leading to a Desmond rebellion, the Earls of Kildare were left with the upper hand. Their strategic position in the lands of the Pale did them no harm, either.

In 1494 the Great Earl of Kildare was removed from his position as Lord Deputy of Ireland and replaced by a man sent from England, Sir Edward Poynings; but in 1496 the Earl had to be restored to his position, and he ruled as Lord Deputy until his death in 1513, when he was succeeded by his son.

Opposite page: the little tower house at Dysert O'Dea is typical of the many such towers that sprang up all over Ireland in the 1400s.

The crown seeks to impose English law, and plantation starts, 1513 to 1607

Henry VIII and Elizabeth

ROYAL POWER IN IRELAND continued to be in effect placed entirely in the hands of the Fitzgerald Earls of Kildare right up until 1534. However, in that year what sounds like a minor misunderstanding between Henry VIII and the latest Fitzgerald of Kildare to hold the position of Lord Deputy got blown up out of all proportion and the situation changed radically.

The Lord Deputy of the time was Thomas Lord Offaly, son of the ninth Earl of Kildare. He responded to a threat to his authority by doing something his predecessors had done several times before: he withdrew cooperation and waited to be invited back.

Unfortunately, the young and inexperienced Thomas also made the mistake of criticising Henry's recent split with the church in Rome. When Henry's new appointee as Lord Deputy, Sir William Skeffington, arrived at the head of a well-equipped army of 2,300 men, support for Thomas melted away. The eventual result was that the Fitzgerald lands were declared forfeit, and all the male members of the family except for Thomas's infant half-brother were executed.

Harsh treatment, perhaps, but Henry was very sensitive about his position, since the Reformation which had just taken place in England had no legal force in Ireland. He set about gathering an Irish parliament, and in 1536 and 1537 it passed exactly the same legislation for reforming the church that had recently been passed in England.

The problem now, though, was that the sudden removal of the Earls of Kildare had unbalanced the political scene. First the Gaelic lords of the area took up arms on the pretext of restoring the Fitzgeralds, and then they continued to raid the counties of the Pale just because it was a profitable enterprise. In the end, the only solution was to bring back the surviving Fitzgerald heir and restore at least part of his lands, at the same time replacing some of the Gaelic lords of the midlands with English army captains, with garrisons at their command, who took the revenue from the lands around their fortified bases. In this way, the dispossessed Irish lords were pushed back into the boggy land further west. However, any lord who submitted to the crown and gave up his lands could, after his loyalty had been demonstrated, have them given back to him in a system known as 'surrender and regrant'.

For the next 20 years and more, it was not at all clear exactly what royal policy in Ireland was. At times, it seemed that the English crown was determined to get the Irish lords to submit to English rule, and to bring to them the civilising influence of English laws and customs; and at other times it seemed happy to let them get on with it. The result was that sporadic interference here, there and everywhere stirred up all sorts of resistance, and made the country increasingly difficult and expensive to govern.

BY THE TIME OF QUEEN ELIZABETH, the situation was seen as a problem in search of a solution, and there were two main candidates willing to provide that solution. The first to try his scheme was Thomas, Earl of Sussex. His idea was to build on the start that had already been made with the military settlement in Gaelic lands in the midlands, and the surrender and regrant agreements that had previously been arranged. He soon became bogged down in the pursuit of Shane O'Neill, who had chosen to disregard the surrender and regrant agreement for the lordship of Tyrone. Sussex built up a huge military force to pursue O'Neill in Ulster, but the campaign proved futile, and finally Sussex was ousted after protests about the taxes he had imposed to pay for his military force.

In 1565 Sir Henry Sidney took over. His plan was to dispossess any Gaelic lord who took up arms against the crown, granting the lord's lands both to his kinsmen and to English settlers who would develop the land at their own expense and impose English law. He also intended to confiscate any Gaelic land to which there was an English claim, however old. This brought all kinds of adventurers to Ireland, some of whom raised their own private armies. The chaos that ensued provoked an insurrection amongst some of the more powerful Anglo-Irish nobles.

Since three of the most prominent members of this insurrection were brothers of Thomas, Earl of Ormond, a favourite of Queen Elizabeth, the queen made sure that all the leaders of the insurrection were pardoned – all except for James Fitz Maurice Fitzgerald, who had stated religious reasons for his involvement. James now fled abroad; Sidney was forced to abandon his schemes for colonisation of Gaelic lands.

In 1579, however, James returned to Ireland with a small military force, planning to start a rebellion against the Protestant heretic queen. Surprisingly he raised considerable support in Munster, and before long the Earl of Desmond himself had joined in. The queen sent an army of 8,000 men under Arthur Lord Grey de Wilton, and soon the rebellion was suppressed. In the aftermath, more than 4,000 English settlers were given land that had previously belonged to the Earl of Desmond and his allies.

ONE CONSEQUENCE OF the Desmond rebellion was that government officials wished to impose heavy fines on all landowners who refused to conform in religion, which would inevitably have meant many Gaelic lords being dispossessed. The queen, wary of provoking a military uprising in Ireland at a time when Spain was such a threat, withheld her approval.

It had become clear by this time that the most determined resistance to English ways would be in the O'Neill heartlands of Ulster, and no plan had yet been suggested that could solve this problem. Fortunately for them, the O'Neills themselves now made it happen.

Hugh O'Neill, who became earl of Tyrone in 1585, decided in the early 1590s to expel all the Protestant officials from Ulster, and ended up locked in a battle of wills with the Lord Deputy. Hugh raised an army, equipped it in the English style, and enjoyed a few early successes. He gained the support of discontented lords across Ireland, called for the help of all Catholics against the Protestant queen, and gained the support of King Philip III of Spain, who in 1601 sent a 4,000-strong army to his aid. Perhaps the fact that they landed at Kinsale in the far south-west wasn't ideal, but it was a welcome gesture.

Even before the arrival of the Spanish force, however, Queen Elizabeth had recognised the serious nature of the challenge and had sent an army of 20,000 men to deal with it. An English victory at Kinsale was practically a foregone conclusion, and duly followed.

With the collapse of the Irish resistance, a determined attempt to impose English law was bound to follow. It was delayed for a while, but in 1607 the Irish Earls fled the country, and the new Scottish-born king, James I, approved plans for extensive new settlements in Ulster. The so-called Plantation of Ulster had begun.

Charles Fort at Kinsale was actually only built in the 1670s, but the need for stronger defences around the important harbour at Kinsale was made obvious by the O'Neill rebellion of 1601, when a small Spanish army landed here and held out until Irish forces from the north could join up with it.

English colonisation, the Irish uprising of 1641, and the crushing response

Plantation and Cromwell

KING JAMES MADE IT CLEAR that the landowners who had taken part in the O'Neill Rebellion should no longer be tolerated; that anyone who held property that rightfully belonged to the crown should be pursued; and that the king would only give his protection to landowners who could prove their right to the land they owned. This meant that the only people who could be certain of keeping their lands were those now referred to as the 'Old English', descendants of the Anglo-Norman families. Even their position was not entirely secure, however, since the king expected them to conform in the matter of religion: though frankly this was not as important to him as loyalty.

The major impact of the religious schisms of Elizabethan times was that the officials who now ran the country had to be Protestant and were, as a result, largely English. They now forged ahead with a series of major schemes of colonisation along the lines of the one that had previously taken place in Munster following the Desmond rebellion.

Plantation schemes, as they became known, went ahead in Wexford, Leitrim, Longford, Meath and Tipperary; but the biggest push was made in the former O'Neill lands of the north, and six of the nine counties that then made up the province of Ulster were colonised. Further schemes were planned for Mayo and Connacht.

Some land was given to newcomers from England and Scotland who had no previous experience of Ireland, and these people were obliged to construct defensible buildings and settle ten British Protestant families on every 1,000 acres. More was given to native Irishmen who had a record of loyalty. Most land, however, went to men described as servitors, who had already served the government in a civil or military capacity in Ireland.

Servitors were allowed to maintain native tenants on their land, and very often did so in the early years to keep a guaranteed income coming in while they built themselves good, strong houses. Later they often displaced their Irish tenants in favour of Scottish or English people who were given long tenancies at cheap rates on condition that they improved the land. The best way to make a lot of money quickly, however, was to exploit the natural resources of their new lands, and huge profits were made from shipping timber to England and Holland.

The face of Ireland was changed forever by the new ideas brought in by the settlers, especially since certain of them were skilful at acquiring new lands. The native Irish also saw the need to bring in new ideas, however, partly because these new ideas were profitable, but also because they were keen to prove that they too could be worthy subjects. Particularly in the south east, they adopted the English language and English dress, they upheld the English laws,

Below: Donegal Castle was the seat of the O'Donnell chief of Tyrconnell, who died in Spain in 1602 following the Irish defeat at Kinsale the previous year. Later it was rebuilt by an English settler, Captain Basil Brooke, who was granted the castle in 1611.

and they built new houses or modified their old ones to conform with the latest English tastes. They paid for all this by bringing in English tenants for their lands, not least because these people were willing to pay high 'entry fines' for the right to take up a tenancy.

This increasing Anglicisation was reciprocated by a certain amount of religious tolerance on the part of the English kings. James was not keen to have his diplomatic relations with Europe soured by overzealous application of the laws against Catholicism, and Charles I went so far as to promise to free Catholic landowners from the threat of further plantation, and suspend the practice of fining landowners who did not attend Protestant church services.

PERHAPS THE BACKLASH was inevitable; perhaps it could have been avoided. But in 1641, after eight years in which governor Thomas Wentworth had screwed the maximum amount of revenue out of all parties and had made Catholics feel that more confiscations of land were on the way, a bloody and brutal uprising broke out in Ulster.

As many as 2,000 Protestant settlers were killed, and many thousands more were stripped of their possessions (and even their clothes) and driven out. The troubles spread throughout Ireland and nearly all Catholic landowners were involved to some degree, though often only under pressure from those who had nothing to lose.

The atrocities were greatly exaggerated in England and Scotland, where it was believed that a general slaughter of all the Protestants in Ireland had taken place. Charles I was in no position to take action, however, with a civil war on his hands, and no response was made until Oliver Cromwell was free to devote his attentions to Ireland in August 1649.

Cromwell came up with a three-point plan. First he would crush all military resistance; next he would remove all priests and landowners who were in any way involved with the 1641 uprising; and finally he would institute an evangelisation drive that would convert the whole of the Irish population to Protestantism.

Whatever his faults, Cromwell was primarily a brilliant military commander, and he had at his disposal a 20,000-strong army that, having had plenty of practice, was the finest fighting force in Europe at the time. The military part of the plan was therefore no trouble at all. The same pattern was repeated all across the country wherever Cromwell's army approached a town or castle. He would send a note to the defenders explaining that they could surrender and be given honourable terms, but if they resisted there would be no mercy. They always surrendered.

Catholic priests were hunted down, and the entire fabric of the church that had enjoyed such growth in the 1620s and 1630s was swept away. It was decided that all Catholic-owned lands would be confiscated, and land west of the Shannon offered in compensation only to those landowners who could show that they had played no part in the uprising. Thanks to the work of the man charged with making it happen, William Petty, Ireland now became the most accurately mapped country in Europe.

As for evangelisation, money was provided to build churches and schools, but not enough clergy could be found – especially ones who could speak Irish. Before long, the zealots gave way to more accommodating figures, and the country sank into an uneasy peace.

Monea Castle, although it has an unusual design which it owes to the Scottish origins of the man who built it, is very much a typical castle of the Plantation era in Ulster. It was taken by the Maguires in the Irish uprising of 1641.

A Catholic king fights a Protestant one in Ireland, 1660 to 1691

William of Orange

THE RESTORATION OF THE MONARCHY and the return of King Charles II in 1660 brought some respite for the Catholic population of Ireland. No longer were they subject to the intense persecution of the Cromwell era, despite an occasional fairly shocking outrage, such as the execution of Archbishop Oliver Plunkett. Quietly, Catholic priests were able to return from Europe and get to work in the community, and in these years the future of the Catholic church was secured.

King Charles restored to their lands any landowners, whether Protestant or Catholic, who had joined him in exile in France, but he was reluctant to do anything more to change the land settlements decided by Cromwell. Consequently, very little land was now in the possession of Catholics, and most of that was in the far west of the country.

For a time, Catholics felt that their fortunes were at a low ebb – their glory was in the past, and nothing but further defeat lay ahead – and their pessimism is very evident in the Gaelic poetry composed at this time. In 1685, however, their spirits were suddenly revived by the accession to the British throne of James II, who just happened to be Catholic.

Unfortunately, one man in particular was to let his enthusiasm carry him away. James now appointed a favourite of his, Richard Talbot, as Lord Lieutenant of Ireland, at the same time giving him the grand title of Duke of Tyrconnell. Richard not only set about appointing Catholics to public office, but also raised a Catholic army to be ready if the king needed it, and tried to convene a parliament in Dublin composed more or less completely of Catholic members, which could set about the task of reversing all the Cromwellian confiscations of land.

THE MAIN EFFECT OF THIS WAS to alarm the Protestants of Ireland and to provide further ammunition to all those in England, Wales and Scotland who thought that a Catholic king at this point in time was not at all a good idea. Shortly afterwards, the English throne was offered to Prince William of Orange jointly with his English wife, Mary, and their claim was validated by the fact that they brought a large army with them. King James fled to Ireland, where he knew loyal support awaited, and where he was joined by a French army.

Inevitably, William came after him. The towns of Ulster, where the Protestant merchants and landowners feared a repetition of 1641, held out for William, thus providing him with a toehold. He landed near the castle at Carrickfergus, which his French commander had already captured for him, in the early summer of 1690, and set off southwards for Dublin.

The armies of the two rival kings first met on the banks of the River Boyne in July 1690. This famous battle was by no means conclusive, but the important thing is that it did not prevent William from continuing his progress towards the south.

The Catholic forces were now on the defensive, and were obliged to defend the line of the Shannon against incursion from the east. The decisive engagements took place in 1691: at the Bridge of Athlone, where the Catholics failed to stop William crossing the Shannon; the Battle of Aughrim, where they failed to prevent his westward progress to Athenry and Galway City; and at a second siege of Limerick.

Right: Enniskillen Castle was one of the focal points for Protestant resistance to the deposed King James II which enabled William to get a foothold in Ireland in 1690.

Before long, this series of defeats prompted the capitulation of James's army and the flight from the country of most of the Catholic officers who had fought with it.

The immediate consequence was yet another confiscation of Catholic lands, followed by the passing of a series of rigid penal laws that restricted Catholics in practising their religion and rewarded them for changing faith.

At the same time, however, the battle had in many ways been won. Although Ireland now appeared to be dominated by the English and the Protestants, the people were still for the most part Catholic in faith.

IRELAND AT THE START OF THE 1700s was, for all the struggles that had rolled across its lands, still a fairly prosperous country. The survey that had been carried out by Sir William Petty at the time of the Cromwellian confiscations in 1687 had shown the population of the country to be about 1,300,000. By the standard of the time, this suggests a density of population in this small country that was the equivalent of the most developed nations in Europe.

The great majority of these people lived on farms or smallholdings and worked rearing livestock or growing crops, the poorer ones supplementing their income by working in the textile industry, weaving woollen or linen cloth. Textiles, meat and animal products made up the bulk of Ireland's exports, and most of the profits went into the pockets of the landowners.

The landowners not only held on to the wealth but also controlled politics, and some of them were members of parliament or officials of the government. To keep up their positions they needed houses at Dublin, which by now was a thriving city with a population of 50,000.

Dublin was also an important port, however, and the inland waterways connected it not just with most of central Ireland but also with parts as distant as eastern Connacht. The town of Derry did a similar job of acting as the main conduit for exports in west Ulster and north Connacht, and the ports of Cork, Waterford and even Youghal acted as an outlet for the farm produce of the rich farmlands of Munster. Towns like Limerick, Galway and Sligo were also of commercial importance, and a network of smaller towns in the inland areas contributed to a remarkably good economic infrastructure.

The great drawback, however, was that Ireland remained dependent on England for its economic well-being; and that was a situation that would not change for a very long time.

Carrickfergus Castle, where William of Orange landed with his men in 1690 to begin his campaign against the ousted King James II.

Dunluce Castle

Castles
& ancient
monuments
of Ireland

South East

Wexford, Waterford, south Tipperary, Kilkenny and Carlow

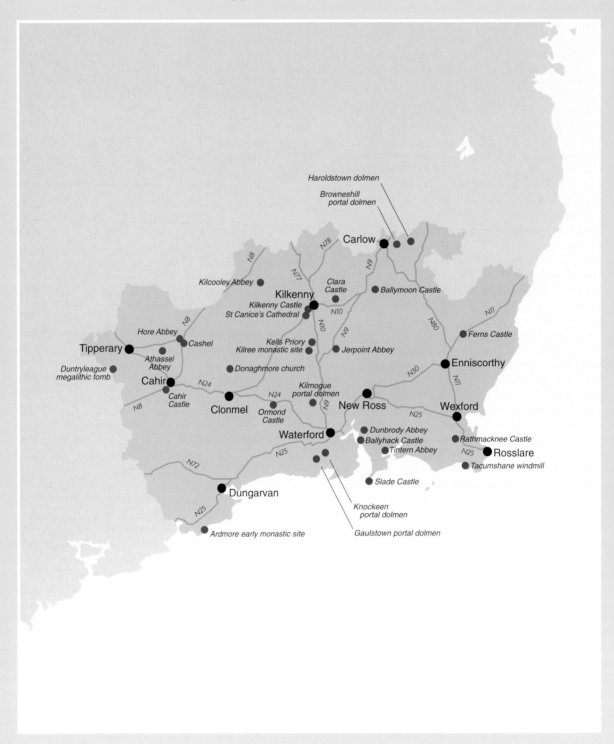

Haroldstown dolmen

Browneshill portal dolmen

Carlow

N78

N9

Kilcooley Abbey

Clara Castle

Kilkenny

Ballymoon Castle

N7

Kilkenny Castle
St Canice's Cathedral

N10

N10

Hore Abbey

N8

Cashel

Kells Priory
Kilree monastic site

N9

Jerpoint Abbey

N80

Ferns Castle

N11

Tipperary

Athassel Abbey

Donaghmore church

Kilmogue portal dolmen

N30

Enniscorthy

Duntryleague megalithic tomb

Cahir

N24

N24

N9

New Ross

Wexford

N11

Cahir Castle

Clonmel

Ormond Castle

N25

Rathmacknee Castle

N8

Waterford

Dunbrody Abbey
Ballyhack Castle
Tintern Abbey

N25

Rosslare

N72

N25

Tacumshane windmill

Slade Castle

Dungarvan

Knockeen portal dolmen

N25

Ardmore early monastic site

Gaulstown portal dolmen

The extensive remains of Athassel Abbey, stretched across a river meadow, include a gatehouse and bridge.

Athassel Abbey

Dúchas, on farmland • Free • Open access at any reasonable time

This attractive ruin stands in a peaceful rural setting, its crumbling stone buildings stretching across a meadow beside the River Suir. Hard to believe that this was once the largest abbey in Ireland, with a whole town standing outside its walls.

Founded by William FitzAdelm de Burgo in the late 1100s, not very long after the Anglo-Normans came to Ireland, and dedicated to English martyr St Edmund, the abbey was so important that its abbot was a peer in the Irish parliament. The town was burned in 1319 by Lord Maurice FitzThomas and again ten years later by Bryan O'Brien, and never recovered after the second attack. There's no trace of it to be seen now.

Although it looks forgotten, the ruin is in fact fairly well looked after, and it's easily accessible, thanks to a stone stile alongside the field gate (and presumably a sympathetic farmer). As so often in Ireland, the interior of the ruined church has been used as a burial ground in more recent times, but this is not as intrusive here as it is in some other places.

Lots of the abbey's buildings have survived, though some of them are more crumbling than might be hoped. As you approach the abbey from the road, the field in which it stands slopes away before you, offering a view over the whole complex. At the front is a broad ditch or moat, crossed by an attractive stone bridge, with the ruin of a large gatehouse

at the far side. This is the only place in Ireland you'll find such structures.

Beyond the gatehouse, the church stands at the far side of a largish compound. Passing through the elaborate west door, you can see by the size of the church and the richness of surviving details that it must have been a grand building. It had a full-sized tower over the crossing, about half of which still stands, supported by a couple of soaring arches. The arch to the south transept has been blocked in with rough stonework, showing that the tower was converted for use as a fortified house (just like *Tintern Abbey* in Co Wexford – *see page 71*). This probably happened after an attack in 1447 which destroyed the church.

The cloister is to the south of the church, and quite a decent amount of the various buildings that surround it has survived, along with a few ramshackle

Inside the ruined church. The tower seems to have been adapted for use as a castle in later days.

pieces of the cloister arcade. From the south transept of the church, you can climb the 'night stairs', down which sleepy monks would have come for services in the middle of the night and early in the morning, to the dormitory on the first floor. Whether the flagstone floor is original or was added in recent times as a roof for the buildings below isn't clear. The lavatory was at the far end of the dormitory.

Looking over the cloister from up here, you can see the church to your right and the refectory, where the monks ate all their meals, to the left. The refectory seems to be in pretty good condition, but the vaulted undercroft below it is locked up. Below the dormitory are the sacristy and chapter house, but again, these rooms are locked up. Beyond them are other vaulted rooms used as workrooms or for storage. On the opposite side of the cloister would probably have been a dormitory for lay people, the non-religious staff of the abbey, but there's not a lot of this left.

Don't leave without taking a stroll round the outside of the abbey, behind the refectory, where there are several more buildings (including the monks' lavatory), then alongside the river and past the rather attractive east end of the church.

Near Golden, Co Tipperary. About 2.4km (1.5 miles) south of Golden, in a field by the River Suir, next to the minor road to Bansha and Lagganstown (on the west side of the river). The abbey can easily be seen from the road. Access is by a stone stile beside the field gate.

Ballyhack Castle

Dúchas • £ • Open June to September daily
(closes for lunch weekdays)

This is a very nice little tower house of the mid-1400s, with lots of interesting features. It's in a picturesque setting in the little harbour village of Ballyhack, near the landing of the Passage East ferry.

If you want to, you can take a guided tour which will point out lots of details that you might not otherwise have noticed. Most of these details are typical of an Irish tower house of this age and size. They

Ballyhack Castle is an appealing little tower house, thought to have been built by the Knights Hospitaller.

include the box machicolation high above the door, the murder hole in the ceiling of the passage just inside the door, and the doughnut-like pierced stone fixtures which acted as primitive hinges for the doors.

Upstairs on the first floor is the main reception room, while the second-floor room has a small chamber and a garderobe toilet opening off it. The vaulted roof shows impressions of the wattle frames used to support the rubble-and-mortar mix during construction. The third floor is now

open to the sky. Again, smaller chambers open off the side, including a chapel and the opening to a windowless prison cell.

Ballyhack probably belonged to the Knights Hospitaller, whose self-imposed responsibilities included safeguarding major routes and offering medical care. They would have guarded the ferry crossing and policed the estuary, which gave access to the country's major port at Waterford.

In Ballyhack, Co Wexford, near the harbour.

Ballymoon Castle

Dúchas, on private land • Free • Open access at any reasonable time

A peculiar castle of unusual design, in fairly good condition considering its age (it dates from around 1300) and that it may never have been finished. Its plain design means it's not vastly interesting to explore, but it certainly deserves a look if you're in the area. It's just standing there in a field, so it's easy enough to get to.

The castle basically consists of a big, almost square, walled enclosure, and the unusual thing about it is that it has no proper towers. It does have projecting sections which might have helped defenders protect the walls from attack – though the fact that they also contain garderobe toilets suggests that they may simply have been latrine towers.

On the west – the nearest side as you approach the castle – is a modest gate which was the main entrance. Inside the enclosure you can see traces of buildings which ran along each side of the courtyard, with just a narrow gap at the entrance. These were two-storey ranges, with cellars below; in the inner face of the enclosing wall you can see fireplaces and openings leading to the garderobes. To the right, on the south side, is the largest of the projections in the wall, which almost

qualifies as a tower, with what appears to be a kind of postern gate below (look out for the groove for a portcullis to run in) and rooms above, from where steps lead to a wall-walk.

Local tradition has it that the castle was never lived in, but nothing concrete is known about its history. It is thought to

Ballymoon is a most unusual enclosure castle of the early 1300s, completely lacking corner towers.

have been built between 1290 and 1310 by the Bigods, a powerful Norman family from Norfolk in England, or the Carews.

Near Bagenalstown, Co Carlow (referred to by its Irish name of Muine Bheag in some maps). In a field by the R724 east of the town; access to the field is across a small timber footbridge.

See also... Ardmore early monastic site

Dúchas, free, open access at any reasonable time. In Ardmore, Co Waterford, signposted for pedestrians.

A fine round tower, a small ruined church which was actually a cathedral, and a tiny, primitive stone chapel are the surviving parts of an early monastery that stands on a hill overlooking the seaside village of Ardmore, which has an excellent sandy beach. As usual, the former monastery enclosure is now in use as a burial ground.

The 29m (94ft) round tower dates to the 1100s, and was one of the last and most elegant to be built. The tiny chapel is four centuries older: it was a shrine to St Declan, and the saint may have been buried inside. The cathedral is from around 1200, and the feature that makes it worth seeing is a series of biblical scenes in the arcades on the outside of the west wall. The carvings are weathered, but one scene you might recognise is the Adoration of the Magi.

Inside the church two ogham stones are displayed. The shorter inscription reads simply, 'Beloved'.

Cahir Castle

*Dúchas • ££ • Open daily all year round
(shorter hours in winter)*

This is the most complete medieval castle
in Ireland, and probably the most
enjoyable to visit. Its picturesque setting
beside the River Suir, with the option of
taking a gentle stroll along the riverbank
to the ornate early 19th century folly
known as the *Swiss Cottage* (*see page 81*)
makes the little town of Cahir an ideal
destination for a pleasant day out.

The castle is an unusual one, clearly too
large to have been a mere tower house,
and yet too small to have been a serious
military base on the pattern of a grand
Norman fortress like the one at *Trim* in
Co Meath (*see page 160*). In fact, it owes
its form to a series of modifications over
the years, and its relative completeness to
a restoration in the 1840s.

Although it's not immediately obvious,
the castle stands on a rocky island: the
weed-filled 'moat' between the castle and
the car park is actually a channel of the
river. There was almost certainly a
fortification on the island before the
Anglo-Normans came, because the Irish

name of the place – in full, *Cathair Dún
Iascaigh* – is translated as 'the stone fort
of the fortress of the fishery'.

In the decades after the Anglo-Norman
invasion of 1169, English control was
gradually imposed across most of
Tipperary, and in 1192 the area around
Cahir was granted to Philip of Worcester.
It is thought that he first set up his
headquarters at the motte-and-bailey
castle of *Knockgraffon*, on high ground
not far from here (*see page 79*), but work
soon started on the new stone castle at
Cahir, and continued under Philip's
nephew and heir, William.

The first castle here was a small version
of the classic castle design of the time,
consisting of a circuit of walls with a
large, powerful gatehouse-tower which
contained all the main high-status
accommodation. Inside the courtyard,
several buildings were set against the
walls, the most important one being a hall
to the left of the gatehouse.

This basic layout has been retained
throughout the castle's many
modifications in later years. The main

gatehouse-tower was adapted into a sort of
keep, with the gate passage that previously
went right through the middle of it
blocked up. You can still see where it was,
though, in the stonework on the outside of
the tower. In the early 1500s a new gate
was built to the right, closed by a
portcullis, the winching mechanism of
which has recently been restored.

You can see the portcullis mechanism
up close if you go up to the room on the
first floor of the keep, where a grand
fireplace and the large windows (later
additions) indicate that this was the main
reception room, designed to impress. The
narrow passage in the far corner of the
room originally led to a garderobe toilet,
but now gives access to the portcullis
winch and then to the small round tower
in the corner. The basement of this tower
can only be reached by a trapdoor and
ladder: lift the trapdoor and take a look,
but you can't go down.

Another major modification to the castle
was the addition of a tower behind the hall
at the north-west corner, probably in the
mid-1500s. It was intended to provide

Cahir Castle's high stone walls, developed and adapted over many centuries, give it a formidable appearance.

Left: The gatehouse-tower, which was the main residence of the original castle, built in the 1200s, was later adapted to become a kind of keep. The gateway through the middle was blocked up.

Above: An outer ward was added at a much later date, with a new gate leading to a small middle ward.

Right: The later entrance to the inner courtyard of the castle is through a gate defended by a portcullis into this small enclosed area, where attackers would have been very exposed.

better reception rooms for important visitors, and the room on the first floor has an elegant window seat as well as a large fireplace and a garderobe toilet; but it was also meant as a defensive gun-position, and the ground-floor room has large 'splays' in which cannon were positioned, probably mounted on wooden sledges.

The course of the north wall was also modified when the north-west tower was built, and a tower was added at the north-east corner. To the left of this, there was a small gate with a machicolation above; this was rebuilt in the early 1600s, when a passage was cut in the rock under the wall, leading to a well in the basement of another small tower.

This is the most fun part of the castle to explore. A narrow stair emerges on top of the well tower, outside the walls, with a good view of the river. But be very careful as you go down the last set of steps on your way back out, or you are almost certain to bang your head on the unyielding stone of the passage's low roof.

In Cahir (also spelt 'Caher'), Co Tipperary.

The later history of Cahir, and the Victorian rebuilding of the castle

A written account has survived, complete with drawings made at the time, of an important siege that took place at Cahir Castle in 1599. The castle's owner, Thomas Butler, had joined the rebellion of Hugh O'Neill, lord of Tyrone, against the English crown. Elizabeth's favourite, the Earl of Essex, was sent with an 18,000-strong army to defeat Tyrone, but he decided to start by capturing the castles of Athy and Cahir.

The siege here lasted three days before the wall was breached by artillery fire and the castle fell with the loss of 80 defenders. Thomas, Lord of Cahir, was pardoned in 1601. Incidentally, on your way out, look out for a cannon-ball embedded in the wall of the north-east tower, near a window. It's been there ever since the siege, 400 years ago.

The castle remained the property of the Butlers of Cahir throughout the 1600s and into the 1700s, but by the middle of the 18th century they were living at a house called Reihill and the castle was slowly decaying. In 1788 the

principal line of the family died out, and the estates went to a distant cousin, Richard Butler, who built a new mansion in Cahir (now a hotel) and the ornate Swiss Cottage just up the river. His son, Richard, 13th Baron Cahir and 2nd Earl of Glengall, rebuilt most of the town with the help of his architect, William Tyndall, who also restored the castle between 1840 and 1846.

The Earl seems to have realised at some point that living in the castle again was not a terribly realistic aim, and that he should attempt to restore it for posterity instead. A note he wrote in 1843 reads: 'There are so many inconveniences in the castle for making it a residence that after long consideration I doubt the prudence of doing so. The Castle of Cahir should always be preserved as the ancient memorial of the family.'

The only building that has a significantly Victorian Gothic revival feel to it is the hall, with its elegant timber roof, which would probably have been difficult to restore accurately in any case. This was the last building to still be in use (as a church) in 1964, when the castle was taken into state care.

Cashel

Dúchas • £££ • Open daily all year round

There's an impressive collection of church buildings on top of the dramatic outcrop of the Rock of Cashel.

Geology and architecture have conspired here to create one of the most dramatic-looking sites in Ireland. The shell of a vast cathedral church stands on a sheer-sided outcrop of rock, topped off by a slender, pointed round tower. But it has to be said that the Rock of Cashel isn't quite as remarkable as it appears in photographs, which somehow cut out the town that rambles untidily up to its foot.

The Rock was a fortified stronghold of the kings of Munster from at least the 300s AD, if not before, and would probably have had some ecclesiastical buildings as well as royal residences. St Patrick is said to have come here and converted Aenghus, the king of the time. He also made Cashel a bishopric. In 1101 the Rock was given over to the church by King Muircheartach O'Brien. After that the buildings you see today were put up.

Those buildings are, in roughly the order they were built: a small stone church of the early 1100s, known as Cormac MacCarthy's chapel after the king who had it built; a round tower of the same age; a large cathedral, built in the mid-1200s on the site of an earlier one; a fortified residence, added on to the west end of the cathedral; and a luxurious accommodation range of the 1400s, with its own kitchen, known as The Hall of the Vicars' Choral.

Visitors enter through the Vicars' Choral, which has recently been restored to give a fair impression of the kind of reception rooms used to entertain lordly visitors in later medieval times. Below is a museum containing a tomb from *Athassel Abbey* (*page 55*) and the original St Patrick's Cross, of the 1100s, a copy of which now stands near the entrance to the cathedral.

The cathedral is notable mainly for its size, with soaring arches over the crossing where the two transepts meet the body of the church. The earliest part is the choir – the eastern end – built in about 1230, and now propped up by ugly modern buttresses on the outside. The rest was completed in the 1250s, and the fact that the nave (the western part) is so much shorter than the choir suggests that the original plans had to be scaled down.

The tower-house-like fortified residence was built on the end of the nave in the late 1300s by Archbishop O'Hedigan, but sadly there is no access to its interior. Perhaps at some stage it will be restored.

As long as the weather is not too windy and there's not a shortage of staff, you can climb the many steps to the top of the cathedral tower. This is well worth doing, not so much for the excellent views from the top, which are only slightly more excellent than the views from the wall at the edge of the Rock, as for the the chance to squint through a tiny hole in the floor of the tower's lowest room and see people looking back up at you from far below. It compensates for there being no access to the inside of the (even taller) round tower.

Best of the buildings by far, though, is the extraordinary Cormac's chapel, completed in 1134 and thought to be the earliest Romanesque building in Ireland. The combination of simple shapes in plain stone, a dark, cave-like interior, and fine carved decoration in the naïve style of the time is hugely appealing.

In the town is the shell of the church of St Dominic's Abbey, thought to have been one of the earliest Dominican foundations in Ireland. There are no traces left of the cloister or other buildings. A key is available if you'd like to see the inside, but there's not much to it beyond a few interesting tombs and some decorative detail in the windows.

In the town of Cashel, Co Tipperary.

Clara Castle

Dúchas, on private land • Free • Access with key from nearby house at reasonable times only

A well-preserved tower house, lived in as recently as 1905 and thought to have been built by the Shortall family. An abundance of gun-loops suggests that the tower dates from no earlier than the mid-1500s.

The road that leads up to the castle ends in the farmyard, so park somewhere discreet a little further back and walk up. The key to the castle is available from a nearby farm cottage, as directed by a sign; when I was there, the key was hanging on the cottage gate, waiting for visitors to collect it, which is handy.

Some towers still have their original floors intact, others have had their floors put back: at Clara, uniquely, the huge oak floor beams are still in place but the floorboards have disappeared, and you can look up between the beams to a stone vault over the third-floor room. It makes the gloomy interior feel a little more like a derelict house than a historic building, but it's good fun all the same.

A stone spiral stair leads to the slightly unappealing first floor, with lots of plaster and paint on the walls and a brick fireplace that looks as if it was a later addition. Presumably this room was in use in 1905. The second floor has a splendid stone fireplace and a large, elegant window with a window seat. A small passage to the right of the window leads to a chute-style garderobe toilet. If you're brave, you can walk across the beams to get a closer look.

However, there's an identical garderobe on the third floor which is easier to reach. The main room up here is smaller, and a corridor-like arrangement with a solid floor leads around it to the garderobe. A small window opens into a chamber in the thickness of the wall which could have been either a strongroom or a prison cell. This floor is vaulted over, to prevent a fire in the roof spreading through the castle, and unusually, the vault is plastered. Where the plaster has fallen away you can see impressions of the wickerwork used to support the vault during its construction.

The fourth-floor room, above the stone vault, is impressively large and well-lit, though its airiness is misleading: there would have been an attic storey above it. In the corner is a trapdoor – peculiarly, set into a seat to disguise it – which gave access to the strongroom or prison below. The roof is a modern replacement, and there is no outside access.

Near Kilkenny, Co Kilkenny. Signposted on a minor road that turns off the N10 (Kilkenny to Dublin) main road east of the town.

Clara Castle is one of the most interesting tower houses in Ireland, and fun if you have a head for heights.

See also... Donaghmore church

Dúchas, free, open access at any time. On a minor road off the R688 north of Clonmel.

This is one of the most attractive examples you're likely to find of a Romanesque church of the 1100s (or possibly earlier), roofless but otherwise reasonably intact, in a pleasant rural setting. Though it's small by later medieval standards, it must have been pretty important in its day. It has a rather good carved door at the west end, nice capitals on the chancel arch inside, and pleasingly simple windows on the south side. Little is known of its history, except that it was dedicated to St Farannán, who died in Germany in 982.

It's a modest building, but Donaghmore is a particularly appealing little Romanesque church of the 1100s.

Dunbrody Abbey

*Dúchas, on private land • ££ • Open April to
September daily*

This big, square, gaunt ruin of a major
Cistercian abbey stands in the middle of a
field, looking impressive but also slightly
forbidding. It's a bit eerie when you get
inside, too, especially if you're exploring
it on your own.

The church is large – at 60m (195ft)
long, it is said to be the biggest Cistercian
church in Ireland – with aisles on both
sides of the nave making it feel even larger,
but it's severe in feel, bare of ornament.
It has two transepts, reached through high,
round-topped arches that were partly
blocked when the tower was added in the
1400s, and each transept has three chapels.
The architect Pugin's Irish church designs
are said to have been greatly influenced by
a visit here, and the pointed arches of the
nave are certainly echoed in his Gothic
revival cathedral at Enniscorthy.

The church is fairly intact (though the
south wall of the nave collapsed in 1852),
but the buildings of the cloister have not
survived so well. It's hard to tell whether
the abbey was adapted as some kind of
fortified house after Henry VIII granted it
to Sir Osborne Itchingham in 1546, or
whether it always had an unusual layout:
whichever is the case, the west and south
sides of the cloister are bounded by a high
wall with few openings. No cloister
arcades survive, but there's a lot of rubble
lying around. It's not a particularly
attractive scene.

The west wall of the cloister is just a
wall, with a porched gate; behind the
south wall are the remains of a large
refectory. The range of buildings on the
east seems to have been modified – the
present entrance to the church is through

Dunbrody Abbey, one of the first abbeys founded by the Normans in Ireland, is a slightly forbidding ruin.

one of the chapels of the transept, which is
a bit odd – but they include a chapter room
and a library.

The abbey is one of the earliest Norman
foundations in Ireland, established
between 1175 and 1178 by Hervey de
Montmarisco, uncle of Strongbow (whose
armed expedition had brought the Anglo-
Normans to Ireland in 1169) and Marshal
to Henry II. Hervey himself became the
first abbot. Dunbrody had a chequered
history in the 1300s: its abbot was deposed
for insubordination in 1342; the lands and
buildings of the abbey were seized by the
king in 1348 after it refused to offer
hospitality or give alms; and there were
accusations of horse theft in 1355.

Access arrangements are unusual but
quite helpful. Although the monument

itself is in the care of Dúchas, the land on
which it stands is private, and in the
summer months visitors must buy a ticket
from a booth beside the track to the abbey.
If you have a Dúchas Heritage Card,
however, admission is free, and they even
give you a leaflet with a plan of the abbey.

Presumably in the winter, or if there's
nobody taking money, access is free.
Additionally, the landowners operate a
'visitor centre' just across the road from
the abbey: this consists of tearooms where
you can get excellent tea and cake, plus a
hedge maze and mini-golf (both pitch 'n'
putt and a putting green) to keep kids and
recalcitrant adults happy.

*Near Campile, Co Wexford. Beside the R733
north of Ballyhack, south of New Ross.*

See also... **Duntryleague megalithic tomb**

*On forestry land, free, open access at any reasonable time.
Near Galbally, Co Tipperary. Signposted up a minor
road from the village square; look out for a parking place
to the right of road after 1.9km (1.2 miles).*

Not the easiest monument to get to, and unfortunately now
buried in a forest which obliterates the views that were
presumably the main reason the neolithic builders of this
tomb chose to put it here. It's a bit wrecked, but worth
seeing all the same. In its denuded state, the tomb looks
not unlike a dolmen of sorts, but in fact it was a passage
grave, covered by a mound. Apparently the technique of
covering a passage with large slabs, each one resting on
top of the previous one so that the roof rises steadily until
it reaches the chamber, is not uncommon in neolithic
tombs in Brittany. To find it, walk uphill on the path from
the parking place and keep straight on, crossing a forest
track, until the path eventually turns left to arrive at the
monument. It's a steepish walk of about 20 minutes.

Ferns Castle

Dúchas • Free • Open daily June to August

Although there's little more than a scrap of the castle left, it's an enjoyable one to visit. It's a good example of how an imaginative approach to access arrangements can open up what might otherwise be just another locked-up, derelict building.

Basically, what they've done is employed a youngster to open the castle to visitors in the summer months, with guided tours on request; but because there's not all that much to see, they don't charge for admission. This seems sensible. The cost of staffing must be minimal compared with the cost of restoring such a building, but its effect is to make the whole effort worthwhile by encouraging people to take an interest. The only thing that lets the side down is the surprising amount of litter around the place.

The castle, built some time in the early 1200s, consisted of a square of high walls surrounding a rather small courtyard, with a four-storey tower at each corner. One of these towers survives intact, along with a fragment of a second and a stretch of wall. The wall is full of windows and arrow-slits, and on the inside of it are obvious traces of the interiors of rooms, including fireplaces and doors.

It's the intact tower that really makes the place worth visiting, because you can climb right up to the roof. Entry is by wooden steps up to the first floor, where

Below: Hore Abbey stands in a field overlooked by the Rock of Cashel, in comparative peace and quiet.

there's a plain storage room; a stair leads down to the basement below, with a very pleasing stone corbelled vault.

Up on the second floor is a fine reception room, with good windows but no fireplace, and a chapel in the alcove to one side. The third floor is a bedchamber: the ceiling of this room would have had fine vaulting ribs, like the room below, but these have now gone. A narrow winding stair brings you out on the roof, where a peek over the battlements reveals that you are surprisingly high up, thanks to the generous proportions of the rooms below.

There's a scatter of monuments at the other end of the town, too, including parts of a cathedral of the 1200s and the early Christian site of *St Mary's Abbey* (more details under *'Ferns'* in the *See also...* section at the end of this chapter).

In the small town of Ferns, Co Wexford.

Hore Abbey, Cashel

Dúchas • Free • Open access at any reasonable time

Get away from the tourist hordes at the Rock of Cashel by strolling down to this pleasant little ruin standing in a field less than ten minutes' walk away from the Rock. It's a decent little ruin: the church is pretty much intact, but there's not much left of the buildings of the cloister except their outlines on the ground.

Benedictines from Glastonbury in England were first to settle on this site, but in 1272 they were replaced by Cistercians

Inside the castle at Ferns. The doorways above the steps in the corner lead to the various floors of the tower.

from Mellifont on the orders of an archbishop, and so this became the last Cistercian abbey to be founded in Ireland. Much of the church is of the late 1200s, and many of the stonemasons who built it also worked on the enormous abbey that dominates the Rock.

Cashel, Co Tipperary. Signposted walk of about 10 mins from the entrance to the Rock of Cashel.

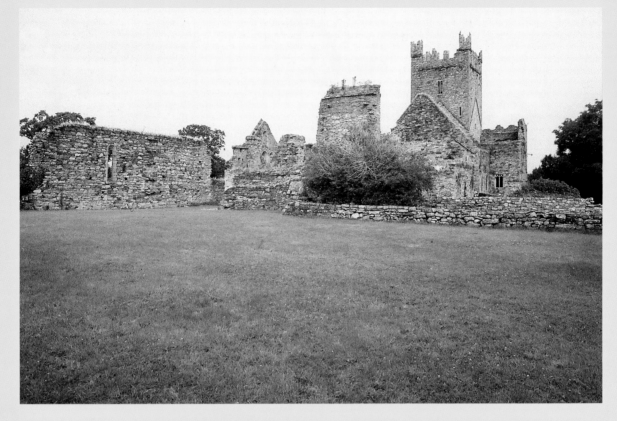

Jerpoint Abbey

Jerpoint Abbey is a pleasant and graceful ruin, with impressive cloister arcades and lovely carved details.

Dúchas • ££ • Open daily except Tuesday in March and November; daily from June to mid-October

Jerpoint is probably the most attractive of Ireland's ruined abbeys. Its remains include substantial parts of the church, with its large tower; most of the buildings on the side of the cloister next to the church; and long stretches of extremely elegant cloister arcade.

The most impressive and memorable feature of the abbey, however, is that it has a number of examples of particularly splendid stonecarving. In the chapels that occupy the transepts of the church there are tombs of various ages from the 1200s

The figures carved on this tomb, called 'weepers', are the work of the famous carvers the O'Tunneys.

to the 1500s, the best of which are carved with lively, cartoon-like figures of angels, bishops and soldiers. These figures, the work of a famous family of stonecarvers of the 1400s and 1500s, are pleasing in themselves as works of art, but they are also highly detailed records of the costume and regalia of high-ranking people in medieval times.

There are other interesting carvings too, including the figures of a bishop and a knight, on the pillars of the cloister arcade, which is said to be the most decorative in Ireland. Most of it had collapsed, and was put back up in 1953.

From the south transept of the church you can climb the night stairs, which the monks would have used when coming down to take part in night-time services, to reach the dormitory on the first floor of the cloister's east range. Below the dormitory, on the ground floor, are the sacristy and the chapter house.

In the south range of the cloister were the kitchen, the refectory and, deliberately placed right next to the dormitory, a room known as the calefactory, which was the only place where the monks were allowed to light a fire to warm themselves by. The fireplace was enormous.

It's worth taking a stroll around the outside of the abbey to see round the back of the cloister ranges. On the end of the dormitory was the toilet block, and you can see the drain underneath through which a stream would have run to 'flush' the toilets.

The abbey was established in 1160 and was colonised by Cistercian monks from Baltinglass, Co Wicklow, in 1180. It flourished in the 1300s and 1400s under the patronage of the Butler family of Kilkenny, and a large town – now long vanished – grew up outside its walls. The abbey was dissolved in 1540 and its lands and buildings leased to James Butler, Earl of Ormond.

Near Thomastown, Co Kilkenny. Beside the N9 (to Waterford) main road just south of the town, and well signposted in the area.

High crosses and early churches near Jerpoint

One extremely useful thing about a visit to Jerpoint Abbey (opposite) is that, inspired by the fact that there's so much fine stonecarving in the abbey, Dúchas has set up a useful display in the ticket office which shows many other interesting examples of carved stonework – high crosses, tombs, church doorways and so on – which can be found at early Christian sites in the surrounding area. If, for example, you are planning to visit the well-known high crosses at Ahenny and Kilkieran, in the south of County Kilkenny, near Clonmel, it's worth stopping at Jerpoint first to get a better idea of what to look out for.

Ahenny high crosses

Dúchas, in churchyard • Free • Open access at any reasonable time

Two classic examples of the Irish high cross from around 700 or 800AD stand in a small burial ground. Both are large, with bold, deep carving, and have odd conical caps. The crosses are decorated with elaborate flowing patterns. Worn scenes on the bases are said to include clerics with croziers, a procession with a ringed cross, a pony carrying a headless man, and a chariot with riders.

Signposted off the R697 south of Tullaghought, Co Kilkenny. Turn left through the village.

Left: there are two very similar crosses in the churchyard at Ahenny, both deeply carved with dramatic geometric patterns.

Kilkieran high crosses

Dúchas, in churchyard • Free • Open access at any reasonable time

Not far from Ahenny. A burial ground on a hillside contains three crosses: one very odd, gaunt, stretched affair; one very large and fine example, similar in style to the pair at Ahenny, with horsemen on the base; and another similar cross, but smaller and plainer. On the largest cross you can see places where the intricate interlace design has gone slightly wrong!

Off the R697 south of Tullaghought, Co Kilkenny. Signposted along minor road to Owning.

Killamery high cross

Dúchas, in disused churchyard • Free • Open access at any reasonable time

Just one cross in a quiet, out-of-the-way setting, but an interesting one. Scenes on the west face include a crucifixion, a stag hunt and chariot procession, and David playing a harp. Designs on the east face represent serpents and marigolds. Scenes on the arms of the cross are thought to be Jacob wrestling an angel, David killing a lion and the death of Goliath. Uniquely, it has an inscription, which reads: 'Pray for Maelsechnaill'. Nearby is an early grave-slab with a similar inscription.

Signposted on the N76 at Killamery, Co Kilkenny.

Ullard church and high cross

Dúchas, in churchyard • Free • Open access at any reasonable time

A small ruined church of the 1100s with an elaborate but badly worn doorway. Heads over the door, now mere outlines, are said to be St Moling, founder of the church, and St Fiachra. There's a cross behind the church, with a crucifixion and a number of Old Testament scenes.

By the road from Graiguenamanagh to Borris.

There are unusual designs on the Killamery cross, such as the beast with a fish in its mouth at the top.

The church at Ullard is a charming little building, but its elaborate doorway is very badly worn.

☐ *See also...*

Also mentioned in the stonecarving exhibition at Jerpoint Abbey are the following…

Gowran church, **Kilfane church**, and **St Mullins early monastic site**, all of which are covered in the 'See also...' section at the end of this chapter.

Kilree early monastic site, which appears in its own 'See also...' panel on page 69.

Knocktopher church is a ruined Gothic church of the 1100s, now mostly demolished. Inside the tower is an interesting tomb of the 1400s, but it is kept locked up. Knocktopher is a minor site, and not terribly interesting.

Kells Priory

Dúchas, on private land • Free • Open access at reasonable times only

It's a remarkable place, this, looking thoroughly impressive when you first set eyes on its circuit of walls and towers, but unfortunately neglect and vandalism make it disappointing to visit. The site consists of a large Augustinian priory, sadly too ruined to be of great interest, accompanied by an extraordinary walled enclosure with a number of towers. It's almost like a small fortified town, and in effect that's exactly what it was.

The priory was founded in the 1190s by Geoffrey FitzRobert, who was given lands in the area in 1192 by William Marshal, Earl of Pembroke. (Marshal had married Isabelle, daughter and heiress of Strongbow, and consequently held most of Leinster and Kilkenny.) Geoffrey established a castle and a borough town at Kells, and he gave land for the priory, bringing four Augustinian canons from Bodmin in Cornwall, England, to set it up.

The Augustinians were allowed by their rules to run parish churches, acting as

Below: The remarkable series of walls and towers at Kells Priory – in effect, this is a fortified town.

priests and accepting the tithe income. Geoffrey and two neighbouring lords contributed the tithes from 42 churches and chapels to the priory's income, as well as land for farms. The priory grew rapidly.

Initially all the Priors who ran the place were brought in from Bodmin, but from the early 1300s they were mostly local men. The priory church was the parish church for the town, and townspeople worked in the priory's farms and around its precincts, so links between priory and town were inevitably close. When things got difficult, they stuck together.

In the early 1400s the tendency for local lords to maintain large armies of professional soldiers at the expense of their tenants made for an increasingly unstable political climate. This was compounded by the absence of local lord James Butler, Earl of Ormond, and his successors after his death in 1452, so that the region was governed by deputies from junior branches of the Butler family, most of whom were constantly feuding.

This was probably what decided the Prior of Kells to build the fortified enclosure between 1460 and 1475. The town had no walls and was vulnerable to raids, but the Burgess Court – so named because it was used by the townspeople – would be a

refuge in all-too-common times of trouble. It could also be used to keep all the local cattle safe at night. Similar enclosures were built at Fore, Co Westmeath; Navan, Co Meath; and Baltinglass, Co Wicklow.

There was probably a small full-time garrison, perhaps billeted in the two smaller towers. Its commander may have occupied one of the two larger towers of the enclosure, both of which are proper tower houses. The second, which stood by a gate facing the town, is thought to have been granted to a former prior in 1470 and to have remained in his family.

At the same time that the Burgess Court was built, the priory church had a tower added, and a new tower house was built alongside the choir as the Prior's residence. This is now the best-preserved part of the priory complex, but unfortunately there is no access to its interior. The same goes for the tower houses of the Burgess Court, and this, along with the ruinous state of the church and cloisters of the priory, makes Kells Priory a less than inspiring place to visit.

Its story remains intriguing, however, and it is told in detail in an excellent guidebook available from local shops.

Near Kells, Co Kilkenny, by the road to Stonyford.

Kilcooley Abbey

The remains of Kilcooley Abbey are in a peaceful setting, in a field behind the gates of a grand estate.

Dúchas, on private land • Free • Open access at reasonable times only

The substantial and attractive ruin of a Cistercian abbey, standing in a peaceful and secluded location in a cowfield behind the walls of a large estate. To reach the abbey you have to go through the gate of the estate and up its wide drive, veering off up a track to the right just before another gate, and passing the tied church. Through a gate at the end of the track is the field in which the abbey stands, with an interesting round dovecot nearby.

Kilcooley was founded in 1182 by Donal Mór O'Brien as a daughter-house of *Jerpoint (see page 64)*, and just like Jerpoint it is particularly notable for its carved stonework. The original buildings of the early 1200s were mostly destroyed in 1445, and afterwards the abbey church was rebuilt on a slightly altered plan, with the aisles of the nave removed, but with a new tower and north transept added. Perhaps there was a lot of money floating around at this time, but certainly much of the most attractive stonework is from the time of this rebuilding.

The ornamental stonework includes a pair of highly decorated seats at the top of the nave, probably one for the abbot and one for his deputy, and, more surprisingly, a series of carvings on the wall leading to the sacristy, inside the south transept. This shows a crucifixion, St Christopher, a bishop (possibly St Bernard, who shared the dedication of the church with the Virgin) and, rather oddly, a mermaid with a mirror. Along the top, there are the arms of the Butler family.

There are some fine tombs in the choir, including one – that of Piers Fitz Oge Butler, who died in about 1526 – signed by Rory O'Tunney (it reads, 'Roricus O Tuyne scripsit'), a member of the famous family of stonecarvers who produced so much fine work at Jerpoint. Arguably the highlight, though, is the flowing, organic, tree-like tracery in the window at the east end of the church. It's beautiful.

There's not much left of the buildings around the cloister, which is slightly disappointing, but the walls that enclose the grassy square give a sense of what it might have been like, and add to the peace and quiet of a sheltered, pleasant spot.

On the Kilcooley estate, near Gortnahoo, Co Tipperary. Turning into drive is signposted on the R690 (Ballingarry road), off the R689 and N8 south of Urlingford, Co Kilkenny.

This unusual carved screen separates the sacristy from the south transept of the church at Kilcooley.

Kilkenny Castle

Dúchas • £££ • Open all year (closed Mondays, and shorter hours from October to March)

Deep down, Kilkenny still has the massive round towers and thick walls of a serious castle of the early 1200s, but most of what you see today is layer upon layer of rebuilding and restoration. In its present form, the castle is an imitation of a sham – that is to say, it's a modern version, recreated from photographs and restorer's clues such as scraps of old wallpaper, of a Gothic-style stately home built by the wealthy Butler family in the 1830s.

In fact, the present buildings still follow the pattern of the original, proper castle built here in about 1204 by Strongbow's heir, William Marshal – though instead of four big, round corner-towers, the present castle has just three, and instead of having a circuit of walls enclosing a courtyard, the castle is now open on the east side. The castle came into the possession of the Butlers in the early 1400s and was remodelled as a Restoration mansion by James Butler, Duke of Ormond, in the 1660s, before being rebuilt in a more castle-like form in Victorian times.

Below: Despite having been rebuilt several times, Kilkenny Castle still retains its original layout.

The grand Victorian house was abandoned in the 1930s and had become derelict by the time the castle was given into state care in 1969. It is now slowly being restored, with great care and at great expense. Admission is by guided tour only; the castle gets very busy in summer, and tour groups tend to be large. Visitors are made to sit through an audio-visual show, and the first few rooms are dull, but things improve with the elegant upstairs drawing room, an impressive cantilevered stair, and the amusing Gothicky stairs at the other end of the range.

The best, though, is saved till last: the tour ends in the long picture gallery that occupies the whole of one wing of the castle, its flamboyantly carved and painted roof adding the finishing touch to a satisfyingly silly and ostentatious showpiece typical of the Victorian era.

There's a small modern art gallery in the basement below, along with a tearoom, both of which are open free of charge to anyone, even if they're not taking the tour of the castle. The same goes for the extensive grounds, with sweeping lawns, woodland walks and an artificial lake, which are now a national park.

In Kilkenny, on The Parade, at the southern end of the High Street.

See also... St Canice's Cathedral

Church authorities, £, open daily all year round. In Kilkenny, off St Canice's Place, on the north-west side of the town centre.

Kilkenny is a lively, bustling little town which in truth is probably more interesting for its shops and pubs than for its much-vaunted medieval remains; but it does have more than its fair share of historic buildings, including three abbeys and a medieval merchant's house (Rothe House, which now contains a rather stuffy and pointless museum).

The best of the lot, though, is this cathedral, not just for the fine church of the late 1200s, but also because alongside it is the only round tower in Ireland that you can climb to the top of. It's hard work, but the views are great.

Ormond Castle

Dúchas • ££ • Open mid-June to September daily

Technically, there *is* a castle here. In fact, there are two earlier tower houses hidden by the later building. But by far the most interesting thing here is the later range at the front, which is certainly not a castle.

Rather, it's a very rare example of an Irish manor house in the classic style of Elizabethan England, with barely anything in the way of fortification. It was built by Thomas Butler, 10th Earl of Ormond, who because of his close English connections was the most powerful man in Ireland throughout the Elizabethan era.

Born in 1531, Thomas was brought up at the English court, where he shared a tutor with the future king Edward VI. Thomas attended Edward's coronation in 1546, and his career at court continued to prosper during the reign of Queen Mary and after Elizabeth was crowned in 1558. In 1559 he was made Lord Treasurer of Ireland and returned to his native country.

Throughout the 1560s, Thomas rebuilt his family's castle at Carrick-on-Suir and turned it into an English-style manor house. He added a grand new range on the front, plus two shorter wings on each side, and he incorporated the two older towers at the

Elegant Ormond Castle is Ireland's only Elizabethan manor house, converted from an earlier tower house.

back into a fourth range, creating a house of four ranges around a rectangular yard. The new blocks, just two storeys high, incorporated all the latest advances in architecture and interior design, but they were also more than that: they became a hymn in stone, wood and plaster to the glory of Elizabeth, whose portrait, arms and monogram appear all over the place.

Bizarrely, the house had been left to go derelict in the early 1900s, and so it has had to be restored with the greatest of care over the course of more than 50 years. Admission is by guided tour only, but this is one of those places where you simply wouldn't get the full story any other way. It's a surprise to find that the place gets hardly any visitors: when I was here at the height of the summer season, I had a guide all to myself.

There are some fascinating pieces of furniture and paintings in the house now, but the highlights of the tour are the many-windowed long gallery — which runs along the whole upstairs floor of the front range and is superbly decorated with plaster and wood panelling — and a visit to the attic.

In Carrick-on-Suir, Co Tipperary.

◾ *See also...* **Kilree early monastic site**

Dúchas, on farmland, free, open access at any reasonable time. Not far from Kells Priory.

Another of the region's intriguing little early monastic sites. A badly ruined church stands in a graveyard on a small wooded hill; nearby is a ruined round tower, and in a field beyond is a worn but classy high cross. Depicted on the cross are a stag-hunt and a chariot scene, as well as the usual biblical highlights. You can get inside the door of the round tower.

Rathmacknee is odd in having a cottage built in its courtyard, but it's a splendid example of a tower house.

Rathmacknee Castle

Dúchas, on private land • Free • Open access during usual hours only

Hidden away in a little-visited piece of countryside just a short distance from the ferry port of Rosslare, this intriguing little tower house of the mid-1400s is well worth seeing. Not only is the tower itself in good condition – intact right up to the typical Irish multi-stepped battlements – but also the surrounding walled courtyard, or 'bawn', is almost complete. It's rare to find a bawn so well-preserved.

The only slight drawback for visitors is that a cottage has been built against the far wall of the bawn, and the whole courtyard area is its garden, so you can't just wander around peering into every corner: this is private property. But as long as you're discreet, nobody will mind if you walk through the arched gateway in the bawn (note the box machicolation above the arch, for defenders to hurl missiles down on anyone trying to break down the gate) and make your way to the door of the tower. This, thanks to a decidedly unofficial access arrangement, usually turns out not to have been properly locked, and you are free to go in and take a look round.

Inside, the basement on the ground floor has a stone vaulted roof and tiny windows. It's now used as a shed, a role which is not very different from its original one as a store-cum-cellar. To the left of the door, which is in the narrower side of the rectangular tower, a straight stair leads up to the first floor.

Upstairs, there's a stone floor and lots of daylight, because the roof and the upper floors have all disappeared. It appears that all the upper floors were made of wood. The stair turns through 90 degrees and climbs steeply up the wider side of the tower, past what would have been two upper floors, all the way up to roof level.

If you don't mind it being a little precarious – there's no hand-rail to stop you falling off – you can easily climb the stair to the roof-walk behind the battlements, which is rather good fun. The way the wall-walk is built from big, overlapping stone flags that provide excellent drainage is a typical construction technique in Irish tower houses.

It is thought that the tower house was built by John Rosseter, Seneschal of the Liberties of Wexford, in the mid-1400s, but apart from that piece of speculation, nothing is known of its history.

Near Rosslare, Co Wexford. Signposted along a minor road from the R793 to Kilmore Quay, off the N25 south of Wexford.

See also... Slade Castle

Dúchas, free, open access to view exterior only. At the southern tip of Hook Head: turn right for Hook lighthouse; turn left for the castle.

It's a shame that this small tower of unusual and intriguing appearance is currently derelict, with signs warning that the structure is unsafe, because it looks like it could be a most interesting place to visit.

The castle consists of an older tower house, built by the Laffan family in the late 1400s or early 1500s, with a later house built on the side. There's also an odd annexe on the end with a corbelled roof, which is thought to have had something to do with the manufacture of salt in the 1700s.

Tintern Abbey

Dúchas • ££ • Mid-June to late September daily

When his ship was spared in a dangerous storm at sea, William Marshal vowed to grant lands for the founding of an abbey. It was set up by Cistercian monks from the famous Tintern Abbey in Wales, and named *Tintern de Voto*, or Tintern of the Vow.

Although it's big, the ruined church is not particularly attractive, looking slightly derelict and having a kind of purposeful plainness about it. But in fact, it has a very good excuse for this. A few years after the abbey's dissolution in 1536, its estates were given to a man named Anthony Colclough, who had fought in Henry VIII's army in Ireland and was later knighted by Elizabeth. He made the tower into a fortified residence, also modifying the chancel for use as living accommodation. In the early 1800s, the nave of the church was also adapted into a domestic wing; and remarkably, the place was still lived in until 1960.

Currently, a good deal of the later work has been stripped away, and the slow process of restoring the abbey has begun. Rather wisely, the decision has been made not to attempt to rebuild the original church, but instead to recreate the fortified house of the late 1500s.

To that end, the tower and chancel are closed while the work goes ahead; so all you can visit is the stripped-back nave, which is really very plain, and the roofed-over chapel in the south transept, which is used as a small museum displaying some of the ornamental stonework found lying around the place. There is very little left of the buildings of the cloister, which were adapted into stables and suchlike, and the cloister itself was paved over as a yard; but there is a rather interesting drain that is almost like a secret tunnel under the yard.

It's impossible to guess how long the restoration will take; but in 2000 it was said that it would certainly be a number of years before it was finished.

The tower and chancel of the church at Tintern Abbey were converted into a fortified house after the dissolution.

For the time being, then, the most enjoyable way to pass a little time here – beyond taking a quick look at the exterior of the church, and popping your head into the south transept – is to take a stroll in the extensive grounds that surround the abbey. At the very least, you should wander down to the elegant old stone bridge that crosses the inlet of Bannow Bay, near which the abbey stands, and up to the ruin of a small medieval church, where Sir Anthony himself was buried. In addition, though, there is a series of longer walking trails to follow, details of which can be obtained from the ticket office here.

Near Saltmills, Co Wexford. Signposted from the R733 west of Wellingtonbridge.

See also... Tacumshane windmill

Dúchas, free, access with key from neighbouring shop during usual hours only. Off the R736 near Rosslare.

This charming little building was the first structure from the industrial era to be taken into state care, in the 1950s, at which time it was the last intact windmill in Ireland. It was built in 1846, but on the pattern of a typical windmill from the century before – though it also incorporates parts of the mechanism of a mill of newer design which was used to update it in the 1930s. The thatched roof is most unusual.

The mill has been restored, and you can pick up the key from the shop-cum-pub next door and let yourself in to have a look around.

The fat capstone of Browneshill dolmen is enormously heavy – it is estimated to weigh 150 metric tonnes.

Portal dolmens in the south east

Perhaps it's the contrast between the huge, heavy stones and the delicate, precarious way they are balanced that gives these distinctive monuments their appeal, but certainly photographs of them are perennial favourites on postcards and the covers of tourist brochures. They are found all over Ireland – the most famous of all is *Poulnabrone dolmen*, Co Clare (*see page 114*) – but nearly all the best ones are here in the south-east. In Britain, incidentally, they are found exclusively in west Wales, Devon and Cornwall.

The word 'dolmen', from the Breton meaning 'stone table', was popularised by antiquarians who thought these were druidical altars. But in fact they were burial monuments used by neolithic people at about the same time that passage tombs and other chambered tombs were in use elsewhere in Ireland.

The typical portal dolmen has an arrangement of two upright slabs of stone like gateposts, and the gap between them is blocked by a third stone set sideways, like a gate – so from above the portal looks like a capital letter 'H'. On top of it rests a capstone, often of imposing size and weight and frequently tilted so that it looms dramatically over the front of the monument. There's usually a chamber of some kind behind the portal.

The evidence suggests that portal dolmens were probably not covered by mounds, though they often seem to have been surrounded by a low, cairn-like 'platform' of stones. Because the monuments were not covered, it is rare for evidence of burials to be found during excavation. There is one in Wales which was incorporated into the mound of a later chambered long barrow, and here evidence of cremation was found, which would fit in with practices at passage graves in Ireland.

Left: Gaulstown is one of the smaller dolmens in the region. It looks more impressive from the front.

Browneshill portal dolmen

Dúchas • Free • Open access at any reasonable time

This surprising and eccentric dolmen is very much on the tourist trail, and at summer weekends it receives a steady stream of visitors, though most only stay a couple of minutes. It's not in the best of locations, however, and its prosaic setting is made to seem even more humdrum by the fence that hems it in.

Presumably the dolmen is such an attraction because of its odd appearance. It's made out of huge, fat, round boulders, rather than the usual flat slabs of stone, and the angled capstone is enormous: it is said to weigh 150 tonnes and is the biggest in Europe, and it looks quite impressive close to, if a bit silly from a distance.

The rock of which the capstone is composed seems to have more glinting crystal bits in it (I believe it's either mica or quartz, but I'm no geologist) than the other stones. Such careful selection of materials is common in ancient monuments and occurs repeatedly in local dolmens.

The stones at the front of the monument have been carefully chosen for their shape, with a square-topped 'gate stone' in the middle flanked by two pointed 'portal stones', echoing the standard design of a portal dolmen even though this is a far from standard example. Smaller stones scattered around might be part of a cairn or a stone kerb around an earthen platform, or possibly even a mound.

Near Carlow, Co Carlow. Just outside the town on the Hacketstown road.

Gaulstown portal dolmen (Cnoc an Challaig)

Dúchas, on farmland • Free • Open access at any reasonable time

It's not one of the largest examples, but this is still a classic portal dolmen with an impressive tilted capstone. Standing in front of it, you're very much aware of its size and weight.

The monument is partly ruined, but there are traces of what could be either a raised platform or the remains of a mound.

It's a good one for access: park at the roadside at the end of the farm track and walk up, and a short way up you'll see a gate leading to the monument, which is quite overgrown and stands among bushes and trees in the corner of a field.

Near Ballymorris, Co Waterford. Signposted on a minor road off the R682 north of Tramore.

Kilmogue portal dolmen (Leach an Scaill)

Dúchas, on private land • Free • Open access at reasonable times only

This is the most impressive of the lot, with its huge capstone set at an astonishing angle. It looks a bit silly from the side, which is where you first approach it from, but once you're in front of the monument you get a real sense of the size and weight of the massive capstone looming over you.

A unique feature of its design is that the smaller secondary capstone at the back is 'cantilevered' – that is, delicately balanced, and held in place by the weight of the main capstone resting on its rear edge. You don't notice this at first, but when you think about it, it's quite a feat.

Again, it appears the capstone has been selected for the abundance of glittering crystals in the rock as well as for its size.

Signposted on a minor road north of Milltown, off the N9 at Mullinavit, Co Kilkenny.

The Knockeen dolmen has an interesting design with two capstones, the front one resting on the one at the back.

Knockeen portal dolmen

Dúchas, on famland • Free • Open access at reasonable times only

If Kilmogue is the most impressive of the region's dolmens, then this one is probably the most interesting. It's of a slightly different design, with a large main capstone set almost level and resting on a secondary capstone that's almost as big, with an excellent chamber beneath.

Again, there seem to be traces of what might be a raised platform or a mound around the monument, but this is not at all clear, thanks to the tendency in these rural parts to hide these monuments in hedges or build them into the walls of fields, which rather reduces their grandeur.

South of Waterford, off the minor road to Dunhill. Take the Dunhill road from the N25 on the south side of Waterford, then take the third left turn (signposted to the monument). Carry on to the next left turn, then turn round, go back the way you came, and park near the farm entrance. Go through the gate opposite the farm; head for the right-hand gate across the field; then go left around a wood with a ruined church in.

With its two overlapping capstones, Haroldstown dolmen is very similar in design to the example at Knockeen.

See also… Haroldstown dolmen

On private land, no official access arrangements. North of Tullow, Co Carlow. Signposted on the R727 Carlow to Hacketstown road, in a field next to the road just after it crosses the bridge over the Derreen River.

A very neat little tomb, similar in design to the one at Knockeen (*left*), standing in a field on the banks of a river. It shows all the classic features of a portal dolmen, with a distinct portal at the front. Its ten uprights support two level capstones, the larger one at the front resting on a smaller one behind. The only drawback from the visitor's point of view is that access is not encouraged: the gate is locked and there is no stile into the field.

Left: Kilmogue dolmen is the most impressive of the lot, its huge capstone tilted at a crazy angle.

See also…

Baginbun Norman fortifications

Dúchas, on farmland, free, open access at any reasonable time. On the Hook Peninsula, signposted from the R734 south of Fethard, Co Wexford.

A promontory near the mouth of Bannow Bay is where one of the first small groups of Anglo-Norman soldiers landed, in advance of the larger force led by Richard FitzGilbert de Clare, better known as Strongbow. The advance party of about 90 men that landed here at Baginbun in May 1170 was led by Strongbow's brother-in-law, Raymond FitzGilbert Le Gros, and their first move was to dig a large defensive earthwork, consisting of a bank and ditch, to cut off the promontory. It's not much to look at, but this is a place where a very significant historical event took place. There are good sandy beaches on either side of the headland, too.

Ballyloughan Castle

On private land, no official access arrangements. Near Ballymoon, east of Bagenalstown, Co Carlow; from Ballymoon Castle (see page 57), travelling away from Bagenalstown, take the first right turn, ignore a right turn, go left and right at a staggered junction. After about 2.4km (1.5 miles), near a small group of houses, the castle is in a field to your right.

Intriguing remains of a large courtyard-style castle (that is, one with walls and towers but no keep)

Right: Callan church (see opposite page).

dating from the late 1200s. The surviving buildings, constructed from large blocks of local stone, are a big gatehouse with two round-fronted towers and a square corner tower with what would have been a very respectable hall-like room on the first floor.

These buildings were once part of a circuit of walls fortified by several other towers, which enclosed a fairly large courtyard. Most of this circuit of walls has now disappeared. Later, a large house

Above: Ballyloughan Castle.

was built in what would formerly have been the rear of the courtyard, presumably using stone from the earlier castle. This too is now ruinous.

The buildings are in a field but, sadly, the gates are kept locked, and the lack of a stile suggests that access is not encouraged.

Burnchurch Castle

Dúchas, free, open access to view exterior only at any reasonable time. In the village of Burnchurch, off the N76 or R697 south of Kilkenny.

This rather excellent tower house, built by a local branch of the Fitzgerald family in the 1400s, is in practically complete condition, though it is said to lack a roof. Unfortunately, the tower is kept locked up, and there is no obvious way to get a key, as you can at the similar tower house of *Clara Castle*, not far from here to the north-east of Kilkenny (*see page 61*). The lack of access is frustrating, since the six-storey tower is said to have an unusual number of chambers and passages within its walls. The castle was occupied until 1817.

Burncourt Castle

On private land, no official access arrangements. Just east of the village of Burncourt, off the N8 west of Cahir, Co Tipperary.

The Irish countryside is littered with the shells of many large houses, some of them destroyed as recently as the 1920s, but this is one of the oldest and most interesting. It's the ruin of a castle-like mansion which was built in 1641 but burned down just a few years later, in 1650, by Oliver Cromwell. Considering that it has been abandoned ever since, the shell of the house is still very impressive, both in its size and in its relative completeness. It originally had 26 gables and seven vast chimneystacks, and its many mullioned windows must have made it a very grand place to live. The ruin can be seen quite well from the road, but you may be able to get a closer look with the permission of the landowner.

Cahir Priory

Dúchas, free, open access to view exterior only at any reasonable time. Signposted beside the N24 (the Tipperary road) just north of the town centre in Cahir, Co Tipperary.

The choir and tower still survive from the large church of an Augustinian abbey that was founded here in the late 1100s, at around the same time that *Cahir Castle (see page 58)* was built. You will find extensive details of the abbey's history in the guidebook to the castle. Some of the stonework is rather fine, but the building is kept locked up and stands in what is now a light industrial area, so it's really not worth coming to see.

Callan Friary and St Mary's Church

Both Dúchas, free, open access at any reasonable time (but to exterior only in the case of the friary). In Callan, on the N76 south of Kilkenny; the church is by the high street, while the friary stands in the mini-golf course just north of the river.

Only the church remains of the Augustinian friary founded in 1462, and it's a very plain building, long and narrow, with no transepts. It is said to have some interesting ornamental stonework inside, but it is generally kept locked up. Far more interesting is the ruin of St Mary's Church, a large building with some extremely attractive carvings. The oldest part of the church is the tall, square tower at the west end, which dates from about 1250, but the majority of it was built in about 1460. There are doors on the north and south side of the nave, with interesting carved details on both; above the north door is a representation of the head of a lady wearing a head-dress in the style of the 1400s. There's a collection of carved tombs inside the church.

Above: Burnchurch Castle.

Carlow Castle

Dúchas, free, open access to view exterior only at any reasonable time. In Carlow, near to the N9 (Waterford road) just south of the city centre.

There was once a large and important castle here, but there's not a lot of it left. It was built by William Marshal between 1207 and 1213 and is thought to be the earliest castle of its type in Ireland. Its main feature was an impressive keep, consisting of a huge rectangular tower with a smaller round tower at each of its four corners. Unfortunately, only one side of this keep remains; it's impressively big, but it stands like a bizarre industrial folly next to an unappealing patch of waste ground.

Above: Clonmines.

Below: Carlow Castle (see previous page).

Clonmines medieval town

On private land, no access permitted. The ruins can be seen from the graveyard of a ruined church that stands beside the R733 just west of Wellingtonbridge, Co Wexford, where there is a lay-by to park in and a signboard describing the site.

This is potentially one of the most interesting historic sites in Ireland – a whole abandoned medieval town, with the ruins of two churches, three tower houses and an Augustinian priory. Sadly, the landowner does not permit access to the ruins, which are neglected and vandalised even though they are in state care; however, there is a burial ground on the site, to which public access is allowed. The town slowly died out following the silting-up of its harbour in the early 1600s, though there was still an Augustinian presence here in 1794.

Duiske Abbey, Graiguenamanagh

Church authorities, free (voluntary contribution to upkeep appreciated), open during usual hours all year round. In Graiguenamanagh, Co Kilkenny.

This Cistercian abbey founded in 1204, which is said to have been the largest in Ireland, was suppressed in 1536 and fell into ruin thereafter. It was rebuilt in 1813, but with no consideration at all for its original appearance; so the brave decision was taken in the early 1970s to rebuild it all over again in a more sympathetic style. It's now a very plain building, but of impressive size inside, with just slight traces of original grandeur in the ornamental stonework at the eastern end.

The abbey stands not far from the River Barrow, and a short walk away along the riverbank is the ruin of a defended mansion of the 1600s.

Duncannon Fort

Wexford County Council; access to courtyard is free; guided tours to other buildings, ££; both open from June to mid-September daily. At Duncannon, Co Wexford, off the R733 south of Ballyhack.

A very well-preserved example of an Elizabethan artillery fort, built in the 1580s, when fears of a Spanish invasion were rife. Its seaside location is pleasant, with an excellent sandy beach nearby. The fort is quite interesting, but its brick walls and gun emplacements do not offer many opportunities for enjoyable exploration. The largest buildings now house a cafe and craft galleries.

Dunhill Castle

Local council, free, open access to exterior only at any reasonable time. Between Dunhill and Annestown, Co Waterford; signposted on a minor road off the R675 Tramore to Dungarvan coast road east of Annestown.

This ivy-covered stump of a tower, on a hill by a river estuary, looks pretty but is not very interesting.

Enniscorthy Castle museum

Wexford County Council, £££, open from May to September daily (but afternoon only on Sundays). In Enniscorthy, Co Wexford.

Although it still follows the ground-plan of the original Norman keep, the castle has been rebuilt many times, and in its present form is essentially a rather unusual house of the early 1900s. It is now in use as a dusty museum, with a thoroughly eccentric collection of bits and bobs which might be of great interest locally but is rather dull for the rest of us.

Above: Enniscorthy Castle.

Below: Duncannon fort.

Enniscorthy St Aidan's cathedral

Church authorities, free, open access during usual hours. In Enniscorthy, Co Wexford.

One of the largest and finest of the many churches built in Ireland by the architect Augustus Pugin, who designed the Houses of Parliament in London and was one of the leading figures in the Victorian Gothic revival movement. The cathedral has recently been carefully restored, with the damage done to it in earlier generations – such as the lino stuck down on top of its custom-made floor tiles – now all made good. A photographic exhibition on Pugin's other churches in Ireland is held inside the church in the summer months.

Ferns St Mary's Abbey

Dúchas, free, open access at any reasonable time. In Ferns, Co Wexford, at the opposite end of the town to the castle (see page 63).

In a field stands the remains of a tiny abbey church founded in 1152 by Diarmit MacMurrough, whose grave is in the nearby churchyard; it is notable for its tower, square at the bottom and round at the top. There are fragments of later churches here too.

Fethard medieval town walls

Free, open access to view exteriors only. In the town of Fethard, Co Tipperary.

There is an almost-complete set of medieval town walls encircling this small town, plus two surviving towers and one gate. The walls have been restored, but there is no access to the towers. There's also an Augustinian abbey here which is still in use; parts of it date to the 1300s.

Granny (or Granagh) Castle

Dúchas, free, open access at any reasonable time. Beside the N24 (Carrick road) west of Waterford.

The focus of interest is not the largish tower house, which is a later addition and is kept locked up, but a well-preserved circuit of curtain walls, with round towers at the corners, which belonged to the original castle built in the 1200s. The castle was the property of the Butler Earls of Ormond from 1375, and the ornamental stonework in the remaining part of a two-storey hall that once stood alongside the tower includes an angel, a favourite symbol of the Butlers which also occurs at *Ormond Castle (see page 68)*.

Gorey church

Church authorities, free (voluntary contributions appreciated), open access in usual hours. On the south side of the town centre in Gorey, Co Wexford.

This plain Victorian church deserves attention for its stained glass windows, produced in the 1920s by the well-known Irish artist Harry Clarke, breathtaking in their subtle use of colour.

Grangefertagh round tower

Dúchas, in churchyard, free, open access at any reasonable time. Off the N8 Cashel to Port Laoise main road north of Johnstown, Co Kilkenny.

A tall round tower in very good condition stands not far from a ruined church with a chapel attached; inside the chapel is a rather fine tomb with stone effigies of a knight and his lady. The tomb is thought to be that of John Mac Gillapatrick, who died in about 1511. It was carved by a member of a famous family of sculptors, the O'Tunneys.

Above: Hook lighthouse.

Gowran St Mary's Church

Dúchas and church authorities, free, open access to exterior at any time, and to interior with key from nearby house during usual hours only. In the centre of Gowran, Co Kilkenny.

Large but unattractive ruin of a collegiate church founded in 1312 by Edmond Butler, Earl of Carrick, to provide a living for four priests or vicars. Half of it was restored in Victorian times and is still in use as a church; inside, there's an array of carved tombs of varying dates from the 1300s to the 1600s.

Below: Granny Castle.

Hook lighthouse

Privately owned by Hook Heritage, £££, open daily from March to October. Signposted from the R733 at Hook Point, Co Wexford.

A lighthouse might not seem an obvious candidate for inclusion in this book, but in fact the Victorian structure you see today owes its unusual appearance to the fact that it is based on a round stone tower built here in the early 1200s by William Marshal. It's a massive structure of three storeys, each one covered by a stone vault. The Tower of Hook probably had a defensive function too, but even then its main purpose was to show a light to guide ships. It remained in use for more than 400 years, only falling out of use in the 1600s, but its original purpose was revived in 1677. Guided tours can be taken of the lighthouse which, as you might expect, is in a splendid coastal location.

Kilcash Castle and church

No access to castle; church is free, open access at any reasonable time. In Kilcash, Co Tipperary, off the N76 north-east of Clonmel.

Standing in good farming country not far from the foot of Slievenamon mountain, this six-storey tower house of indeterminate age (probably early 1500s, but with later modifications) seems at first glance to be in reasonably good condition, but there is no access since in fact its structure is unsound. There are the remains of a two-storey hall block next to the tower. Nearby, beside the minor road that leads back to the main road in the direction of Kilkenny, is the ruin of a small church, probably of the 1100s, with a very weathered Romanesque doorway.

Above: Knockgraffon motte.

Below: The Cantwell 'Fada'.

Kilfane church and the Cantwell 'Fada'

Dúchas, in churchyard, free, open access at any reasonable time. Signposted from the N9 north of Thomastown, Co Kilkenny; travelling south, turn left after the Long Man pub.

The small ruined church here is famous mainly for the Cantwell 'Fada' (or 'Long man' – hence the name of the pub on the main road nearby), which is a larger-than-life-size effigy of a knight, now set upright against a wall. It is thought likely that the effigy represents Sir Thomas de Cantwell, the founder of the church, and dates from about 1320.

The church itself, which dates from the late 1200s or early 1300s, is also interesting. It has an unusual fortified tower with a machicolation over its doorway; there was a sacristy on the ground floor of this tower, and steps still lead to the living accommodation on the first floor. There are a number of nice details in the church, including a cute type of ogee window made up from two cleverly carved pieces of stone, and traces of red paint on the piscina.

Knockgraffon motte

Dúchas, on farmland, free, open access at any reasonable time. North of Cahir, Co Tipperary; from the centre of the town, take the Cashel road (the R670); when it meets the N8, go over the main road and turn left onto the minor road rather than joining the N8; and then turn first left.

One of the best Anglo-Norman motte-and-bailey castles in Ireland, built in the 1190s, with traces of a stone gatehouse added later. Nearby are the ruins of a later church and tower house.

Matthewstown wedge tomb

Dúchas, on farmland, free, open access at any reasonable time. Near Tramore, Co Waterford; from the R675 west of Fennor, take the first minor road on the right (for Ballymorris and Waterford), and the tomb is signposted up a farm track.

An interesting variation on this early bronze age type of tomb, with ten uprights forming a long chamber covered with three capstones. The tomb is part of an archeological trail in the area; details from the tourist office in Tramore.

Moor Abbey

Dúchas, free, open access at any reasonable time. Beside the R633 east of Galbally, Co Tipperary.

Ruin of the small and modestly ornamented church of a Franciscan friary, notable mainly for its scenic location in the beautiful Glen of Aherlow.

Reginald's Tower, Waterford

Dúchas, ££, open daily from Easter to October. Towards the eastern end of The Quay, Waterford.

The Vikings, who established the port of Waterford as a major trading centre, defended their town with an extensive set of walls built of earth and timber. These were replaced in medieval times with an even more extensive set of stone walls. Some fragments of the walls have survived, along with a few pieces of gate and tower, but the only really interesting remnant is this plump four-storey tower on the quay. Its base dates to the early 1200s, but the rest was built in the 1400s as a residence. It was later used as a jail. It now houses a small local museum, worth visiting for the excellent dioramas of ancient Waterford.

Lismore Castle

Privately owned, gardens ££, open afternoons only in summer. In Lismore, Co Waterford.

This large and very grand Victorian mock-castle was partly designed by Joseph Paxton, the creator of the Crystal Palace, and some of its Gothic-revival interiors were created by the architect Augustus Pugin. The house is now hired out to wealthy clients at a rate of £10,000 per week, but the gardens are open to the public at a far more reasonable price.

Above: Lismore Castle.

Below: St Mullins early monastic site.

St Mullins early monastic site and Norman motte

Dúchas, in churchyard, free, open access at any reasonable time. At St Mullins, Co Carlow; signposted from the R729 north of New Ross.

In a still-used churchyard, in a quiet, rural location, is a very extensive collection of ruined churches associated with a monastery here that was founded by St Moling in the late 600s. The remains are from very much later, and unfortunately are mostly in poor condition: they include a large church of nave-and-chancel type, the stump of a round tower, a tiny oratory known as St James's Chapel, and a small high cross, broken and very weathered, carved with a crucifixion scene.

Somewhat more interesting is a stone well-chapel of indeterminate age, with a stream flowing out of it; it stands in the valley below the monastery, and is reached most easily by walking back down the road and following it to the right. By far the most striking remains in the village, however, are the earthworks of a Norman motte-and-bailey castle.

Swiss Cottage, Cahir

Dúchas, ££, open daily mid-March to November, but closed Mondays (except bank holidays) in March, April, October and November. At Kilcommon, near Cahir; signposted from the R670 (Ardfinnan road) south of the town, or reached by a 20-minute walk from Cahir Castle (see page 58).

Though its brand of pastoral twee-ness may not be to everyone's taste, this fine *cottage orné* – a folly of the early 1800s in which sophisticated rich people could play at being simple goatherds and shepherdesses – is fascinating as a piece of social history as well as an impressive artistic achievement. The building might be the work of John Nash, who was the architect of the Brighton Pavilion.

Until recently the Swiss Cottage was derelict, and that neglect is astonishing when you look at the sheer quality of some of the silk wallpaper and engraved glass that has survived. The decay has been swept away by a careful restoration in which imaginative use of colour in the soft furnishings helps create the ultimate country cottage interior.

Entry is by guided tour only, but it's one of the few places that would be hard to appreciate without the extra information a good tour supplies.

Tullaherin early monastic site

Dúchas, in churchyard, free, open access at any reasonable time. At Tullaherin, off the N9 north of Thomastown, Co Kilkenny.

Behind a modern graveyard stands a typical set of monastic remains: a very ruinous church, a tall round tower with its door blocked by a pillar that holds it up, and an ogham stone that has clearly been used as a gatepost. It's not thrilling.

Wexford Westgate and Selskar Abbey

Local authority, £, open daily May to September. On the west side of Wexford town centre (not far from the railway station).

A large, tower-house-like gate-tower that guarded one of the entrances to this medieval walled town has recently been restored as a local heritage centre. Through the heritage centre, visitors can gain access to the ruined church of Selskar Abbey, an Augustinian priory founded in the 1200s.

Right: The Swiss Cottage, Cahir.

And…

Clochaphoill pierced stone *(on private land, no formal access arrangements), near Aghade, south of Tullow, Co Carlow* – A stone with a 12cm (6in) hole through it is thought to have been part of a neolithic tomb. There are stories that mothers passed sick babies through the hole to have them cured.

Clonmel historic town *(monuments mostly owned by local council, free, open access to view exteriors only at any reasonable time), Co Tipperary* – This lively, prosperous town still has parts of its medieval walls and a rather good gateway, as well as the church of a Franciscan friary, restored in Victorian times and still in use. The most interesting buildings in the town, however, are the Main Guard – an unusual courthouse-like affair which is in the throes of a painfully slow restoration – and the church of St Mary's, with its odd octagonal tower. Parts of the church are as old as the 1200s, but it was rebuilt in the 1400s and 1800s. A new version of the existing historic trail and better access to the buildings would make Clonmel fascinating to visit.

Coolhull Castle *(on farmland, no formal access arrangements), by the R736 near Carrick, east of Wellingtonbridge, Co Wexford* – An unusually long, low tower house built in the late 1500s. It is now just a shell, but is interesting all the same. It stands amongst farm buildings, and visitors are tolerated.

Donohill motte *(Dúchas, on farmland, free, open access at any reasonable time), by the R497 north of Donohill, near Tipperary* – Sizeable Norman castle mound standing in a field.

Duckett's Grove *(on private land, free, open access at any reasonable time), signposted from the R726 east of Carlow* – Fascinating ruin of a vast rambling Gothic-revival mansion burned down in 1933.

Dungarvan Abbey *(in churchyard, free, open access at any reasonable time), in Dungarvan, Co Waterford* – Surviving fragments of the abbey church include a chancel of the 1200s and a tower of the 1400s.

Dunmore cave *(Dúchas, ££, open mid-March to October daily, weekends only rest of year), off the N78 at Ballyfoyle, Co Kilkenny* – Limestone cave notable not just for its rock formations, but also as the site of a Viking massacre in 928.

Ferrycarrig Castle *(Dúchas, free, open access to exterior only at any reasonable time), next to Ferrycarrig bridge, on the N11 north of Wexford* – A picturesque, slender tower house overlooking the River Slaney is said to be on the site of one of the first Anglo-Norman castles in Ireland. Nearby is the Irish National Heritage Park *(£££, open March to October daily)* which features reconstructions of all sorts of ancient monuments, including a crannog.

Foulksrath Castle *(now a youth hostel, access limited to residents) signposted from the N77 north of Kilkenny* – A restored tower house of the 1400s is now in use as youth hostel. If you've always wanted to stay in a castle, this is a cheap way to do it.

Giant's Grave standing stone *(on farmland, no access permitted), signposted off the N24 west of Clonmel, Co Tipperary* – A 3m (9ft) high stone pillar in a field is thought to have been placed here in neolithic times, and was later carved with Christian crosses. Sadly, access is discouraged.

Johnstown Castle Gardens and Irish Agricultural Museum *(gardens ££ in summer only, museum £££, both open all year), signposted off the N25 south of Wexford* – The gardens of this elegant Victorian Gothic mock-castle are open to the public, and its outbuildings contain the very informative national museum of agriculture and rural life.

Leighlinbridge, *Co Carlow* – A fairly ruinous tower house stands by the river in the middle of the town, and there's also a large Norman motte outside on a site that may have been Dinn Righ, the residence of the ancient kings of Leinster. Unfortunately the latter is on private land and access is not permitted.

New Ross Old St Mary's church *(in churchyard, free, open access to view exterior only), on Mary Street* – Built in 1210-20, this large church, now a shell, is said to be the earliest pure Gothic building in Ireland.

South West

Cork and south Kerry

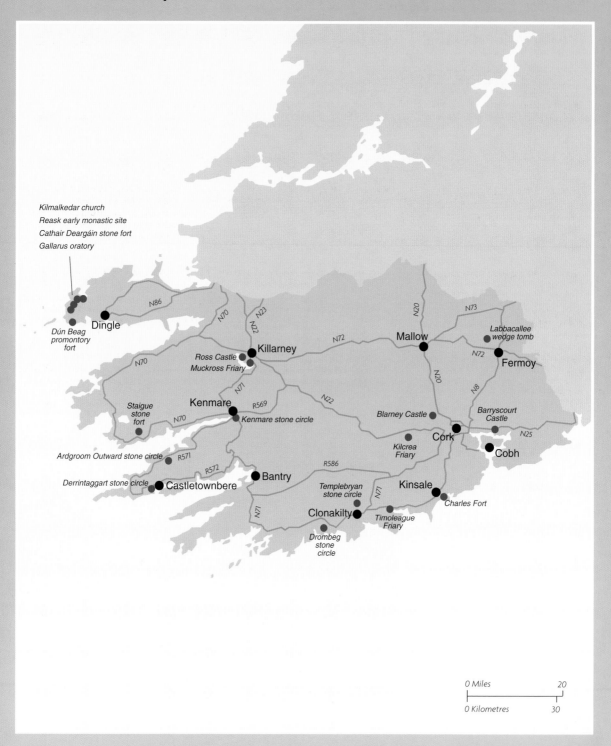

Kilmalkedar church
Reask early monastic site
Cathair Deargáin stone fort
Gallarus oratory

Dún Beag
promontory
fort

Dingle

N86

N70

N23

N22

N20

N73

Labbacallee
wedge tomb

Mallow

N72

Fermoy

Ross Castle
Muckross Friary

Killarney

N72

N70

N71

Staigue
stone
fort

Kenmare

R569

N22

N20

N8

Blarney Castle

Barryscourt
Castle

N70

Kenmare stone circle

Cork

N25

Ardgroom Outward stone circle

R571

Kilcrea
Friary

Cobh

Derrintaggart stone circle

R572

Castletownbere

Bantry

R586

Templebryan
stone circle

N71

Kinsale

Charles Fort

N71

Clonakilty

Timoleague
Friary

Drombeg
stone
circle

0 Miles   20

0 Kilometres   30

Four corner turrets and elaborate battlements give recently restored Barryscourt a flamboyant appearance.

Barryscourt Castle

Dúchas • ££ • Open June to September daily

Opened to the public only recently following a major restoration, Barryscourt is an impressive-looking tower house of an unusual design, its corner-towers and exaggerated multi-stepped battlements giving its roofline a dramatic appearance.

The tower owes its flamboyant look to a short-lived rebuild in the late 1500s, but it was built over a hundred years before on a site that had been the seat of the Barrys since 1206. These were the descendants of Philip de Barri, who came to Ireland in 1180 and whose brother was Gerald of Wales, the famous chronicler of Norman Ireland.

In the 1550s, the main branch of the Barry family died out and a distant cousin, James FitzRichard, gained control of the family estates. His downfall came after he supported the Desmond rebellion in 1580, and James died in Dublin Castle the following year. His son David burned down the castle to prevent it falling into the hands of Sir Walter Raleigh, but he was obliged to make peace with the English not long after, and then rebuilt the castle again in its present form. He died in 1617, and was the last head of the Barry family to live at Barryscourt.

The tower has now been greatly restored. In the summer of 2000, there was still a lot of work in progress on the gardens and outbuildings, and some of the upper parts of the castle were not yet open. At the time, access to the castle was by guided tour only, and the example of *Ross Castle*, near Killarney (*see page 88*) suggests that this policy will probably continue. Inside, the contrast with less grand tower houses is obvious in the way the main central block is divided vertically into just three high-ceilinged rooms. There are lots of smaller chambers in the corner-towers, including toilets, a chapel and, unusually, a kitchen. The tour is not without interest, but frankly this is not the most fascinating castle in the country.

Near Carrigtwohill, Co Cork. South of the N25 (Midleton to Cork) main road, which bypasses Carrigtwohill village; clearly signposted from the N25 or from the centre of the village.

Blarney Castle

Privately owned • ££££ • Open daily from April to October, Sundays only rest of year

There are two contradictory facts about Blarney Castle. On the one hand, it's a big, brutal, fascinating example of a major tower house of the mid-1400s. On the other, the bewildering popularity of a legend that says being held upside-down to kiss a particular stone of the parapet will confer eloquence on the kisser has made it a tourist trap without equal.

If you come at a quiet time and you can overlook the tourist trappings (there's a gift shop right at the foot of the tower, which is desperately tacky), the castle is well worth seeing. It consists of a main block housing several storeys of big rooms (there's a stone vault over the first floor, but it's now open to the sky from there on up), plus an extension on the end, almost like a separate tower, which contains stairs (one main spiral stair, one smaller one) and also lots of narrow corridors and small chambers. It's this part of the castle which is great fun to explore, but it's totally impossible when the place is busy.

The extension incorporates a projecting turret at the north-west corner which is actually the oldest part of the castle, built in the early 1400s as part of an earlier tower. The vast main block was added on in about 1450 by Cormac Láidir MacCarthy, but the striking parapet and machicolations at the top are from a century later. A Gothic-style mansion was built beside the castle in the early 1700s, and the odd little folly-like tower was part of its facade.

At Blarney, off the N20 north-west of Cork city.

Blarney Castle is one of Ireland's most impressive tower houses, but don't go kissing any strange stones...

Charles Fort

Dúchas • ££ • Open mid-March to October daily, rest of year at weekends only

This is a splendid large artillery fort of the 1600s, in a fine setting overlooking the last stretches of Kinsale Harbour as it meets the sea. It's far and away the best example in Ireland of a fort of this type, built at a time when advances in 'military science' in Europe – particularly the ideas of Sebastian de Vauban (1633–1707), chief engineer to French king Louis XIV – had radically altered the appearance of defensive fortifications.

Thick ramparts of earth, faced with stone, were designed to absorb the impact of artillery, and there were vaulted bunkers ('casemates') underneath for the soldiers to shelter in. The external walls were set at carefully judged angles, with 'bastions', like miniature forts, at the corners, to ensure that every inch of the wall was protected by crossfire from the defenders' guns.

These features remain impressive today, the sheer scale of the exterior walls and the gentle sweep of the grassy ramparts combining with the fine views out to sea to make this a memorable place to visit. There's a surprising number of buildings inside the fort, including a fine

The massive earthen ramparts of Charles Fort were built to safeguard the approach to Kinsale Harbour.

barracks square, but currently too much of it is ruinous to paint a picture of daily life in the fort. There is, however, a very good display on the historical background in the elegant restored barracks stores. And the teashop is welcome, too.

The fort was built in the 1670s as the last element in a series of defences which protected the natural harbour of Kinsale, then the region's major port. A pentagonal fort with bastions had already been built on a peninsula known as Castle Park, on the far side of the harbour, following the O'Neill rebellion of 1601. During that rebellion, a tower on the same site had been held by Spanish troops, preventing the English from using the harbour. The Castle Park fort, renamed James Fort, was now strengthened with the addition of a shoreline gun battery in the late 1660s. Both James Fort and its shoreline battery can be seen from Charles Fort.

A large set of earthworks was built where Charles Fort is now, but these were not easy to maintain, so in 1671 the decision was made to create a proper fort here. It was completed in August 1681, and named in honour of King Charles II. Its weakness, however, was that it could be bombarded from higher ground nearby.

In 1689 James II landed at Kinsale as he launched his attempt to regain the throne, and the following year both forts were besieged by King William's forces. James Fort surrendered after a cask of gunpowder exploded, killing many of the defenders. Charles Fort held out for 13 days against artillery fire from that higher ground, but surrendered when the ramparts were breached.

The fort was later strengthened, and remained in use, with modifications, throughout the 18th and 19th centuries. Not until 1922, when the British were kicked out, were most of the buildings inside the fort destroyed.

Incidentally, a good way to get here is to walk from Kinsale, a distance of just over 3km (2 miles). It takes about 40 minutes. The path follows the shoreline all the way: it starts out along the road, but leaves it after the headland at Scilly. It's a pleasant walk, but steep towards the end, where it climbs to meet the road, which then dips through Summer Cove before climbing again to the fort. A coast path also carries on from the fort right out to Prehane Point.

Near Summer Cove, to the south-east of the town of Kinsale, Co Cork.

Drombeg stone circle

Dúchas, on private farmland • £ • Any reasonable time

Admittedly this is a very tidy little stone circle with a number of interesting features, but it's really too insignificant to justify the entrance fee that is charged. Access arrangements in the summer months, when the site is at its busiest, are frankly poor: visitors are buttonholed as they approach the gate and led to an amateurish museum-cum-gift shop, where they are relieved of a modest entrance fee and subjected to a brief lecture by a youngster who seems to have learned the words by rote. It's rather depressing.

Out of season, presumably access is open, with an honesty box for fees: a far better arrangement.

The monument itself, however, is not without interest. It's a small circle, 9m (29ft) across, consisting of 17 closely spaced stones. As is typical of the region's stone circles (the 'Cork-Kerry type'), a pair of taller 'entrance stones' stands opposite a recumbent 'axial stone', giving the monument an axis which points to the south-west, in the direction of the setting sun on the day of the midwinter solstice – the shortest day of the year. The top of the axial stone is decorated with a hollow, or 'cup mark', and an outlined shape that looks like a bronze axe.

The tidy appearance is owed to the fact that the monument was restored after excavation in 1958. At the centre of the circle, a pot was found containing the cremated remains of a young adolescent. Dates of 945BC and 830BC for samples from the site agree with evidence from

The stone circle at Drombeg is the most distinctive of the region's stone circles, but it has been restored.

another similar circle, which seems to have been in use from about 970 to 715BC.

Just a few metres away are the foundations of two round, stone-walled huts, thought to be of rather later date. There's also a bronze age cooking place, or fulacht fiadh, where a tank of water would have been heated by throwing hot stones into it. There's even a ready supply of fresh running water.

West of Ross Carbery, Co Cork. Signposted on the R597 Ross Carbery to Leap road.

Kenmare stone circle

On private land • £ • Any reasonable time

Another fairly small stone circle of the Cork-Kerry type, though rather different from Drombeg. This is actually the largest of the region's stone circles, consisting of a number of rounded boulders (it is thought that there were originally 15) set in an egg-shaped formation rather than a true circle, some 17m (55 ft) across. In the middle is a boulder burial – a simple variety of megalithic tomb that dates from the same late bronze age period as the circle.

Again, access arrangements really ought to be better. The monument stands just on the outskirts of the lively little town of Kenmare, two minutes' walk from the high street, in an entirely undramatic setting that looks like a suburban garden, all clipped lawns and dwarf conifers. Still, at least it's well tended. There's a ticket booth, and you're asked to pay a small fee if it's manned, or drop the coins in an honesty box if it's not. It's hard to begrudge such a minor sum, but on the other hand this is not a major monument, and the eagerness to make a few quid from the summer visitors hardly does anything for the dignity of Ireland's heritage.

In Kenmare, Co Kerry. Signposted along a lane from The Square in the centre of the town.

Left: A type of tomb known as a 'boulder burial' stands in the middle of the stone circle at Kenmare.

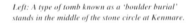

Kilcrea Friary

*Dúchas • Free • Open access at any
reasonable time*

It's always intriguing to find such a large
and complete ruin as this standing among
fields in a peaceful patch of countryside,
and it's always a pleasure to come across
somewhere that is so well looked after and
so easily accessible.

The friary was founded in 1465 by
the Franciscans under the patronage of
Cormac Láidir MacCarthy, Lord of
Muskerry. Friars still lived here in the
1580s, when the place was raided by a
company of English soldiers from Cork,
and they restored the friary again in 1604,
but were finally ousted ten years later.
Cromwell's men occupied the buildings
in 1650, making alterations to suit their
own purposes, and most of the decorative
stonework was robbed in the following
two centuries.

As is often the way, the friary has
remained in use as a burial ground, but
this is by no means as intrusive here as in
some other places. The layout is on the
usual Franciscan pattern, with an aisle and
a transept on the south side of the church,
and the cloister on the north.

From below the narrow tower a set of
steps leads upstairs to the dormitory on the
east side of the cloister. The rooms on the

*Below: Kilcrea Friary stands in a tranquil
countryside location, seldom disturbed by visitors.*

The wedge tomb of Labbacallee is the largest and finest example in Ireland of this kind of chambered tomb.

north side of the cloister would have been
the kitchens, while the west side would
have contained a range of day-rooms or
accommodation for lay people.

But the most interesting and unusual
feature of the friary is down at the east end
of the church, through a door to the left.
There's a two-storey room here: the
ground floor was the sacristy, where the
valuable vessels and clothes used in
services were kept safe; but the interesting
bit is upstairs. This was the scriptorium,

where monks worked writing documents
and copying books: the large windows
gave them plenty of light to work in, and
the big fireplace kept them warm as they
sat at their desks.

Nearby is Kilcrea Castle, a ruined tower
house, but there is no path to it – you have
to tromp across fields – and it's just a shell,
the ground floor used as a shelter by cows.

*Near Aherla, west of Ballincollig, west of Cork.
Beside a minor road south of the N22 main road.*

Labbacallee wedge tomb

Dúchas • Free • Open access at any time

This is the biggest and finest example in Ireland of a burial monument of this type. It's very easily accessible, too, standing in a glade of trees right by the road, with access via a stile over the fence. It is what's known as a wedge-shaped gallery grave, a kind of chambered tomb that was built in the early bronze age, circa 1500BC.

This one is not only of impressive size, but also has a particularly interesting design, with a long, rectangular chamber at the back and a smaller collapsed one in front, covered by three huge capstones. There are three smaller chambers at the back of the monument, too, and the whole thing is surrounded by the remains of a stone cairn, kerbed with upright slabs in a 'U' shape.

Excavations in 1934 found inhumations (complete burials, rather than cremated remains or separate bones), fragments of pottery, animal bones and stone tools.

North of Fermoy, Co Cork. Beside a minor road, signposted from the R512 north of the town.

Muckross Friary

Dúchas • Free • Open daily during usual hours from mid-June to early September

The Muckross Estate is a large slice of land in a lakeside setting near Killarney. Owned wholly by the heritage service, Dúchas, the estate takes in the grounds of Muckross House and its estate farms, and is the most popular tourist attraction in the country: second most visited is the Book of Kells exhibition at Trinity College, Dublin, while the Brú na Boinne visitor centre claims third place.

The house is a grand Victorian mansion, open to the paying public all year round. Adjoining it is a massive gift shop and restaurant. Nearby is a working farm employing traditional methods, open to visitors at weekends in March, April and October and daily from May to September (you can buy a reduced-price admission ticket jointly with Muckross House).

The roads in the estate are closed to motor vehicles, but are used by horse-drawn 'jaunting cars' which ferry tourists around at extravagant fares. The paths and lanes of the estate, and the gardens of the house, are open free of charge to anyone who wishes to wander around them. If you stroll down to the lake, you'll see some of the finest mountain scenery in Ireland, all of it part of a huge national park.

Also open to the public is an attractive and remarkably complete ruin of a Franciscan friary founded in about 1448

Muckross Friary has the best-preserved cloisters in the country, and stands in a splendid country park.

by Donal MacCarthy. It stands on the side of the estate nearest to the town of Killarney: there's a car park by the friary, signposted from the main road, but it's more fun to park in the main car park at the house, or in the small car park by the waterfall on the far side of the estate, and walk there. It takes about 15 minutes from the house, and the same again to get to the house from the waterfall.

The most remarkable part of the friary is the cloister, which is in excellent condition. With the upstairs rooms overhanging the arcade in the manner typical of Franciscan friaries, the cloister garth (or yard) would be gloomy even if it weren't filled with an ancient yew tree that blocks most of the light. It's a place to come on a warm, sunny day, when the shade is welcome.

The buildings around the cloister are probably the best-preserved in Ireland. Each side is slightly different because the three ranges were built at different dates. The east side of the cloister would have

had the dormitory on the first floor (with stairs leading directly to the church), and a day-room below (though it looks a bit dark in there for daytime activities). The kitchens and refectory were on the north side, across from the church; and the west side was probably storerooms below, with a house above for the head of the friary.

The church, meanwhile, is on a typical Franciscan pattern, with a transept on the south side only (rather than on both sides) and the cloister to the north. The tower, however, is the full width of the church, uniquely for a Franciscan friary in Ireland. You can climb up to a room in the base of it, just above the crossing of the church.

The friary was suppressed in 1541, but then was reoccupied in 1602 and officially re-established in 1612. By 1626 it had been fully restored. The friars were only finally put out of business by Cromwellian forces in 1652.

In the Muckross Estate, near Killarney, Co Kerry. Signposted from the N71 south of the town.

Ross Castle

Dúchas • £££ • Open daily April to October (but closed Mondays in October)

The effort that has gone into the recent restoration of this tall, powerful tower house is quite remarkable. For example, it's common enough for timber floors to be replaced during restoration; but here the stone vault above the second-floor bedchamber has been completely rebuilt using the traditional method, which involved weaving a wicker mat on site and curving it into a 'former' to support the rubble and mortar of the vault. The flagstone floor above has been relaid using fallen pieces of the original stone.

The tower stands in a scenic location on the shore of Lough Leane, not far from Killarney, the major tourist town of south-western Ireland. Below its walls there are landing stages for boat-trips on the lake (including visits to the early monastic site on the island of Inishfallen). It's a busy spot, yet the inside of the castle is far from overrun, since visits are by guided tour only and are restricted to small groups of about 20 people at a time.

Tours are not generally the best way of seeing a castle, but in this case the system works well. If you have never been on a tour of a similar tower house, it's a safe bet that the guide will point out details that you wouldn't otherwise have noticed; though by the same token, if you have taken a tour of a similar tower elsewhere in Ireland, you might find that certain elements here are very familiar.

Some of the small details supplied by the tour, such as the fact that the windows would have been 'glazed' with waxed animal skins, are certainly interesting, and combined with the attention to detail of the restoration – such as the dished sills and drainholes under the windows, to gather and drain away any rainwater that may have got in through the leaky windows – it all adds up to a tower house that is far more informative than most.

The layout is classic: the high-ceilinged principal chambers are stacked on top of one another in the main body of the tower, but there's also a sort of annexe on one end containing a spiral stair and a series of small chambers, plus a garderobe toilet. There's an extra 'intermediate level' of these smaller chambers between each storey of the main tower.

The way in which the rooms were used was not so typical, however. Above the basement (primarily for storage), the first floor was a reception room, the second a bedchamber, and the top storey was, unusually, the main hall, with the largest windows and the best fireplace. There was

Ross Castle is one of the most impressive tower houses of Ireland, in a very popular corner of the country.

even a kitchen up here – though food would probably just have been warmed after a journey from 'proper' kitchens in the courtyard below – separated from the hall by a reconstructed wooden screen, with a minstrels' gallery above.

The tower has been sprinkled with a few items of precious and delicate oak furniture from the 1500s and early 1600s. These items, some of which are very beautiful, help to sketch the way the room might have been furnished, but it's a long way from a reconstruction, and further yet from a properly furnished period house. The compromise isn't entirely successful.

The castle was built in the late 1400s by local ruling clan the O'Donoghues, but it passed out of their hands after they fought against the Crown – and lost – in the Desmond Rebellion of the 1580s. In 1652 it held out for ages against Cromwell's forces, but surrendered when artillery was brought here by boat via the River Laune – fulfilling, some say, a prophecy that it would only ever be taken by a warship.

A fortified house was built alongside the tower in 1688, but this was adapted into a military barracks at the time of the Williamite wars, then replaced by a proper barracks in the mid-1700s. It went out of use in 1825, and the ruin was 'romanticised' on the orders of Lord Kenmare. A modern visitor centre has been cleverly built into the ground floor of this block.

On the shore of Lough Leane, south-west of Killarney, Co Kerry, signposted on a minor road off the N71 just south of the town centre.

Staigue stone fort

Dúchas, on private farmland • £ (honesty box) •
Open access at sensible times only

This rather splendid round stone fort is the
best example in Ireland of an unusual type
of Celtic stronghold. The only directly
comparable one that survives is *Grianán
of Aileach*, Co Donegal (*see page 144*),
which was rebuilt in the 1800s.

There's a lack of evidence to pin down
when Staigue was built or used, but it's
from the late iron age, around 300 to 400 AD.
It's basically an earlier equivalent of a
medieval tower house, the defended
residence of a local lord – or in those days,
more likely a local king.

The fort is a considerable feat of
engineering by the standards of the time.
It's not easy to build a structure this large
out of dry stone, with no mortar holding it
together. Many experts think that the high
walls would have been more an expression
of status than a practical measure.

It's altogether a very pleasing structure,
despite (or perhaps because of) its partly
ruined state, its ragged wall-tops looking
like a broken eggshell. Up close, the walls
are higher than you might expect – up to
5.5m (18ft) high in places, and as much as
4m (13ft) thick – and very neatly built.

The stone fort of Staigue stands in a sheltered location at the head of a small valley overlooking the sea.

An entrance passage roofed by stone
slabs (there's a similar one at Grianán of
Aileach) leads into the fort, where the
main feature is a series of cunningly
arranged flights of steps, with pairs of
flights crossing at small landings to form
'X' shapes, obviously planned to make it
easier for anyone dashing up or down the
stairs to go the right way more quickly.

Two small corbel-roofed chambers in
the thickness of the wall would have been
for storage: these are not too hard to get
into, and it's worth taking a look inside.
You don't particularly need a torch.
Presumably there would have been free-
standing wooden buildings inside the fort,
and there's plenty of space: the central
area is about 27.5m (90ft) across.

The fort is in a sheltered location at the
top of a long valley that winds up from the
sea. The superb view of the coast which is
so pleasing today must have been a crucial
practicality at the time, since the keepers
of the fort would have owned ships and
relied on them for all their long-distance
travel, and the most likely direction for
any attack would be from the sea.

Access arrangements are pretty good:
the narrow minor road that leads up the

valley to the monument is clearly
signposted from the main road, and there's
a large car park at the top of the road,
which is just as well: it can get busy here
in the summer months. It's a very short
walk to the field in which the fort stands.
The farmer requests that visitors put a
small payment (a pound or so) into an
honesty box for access to the land, and it's
hard to begrudge it for the right to visit
such a fine monument.

*On the south coast of the Iveragh peninsula,
signposted from the N70 west of Sneem, Co Kerry.*

*The flights of steps, which cross in an 'X' pattern,
are a distinctive feature of the fort's interior.*

See also... Templebryan stone circle

On private land, free, open access at any reasonable time. On a minor road off the R588 north of Clonakilty; turn right for Ballinascarty and the circle is in a field to the left of the road.

This ruined example of a Cork-Kerry type stone circle stands in a field near Clonakilty, not far from Timoleague. The monument is not an especially impressive one, and there is no proper access to it, but it's interesting because of the small white quartz pillar in the middle of the circle. It is thought that this type of stone, besides being a distinctive building material, might have been especially significant to the builders of these bronze age monuments because it occurs among the same type of rocks that produce copper ore (alloyed with tin to make bronze) or gold.

Timoleague Friary

Dúchas, church authorities • Free • Open access at any reasonable time

The best thing about this elegant-looking ruin of a Franciscan friary is its setting, on the shore of the tidal river estuary known as Courtmacsherry Bay. Between here and the sea, the bay widens rapidly, with broad mudflats at low tide; but the narrower river near the friary is a particularly good spot for wading birds. There's a footpath along the river which follows the course of an old tramway, and a series of attractively illustrated signboards explains some of the more interesting species of bird found here.

The friary itself is not as well-preserved as it first appears; it just happens that the parts that are in best condition face towards the bridge where the main road crosses the river, which is the direction visitors are most likely to approach from. The buildings of the cloister are largely ruined, the south wall of the church has gone, and the interiors of all the buildings have been very much disturbed by their continued use as a burial ground.

However, enough of it remains to show that this was a fairly typical Franciscan

Timoleague Friary rises majestically above the mud of the estuary. It's a fine place for wading birds.

friary, and even though it was built a fair bit earlier – founded in the late 1200s or early 1300s, with modifications made in the early 1500s – it had a lot in common with the excellently preserved later examples further north, such as *Ross Errily* in Co Galway and *Moyne Friary*, Co Mayo (*see pages 131 and 127*).

As usual, the cloister was to the north of the church. The best-preserved parts of it are all on the east side. The dormitory was next to the church, on the first floor, above a library and a day-room. The refectory was a kind of extension on the end, lit by five large windows which would have had a fine view over the river. Behind it was an infirmary.

Although the friary was initially closed down at the time of the reformation in about 1540, the friars returned and stayed until as late as 1642, when the place was burned down by English soldiers under Lord Forbes.

At Timoleague, Co Cork, beside the river on the south-east side of the village.

Stone circles of the Beara peninsula

The rugged beauty of the Beara is a match for the Iveragh peninsula (better known as the 'Ring of Kerry') to the north, but Beara is smaller and less overrun with tourists. The main thing it has to offer in the way of archeological or historic interest is a scattering of small stone circles of the Cork-Kerry type.

These bronze age stone circles come in two principal varieties: five-stone settings, and larger multiple-stone arrangements, always made up of an odd number of stones. The multiple-stone circles are more common near the coast, and that's the sort you'll find here.

The more notable of the circles are signposted from the roads that loop the peninsula, with a concentration of them near the R571, which leads from the tip of the peninsula along its north coast to Kenmare. Perhaps because they are well signposted, or perhaps because there's not much else to do here, these little circles, none of which is all that

Below: The ruined circle at Ardgroom Outward stands in a ruggedly beautiful moorland setting.

impressive, do seem to attract an awful lot of visitors. Only the two mentioned below are particularly worth seeing.

Access arrangements are generally fairly reasonable, with the farmers on whose land the circles stand usually requesting a fee for access, to be put in an honesty box. Some kind of intervention by the government heritage service Dúchas to improve things like footpaths and fences would be handy.

Ardgroom Outward stone circle

On farmland • £ (honesty box) • Open access at any reasonable time

This is far and away the most impressive of the peninsula's monuments, not so much for the haphazard beauty of the stones as for the superb setting, with views across the bay of the Kenmare River to the mountains of the Iveragh peninsula. The circle is partly ruined, but the stones seem to be graded in size to give it an alignment. There's an outlying

pillar, with suggestions that there may have been other stones in the setting too. Access is good, with space to park cars at the end of the track, from where it's a short walk to the monument. The choice of concrete patio slabs as stepping stones across the bog is an odd one, though.

Signposted from the R571 east of Ardgroom.

Derrintaggart stone circle

On farmland • £ (honesty box) • Open access at any reasonable time

The most accessible of the Beara's circles stands on high ground overlooking the harbour of Castletownbere. It's a fairly handsome example of a Cork-Kerry circle, with an alignment defined by an entrance opposite a recumbent 'axial stone', though the circle is partially ruined. Access is easy, and the landowner promises to contribute fees to charity.

Signposted on a minor road from the R572 on the west side of Castletownbere (also known as Castletown Bearhaven).

The stone wall of Dún Beag cuts off a promontory overlooking the sea, to turn it into a stronghold.

The Dingle peninsula

This outstandingly beautiful part of Ireland is scattered with dozens and dozens of minor archeological monuments and small historic buildings. Many of them wouldn't be of much interest to the average everyday visitor, but a few are real gems.

The great thing about this area, though – apart from the superb scenery – is that the monuments are generally so close together. You can comfortably visit several neighbouring sites in the course of a pleasant walk, or get to a whole lot of them in the course of a busy day on a bicycle.

Dún Beag promontory fort

On private land • ££ • Open daily all year round

Standing in a splendid clifftop location, with extensive views out to sea, this is a very unusual kind of iron age fortification, consisting of a stone wall built across a headland to turn the promontory into a defended enclosure. The only other fort like this in the whole of the British Isles is at Ness of Burgi in the Shetland Islands, way up to the north of Scotland.

The main structure is a stone rampart – very thick but not particularly high – with an entrance passage leading through it. The inner part of the wall was built first, and the outer half was added later to strengthen it. Outside this wall there were four ramparts of earth, only two of which are now obvious. There was originally a lot more of the fort to the right of the entrance, but this disappeared when part of the cliff collapsed into the sea.

In front of the entrance is a souterrain – an underground passage that was probably used for storing food, though in this case it might also have been a kind of sally-port or secret entrance. The large stone slabs that roof the souterrain also act as a paved pathway leading to the fort's gate. You

can't get inside the souterrain, but if you peer through the gaps between the roofing slabs, you can see the drystone construction of its walls.

Inside the entrance passage, to the right, an angled 'squint' means that traffic through the gate can be covered from a guard chamber beyond. On the inner face of the fort wall, to the left, an opening leads to a small corbelled-over chamber, high enough to stand up in, which would probably have been used for storage.

There would presumably have been a number of buildings on the piece of land behind the wall, but most of the space is now taken up by the low ruined walls of a large rectangular building, with fine drawbar-holes at its entrance and a stone drain running all the way round, which appears to be a house of later date.

Excavations that took place here suggested that the fort may have been built as recently as the 900s.

Access is easy, with car parking provided just across the road from the monument. A charge is made for entry in the summer months, but it seems likely that access would be free in the winter.

Beside the R559 west of Ventry.

Gallarus oratory

Dúchas, access via private land • ££ or free •
Open daily all year round

This charmingly simple little building is the best-preserved example in Ireland of a very early kind of stone church or chapel. It's not known when exactly it was built, but between the 700s and 900s is likely.

The unusual shape, often compared to an overturned boat, is clearly owed to a development of the same technique of building with corbelled stone used to create the beehive huts often found on early monastic sites. However, the method is not as well suited to the rectangular shape of the oratory as it is to round huts, and the two longer sides of the roof tend to bow in and collapse under the weight of the stone, which is why this is the only one of its kind to remain intact. You can see the sides of the roof sagging.

Simple though the structure is, the care that has gone into its construction is admirable. Inside, it has an almost cave-like quality, lit only by the light from the door and from a tiny pointed window directly opposite. It manages to retain its dignity even with coachloads of tourists crawling all over it.

The oratory was presumably part of an early monastery on this site: next to it are what seem to be the remains of another building, and a stone cross-slab carved with an ogham inscription. But little is known about the history of this place or, indeed, of any of the early monastic settlements in the immediate area.

Both *Reask monastic site* and *Kilmalkedar church (see page 94)* are very close by, sharing a superb setting in a bowl of hills where the land sweeps down to the sea at Smerwick Harbour. It's a very evocative location, as well as a very beautiful one, and it suggests that there must have been a particular reason for so much religious activity to take place here, on the slopes above Smerwick.

The accepted explanation for there being so many early Christian monuments in the Dingle area generally is that people were attracted here for pilgrimages to the top of Mount Brandon, holy because of its associations with Saint Brendan. His journey across the Atlantic Ocean in a boat made of hides is supposed to have begun from Brandon Creek, a small inlet at the foot of the mountain. As elsewhere in Ireland, however, the tradition of pilgrimage to a mountain top almost certainly owes its origins to pre-Christian customs.

Finally, a brief word about the slightly odd access arrangements. Visitors coming by car or coach will arrive at the car park belonging to the visitor centre, where a

Above: The Gallarus oratory is a tiny chapel built from dry stone in an appealingly simple style.

charge is made for access to the site. Anyone coming by bicycle or on foot, however, may enter the site by a footpath from the minor road that passes to the south of the oratory, and entry is free. Presumably you can use this path in winter or when the visitor centre is closed.

Off the R559 south of Ballydavid, Co Kerry.

☐ **See also... Cathair Deargáin stone fort**

Dúchas, free, open access at any time. By the R559 south-east of Ballydavid.

This intriguing little fort consists of a walled enclosure with the foundations of a number of round stone huts inside. Two of the huts are linked by a passage, and one has a souterrain. It's a good place to visit on a walk from Gallarus oratory to Kilmalkedar church.

Below: the linked circular huts, surrounded by an outer wall, at Cathair Deargáin.

93

Kilmalkedar church

Dúchas and church authorities • Free
• Open access at any reasonable time

There's a striking group of monuments in and around this early monastic site, including a holy well in the field opposite and a ruined oratory of the same sort as Gallarus nearby.

The church is surrounded by an interesting collection of carved stones, including an early sundial, an ogham stone inscribed with the name 'Mael Inbir, son of Brocán' and, inside the church, a stone carved with the Latin alphabet.

The site is named after, and may have been founded by, Saint Maolcethair, who died in 636, but the present church was built some time in the 1100s. By the standards of the time, it's a particularly large and ornate building, and it shows many of the typical features of Irish churches of the time, including projecting walls known as 'antae' on either side of the shorter walls, which were intended to help support the roof. There are carved animal heads at the tops of the antae. An interesting survival is the 'whale-tail' stone at the top of the pointed gable end: barge boards would have been attached to it to prevent rain from getting in under the gables.

Features such as the richly carved arched doorway in the Irish Romanesque style and the fancy blind arcading on the inner wall suggest that the building may have been influenced by Cormac's Chapel at *Cashel*, Co Tipperary (*see page 60*).

Beside the R559 on the hillside east of Ballydavid, less than 30 minutes' walk from Gallarus oratory.

Of the early monastery at Reask, all that remains is low walls (above) and an unusual cross-slab (below).

Reask early monastic site

Dúchas • Free • Open access at any reasonable time

Although there is nothing left of its buildings but low walls, uncovered and excavated fairly recently, this is an interesting site because it shows the layout of a typical little monastery, with a number of buildings set within a surrounding protective wall or cashel.

The compound is divided by a cross-wall. The smaller part contained an oratory, a small round clochan (stone hut) and a large rectangular one, a graveyard, and about ten carved stone slabs, one of which is a very fine example of the curly style common in this area.

The larger part of the compound contained two large round clochans joined in a figure of eight. It is thought that this part of the monastery would have been set aside for the domestic buildings

Signposted from the R559 south of Smerwick Harbour, near the road to Ventry.

Left and above: The mid-1100s church at Kilmalkedar is a nave-and-chancel design, the nave being the main body of the church, and the chancel being the extension on the eastern end. Note the projecting walls, known as 'antae'.

☐ See also… other sites on the Dingle peninsula

Fahan beehive huts

On private land, £, open all year round. Near the R559 between Ventry and Slea Head.

There are several collections of these small round dry-stone buildings alongside the coast road here, with small fees requested by landowners for access. Some of the huts are thought to have been shelters for pilgrims making their way to Mount Brandon. Identical buildings were still constructed as sheds right into the late 1800s, so it is not always clear how old any particular hut might be.

There are several groups of these huts inside enclosing walls. Some of the huts have souterrains beneath, and some of the entrances to the enclosures are guarded by a small hut, like a sentry-box.

Gallarus Castle

Dúchas, free, open access during usual hours only. Near the Gallarus oratory (see page 93).

This neat little four-storey tower house was built by the Fitzgeralds, Knights of Kerry, probably in the late 1400s, and was lived in until 1688. It has recently been restored and you should now find it unlocked, during the summer months at least.

Above right: Rathinnane Castle.

Below: Minard Castle.

Minard Castle

On private land, no access permitted. Signposted from the R561 and the N86 west of Annascaul.

This ruined tower stands on a small headland at one end of Minard Bay. Unfortunately the castle is unsafe, so there is no access to it, but it is such a picturesque affair in such a lovely place that it is well worth making the effort to come here and look at it from the sandy beach below.

Rathinnane Castle

On private land, £, access with permission from farm at reasonable times only. North of Ventry, beside the minor road to Ballydavid.

You have to call at the farm and pay a small fee for permission to visit this interesting site. The remains of a tower house of the 1500s, rather badly ruined, stand in the middle of a round earthwork fort, or rath. There's a souterrain, but you can't get inside it.

See also...

Ballynacarriga Castle

Dúchas, free, open access to view exterior only at any time. By the minor road to the west of Ballynacarriga village, near Dunmanway, Co Cork.

There's something odd and neglected – almost a ghost-town feel – about the village of Ballynacarriga, and this ancient-looking tower house, standing on a rocky outcrop near a stream west of the village, feels equally forgotten. It's in decent condition externally, but looks as if it was locked up and left to rot a long time ago. There's no access to the interior. There are unusual chunky machicolations at opposite corners, fairly low on the wall.

It's a shame you can't get inside, because a room on the fourth floor of the tower is said to have interesting carved decoration around the windows, depicting a woman with three roses – thought to represent Catherine Cullinane, an owner of the castle in the late 1500s, with her three children – and also a crucifixion scene. The room remained in use as a chapel right up to 1815.

Belvelly Castle

Dúchas, free, open access to view exterior only at any time. Beside the R624 on the north coast of Cobh Island.

This small tower house, built by the Hodnett family in the mid-1400s to guard the main bridging point between the mainland and Cobh Island, was owned by Sir Walter Raleigh in the 1580s. It looks to be in good condition, but there is no access to its interior.

It stands on the shore of a tidal channel which is a very good spot for birdwatching: a trail of such vantage points is detailed on a signboard at the site. The attractive old stone bridge nearby is still the main access route to the island.

A nearby Martello tower (also derelict and inaccessible) is one of three built to defend the north side of Cobh Island in Victorian times.

Pictured above: Castlelyons Friary.

Below: Ballynacarriga Castle.

Castlelyons Friary

Dúchas, free, open access at any reasonable time. In Castlelyons, near Fermoy, Co Cork.

The reasonably substantial but fairly plain ruin of a small Carmelite friary, standing in the middle of a tidy, quiet little country village.

Most of the church survives, along with two ranges of domestic buildings (probably the dormitory and refectory) on opposite sides of a small cloister. The structures are mostly of the late 1400s.

The friary was founded in 1309 on lands granted by John de Barry to Carmelite friars from Drogheda, Co Louth. The Carmelites, who were better known as White Friars, were still fairly new to Ireland at the time, having first settled in this country at Leighlinbridge in about 1270.

Just outside the village, near the road that heads south towards Midleton, are the remains of the house-like castle after which the village is named, but it's very ruinous and not accessible.

Cloyne round tower and cathedral

Church authorities, free, open access during usual hours only. In the small town of Cloyne, Co Cork.

The round tower, which stands at the end of a row of houses in the middle of this old-fashioned little town, is a good one. The stonework of its exterior has an archaic, slightly crumbling appearance; the conical top has been replaced at some relatively recent date by battlements.

The good news is that normally you can climb up it: the key is available from the house next door to the cathedral. The views from the top are said to be very fine. The bad news is that in 2000 it was closed for restoration because it had become unsafe, and it it looked likely to remain shut indefinitely.

The former cathedral nearby was restored for use as a church in the 1800s, with an unusual arrangement whereby the new church occupies the choir of the much larger earlier building and uses the old nave as a kind of large vestibule. It's all a bit of a mess, with barely any of the original building of the mid-1200s surviving, but has some interesting monuments and is worth a quick look.

Conna Castle

Dúchas, free, open access to exterior only at any reasonable time. In the village of Conna, Co Cork, standing in a public park to the east of the village, beside the R268 (Tallow road).

This impressive little castle – a tall, thin tower house of the 1500s standing on a small hill next to the River Bride – is in very good condition externally (in fact, it was restored in the 1800s). But there is no access to the interior, which is missing its floors above the first-floor stone vault. However, the tree-girt hill on which the tower stands is a public park, so you can at least wander round the outside and peer in through the windows.

The five-storey tower has lots of interesting details, such as a simple box machicolation – looking a lot like an upside-down fireplace – on the wall above the door, from which missiles could be rained down on attackers. Just round the corner from the door, to the right, there's an opening which is the bottom of a latrine chute. Elegant detailing on the narrow slit windows lower down and the fancier but still small double-lancet windows that light the upper floors suggests that this must have been quite an expensive building when it was constructed.

Conna was the birthplace of Thomas Fitzgerald, 14th Earl of Desmond, who died insane in the Tower of London. King James I later gave the castle to Richard Boyle, Earl of Cork. In 1645 it was captured by Lord Castlehaven; in 1650 Cromwell failed to take it; in 1653 it was burned and the daughters of the occupant were killed.

Coppinger's Court

On private land, no formal access arrangements. Near the R597 west of Ross Carbery, Co Cork.

Though it's on the way to crumbling away altogether, this once-proud fortified mansion is a perfect example of an ivy-covered ruin, with unquestionable picturesque appeal.

Up close it's just a shell, and the interior is used as a pen for animals, so there's not much mileage in having a poke round. But the layout of the building is interesting – it consists of a rectangular central block with projecting wings on either side at the front and a single tower-like projection in the middle at the back. The extensive machicolations are fairly impressive.

The mansion was built between 1620 and 1640 by Sir Walter Coppinger, who surrendered his estates to King James I one day in 1616, and had them granted back to him the next day.

Desmond Castle, Kinsale

Dúchas, ££, open mid-April to early October daily (but closed Mondays until mid-June). In the town of Kinsale, Co Cork.

This attractive little fortified tower was built as a customs house in about 1500, and would have been the place where duties on luxury imports such as wine were paid. From 1630 to about 1800 it was used to hold prisoners of war captured overseas, and it is still often referred to as the French Prison, though it actually held captives from Spain, Portugal, Holland and America as well.

When the decision was taken recently to restore the tower, its original role as a customs house prompted the idea of turning it into an international museum of wine. It's really just a couple of rooms, but the displays give an interesting insight into the surprising Irish contribution to some of France's best-known vineyards and brands.

Above: Desmond Castle, Kinsale.

Below: Conna Castle.

Dunboys Estate

Privately owned, £ (honesty box), open access during usual hours only. On the Beara peninsula, signposted off the R572 west of Castletownbere.

This extraordinary place is worth coming to for several reasons, easily the best of them being the spectacular ruin of a Victorian Gothic-revival house called Puxley Mansion.

The mansion incorporates a medieval tower house, named O'Sullivan Bere Castle after the family that owned it, the top of which has been Gothicised in a comparatively clumsy, angular style. But far more interesting is the eerie ruin of the later added wings, all pointed arches and towering columns of the most exuberant and flamboyant sort. It's utterly fascinating. The house, like many others, was burned down by the IRA in the 1920s, and the ruin is said to have inspired Daphne Du Maurier's novel *Hungry Hill.*

There's another significant monument here, too, in the form of Dunboy Castle. Little more than the foundations survive, with a stair leading to first-floor height on one surviving piece of wall. The tower, built in the 1400s, had a new bawn wall added to it in 1602 by its joint force of Irish and Spanish defenders, expecting an attack by the English; but the attack succeeded all the same, and the castle was destroyed. Later, a star-shaped fort was built on the site, and you can make out the remains of this, too.

Don't fail to walk up to the headland just beyond Dunboy Castle for smashing views out to sea.

Innisfallen monastery

Dúchas, free, open access at any time (but you'll need a boat to get here). Near Killarney, Co Kerry.

This famous monastic site stands in an extremely picturesque location, on an island in the lake of Lough Leane. Boat trips out to the island are readily available from the landing stage next to *Ross Castle* (*see page 88*). The ruins include an oratory of the 1100s and an abbey church, parts of which – the *antae* and flat-lintelled door – are rather older.

Kanturk Castle

Dúchas, free, open access at any reasonable time. Beside the R579 south of Kanturk, Co Cork.

An excellent example of a later type of castle from the Elizabethan era, really a grand variety of fortified mansion. It consists of a large central block with a tower on each of the corners, and it has lots of large, elegant windows and big fireplaces. It was built in around 1601, and probably never finished.

The ruin is very well kept, in tidy grounds not far from the town. The only drawback is that it's just a shell – all the stairs and floors were made of wood and are long gone. Similar house-castles worth looking out for include *Portumna* in Co Galway, *Rathfarnham* in Dublin, and *Raphoe* in Co Donegal.

Kinneigh round tower

In churchyard, free, open access to view exterior only. Off the R588 north of Enniskean, at Kinneigh, north-east of Dunmanway, Co Cork.

A rather splendid round tower, the bottom 5.5m (18ft) of which are in a unique octagonal shape, in the graveyard of a small church in a pretty, out-of-the-way spot. The 25m (80ft) high tower was built in 1015, adapted for use as a belfry in the 1800s, and restored in 2000. There is no access to the interior.

Above: Kanturk Castle.

Below: Coppinger's Court (see previous page).

Leacanabuaile stone fort

Dúchas, on farmland. Near Cahirsiveen, Co Cork.

Ruin of a cashel – a fortified homestead defended by a stone wall – dating from the early Christian period. The surrounding wall has been rebuilt to a height of just over a metre (4ft) but was never particularly high (very different from the fort at nearby *Staigue*).

There are several buildings inside: the largest is a rectangular house, but that is a much later addition. Originally there were several round huts, of which one survives. Inside it is the entrance to a souterrain which leads to a chamber under the wall. Items found here include iron knives and pins, and bone combs, which helped date the cashel to the 800s or 900s AD.

Liscarroll Castle

Dúchas, no access. In Liscarroll, Co Cork, just off the R522 north-west of Buttevant.

An enormous and very plain enclosure-type castle of the 1200s, consisting of a rectangle of high walls, with round turrets at the corners, and with a big rectangular gate-tower in the middle of one of the shorter walls. This was later adapted as a tower house. The castle is locked up, and as run-down as the village.

Mallow Castle

Dúchas, free, open access at any reasonable time. In Mallow, Co Cork, at the south end of the town.

Entertaining ruin of a large fortified mansion of the very late 1500s, well cared-for, in the grounds of a private school. The house is thought to have been built by Sir Thomas Norreys, who died in 1599, and it is interesting for its design, with polygonal turrets on the front corners and a tower in the middle both at the back and at the front, the back tower containing staircases and chimney flues. Its few defences must have been fairly effective: it successfully held out against a siege in 1642, though it fell to an attack by Lord Castlehaven three years later.

Sherkin Friary

Dúchas, free, open access at any reasonable time. On Sherkin Island in Baltimore Bay, Co Cork

Ruin of a Franciscan friary founded in 1460 or 1470, standing on an inhabited island reached easily by ferry from Baltimore. The church is pretty complete, and is unusual in having the main door in the south side of the nave. Parts of the cloister survive.

And...

Buttevant Friary *(Dúchas, in churchyard, free open access to exterior only)*, in Buttevant, Co Cork – Large and complete but not very interesting ruined church of a Franciscan friary founded in 1251.

Bohonagh stone circle *(on farmland), just north of Ross Carbery, Co Cork* – One of the more impressive of the many small stone circles in the region. It's a small circle, but quite complete. An interesting feature is that its stones vary greatly in height.

Derrynane House *(Dúchas, ££, open daily May to September, afternoons only March and October, weekends only rest of year), Caherdaniel, Co Kerry* – Ancestral home of statesman Daniel O' Connell, with parklands and coastline.

Doneraile wildlife park *(Dúchas, £, open daily all year round), signposted on the R522 north-east of Mallow, Co Cork* – Vast country park landscaped in the 1700s in the style of Capability Brown.

Dunamark *(on farmland), near the N71 just north of Bantry, Co Cork* – This early Norman site is said to be one of the finest examples of an early type of earthwork-and-timber castle called a ring-work.

Dunloe ogham stones *(Dúchas, free, open access at any reasonable time), near Killarney, Co Kerry* – Roadside site with eight ogham stones, seven of them taken from the roof of a nearby souterrain, said to be the best collection of ogham script there is.

Above: Mallow Castle.

Glanworth Castle *(Dúchas, free, open access to view exterior only), in the village of Glanworth, Co Cork* – Extensive ruin of a large castle of the 1300s overlooking a historic village with a number of interesting buildings, including a fine old stone bridge and a restored watermill. There is also a ruined tower house of the 1500s, which was built in the castle courtyard.

Kealkil stone circles *(on farmland, no formal access arrangements), near a minor road south-east of the R584 at Kealkil village, Co Cork* – Interesting group of monuments, including a five-stone circle and a ruined circle of small stones, on a hilltop with fine views of Bantry Bay.

Youghal historic remains *(on various sites, open access to view exteriors only at any reasonable time), in Youghal, Co Cork* – This little fishing town has an interesting history: Walter Raleigh was mayor of the town in 1588–9, and he is said to have planted Ireland's first potato here! But the town's monuments are either small or badly ruined. Of **North Abbey**, a Dominican priory founded 1268, only one end wall and window stands. **Tynte's Castle** is a small tower house of the 1500s, standing in the main street; it is intact, but derelict. Near **St Mary's Church**, parts of which are from the 1200s, are the remaining stretches of the medieval **town walls**.

Shannon

Limerick, north Kerry, north Tipperary, Clare and south Offaly

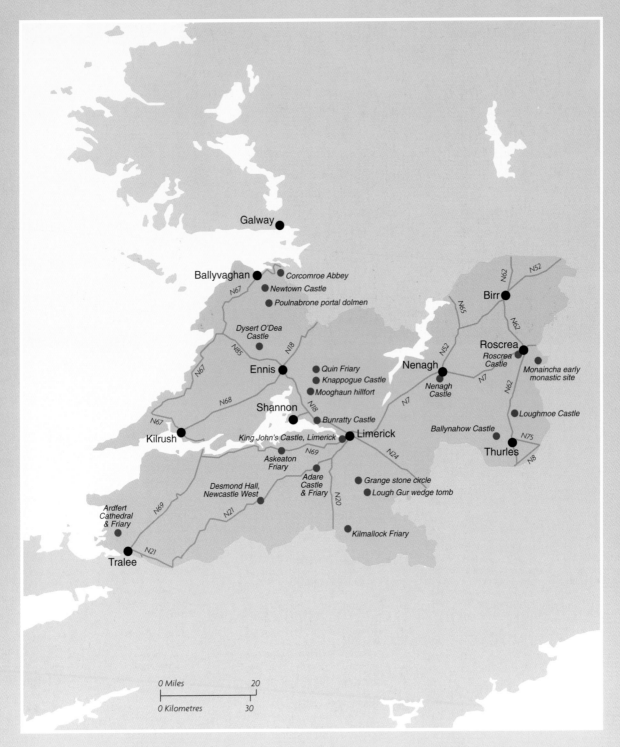

Galway

Ballyvaghan
Corcomroe Abbey
Newtown Castle
N67
Poulnabrone portal dolmen

Dysert O'Dea
Castle
N18
N85

Birr
N62
N52
N65

Roscrea
Roscrea
Castle
Monaincha early
monastic site

Ennis
Quin Friary
Knappogue Castle
Mooghaun hillfort

Nenagh
Nenagh
Castle
N7
N62

N67
N68

Shannon
N18
Bunratty Castle

Loughmoe Castle

Ballynahow Castle
N75

Kilrush
King John's Castle, Limerick
Limerick
N67

Thurles
N8

Askeaton
Friary
N69
N24

Desmond Hall,
Newcastle West
Adare
Castle
& Friary
Grange stone circle
Lough Gur wedge tomb

N20

Ardfert
Cathedral
& Friary
N69
N21

Kilmallock Friary

Tralee
N21

0 Miles   20

0 Kilometres   30

Adare Castle

Dúchas • Access arrangements to be confirmed

Adare is an odd place. It's a picturesque village of old stone cottages with a feel almost like the English Cotswolds. It is inundated with visitors as a result, and there's a large car park and visitor centre to cater for them. It also has a surprising number of historical buildings, but here's the odd thing – most of them are either inaccessible or are left unvisited by the vast majority of tourists who come here.

In all, the village has three abbeys and one castle. Two of the abbeys have been rebuilt as churches and are still in use; the third, a ruin, is the best of the lot, but it's on a golf course and not all that accessible. The castle you currently can't get into at all – but the good news is that it was being restored at time of writing and will open to the public imminently.

The castle should be a good one to visit when it does open, since it was one of the largest medieval fortresses in Ireland, and it has some interesting buildings.

The earliest castle on this important site guarding a bridge over the River Maigue was an earthwork of some kind, possibly a ringfort, which pre-dated the arrival of the Anglo-Normans. When they came, they

Adare Castle was a large one, with a big rectangular keep – now mostly ruined – and two grand halls.

added a timber palisade and then, shortly after, built a grand stone hall just outside the enclosure, by the river. The hall had narrow arrow slits on the basement level, but fine arched windows in its upper walls.

Not long after that, a large, square keep was built inside the original enclosure; unfortunately only one wall of it still stands. In the mid-1200s, a stone wall and a gatehouse were built around it; and in the late 1200s a new, larger hall was built to replace the original one – again, it stood by the riverbank. The buttresses that support its wall are a distinctive feature in pictures of the castle.

It seems that the castle was in a poor condition by 1329. A little more building work was carried out not long after, and there are the remains of a bakery and kitchen built in the early 1400s; yet the place seems never to have been fully restored to its former strength.

Surprisingly little is known about who built the various parts of the castle, but the Fitzgeralds owned it for a long time. It was besieged by the English in 1580 and was made undefendable in 1599.

By the N21 (Limerick road) just north of Adare.

■ *See also...* **Adare Abbey and Priory**

Both owned by church authorities, free entry, open access during usual hours. In Adare, directions as detailed below.

Besides the Friary (*see next page*), Adare has two former abbeys. The one in the centre of the village is the former White Abbey (*pictured*), rebuilt in 1852 as a Catholic church. It was founded in 1230 by the Trinitarians, also known as the Order of the Redemption of Captives, whose main aim was to recover hostages held in the Holy Land after the Crusades. The church is fairly handsome inside, using the body of the original church as an aisle. The formidable tower is also part of the original building.

To the north of the village, near the river, is the former Augustinian Priory, founded in 1315. The church is largely of this period. Restored in the early 1800s for use by the Church of Ireland, it is a handsome building, and worth seeing.

Adare Friary

On private land • Free • Access by permission

The best of Adare's three abbeys (*see also previous page*) is this picturesque ruin of a typical Franciscan friary, with the classic slender tower that marks out Franciscan churches in Ireland. The only drawback is that it stands between the tees and greens of a golf course in the grounds of a rather posh hotel, so visitors must be careful not to disturb the golfers.

In theory, you really ought to ask at the hotel for permission to visit, but it seems to be accepted that there is a certain amount of traffic to the ruin. To find the place, stroll northwards up the main road through the village and you'll see the gates to the hotel on your right; if you take the left fork of the drive and follow it as it first sweeps round to the left, then curves back to the right to head towards the hotel, you will see a footbridge over the river on the left. The friary is just beyond, but you must follow the footpath around the tee, and wait for golfers to play their shots.

The friary was founded in 1464 by Thomas, Earl of Kildare, and its construction is said to have been finished two years later. The interior of the long, narrow church is rather impressive, with some good detail, including elegant sedilia (carved seats for the comfort of clerics who were taking part in ceremonies).

The buildings of the cloister are not in especially good condition, but the arches all round it are still intact, trailed with ivy and looking prettily gothic, with a yew tree in the middle. It's a pleasant spot.

In Adare, Co Limerick. Just north of the river, on the golf course in the grounds of the hotel.

The friary at Adare is the best-preserved of this historic town's three abbeys, but it stands on a golf course.

Askeaton Friary

Dúchas • Free • Open access during usual hours

It's very unusual for the cloisters of an abbey to have survived in better condition than its church, but that's the case here. The buildings around the cloister are in exceptionally good condition, complete right up to the tops of their gables and lacking only their roofs, so that when seen from the other side of the river, the friary almost looks as if it's still in business.

This makes Askeaton one of the best places in Ireland – along with *Muckross* in Co Kerry (*see page 87*) – to get a clearer impression of what the cloister of one of these Franciscan friaries must have been like in its heyday. It's surprisingly dark and gloomy, with heavy arches propping up the buildings above. It's not at all the tranquil garden you'd expect. Look out for a carving of St Francis in one corner.

Sadly, access and maintenance are major problems here. The friary has remained in use as a burial ground and is very untidy as a result, and the buildings around the cloister are all locked up, which is extremely disappointing.

The friary was founded in about 1400, and most of its buildings date from between 1420 and 1440. After being dissolved, it was revived in 1627 and remained in use until at least 1714. Unusually, the cloister is to the south of the church.

In Askeaton, Co Limerick, north of the town centre.

Left and above: The cloister of Askeaton Friary is in remarkably good condition. It looks almost as if it's still complete when seen from across the river.

Ardfert Cathedral

Dúchas • ££ • Open early May to late September

Although very little is known about its early history, Ardfert was clearly a very important religious community from a long way back, primarily because of its associations with St Brendan. There was almost certainly a monastery here in the early Christian period, but the earliest references are to a stone church that was struck by lightning in 1046. Part of the wall of this very same church can be seen built into the north wall of the cathedral.

More significantly, a new church was built here in the 1100s. The main part of it to survive is a superb arched doorway at the west end of the cathedral, carved in the Romanesque style of the period. Like the rest of the building, it has recently been restored very effectively and with the greatest of care by Dúchas.

Of the two small ruined churches that stand near the west door, the smaller and nearer, known as Temple na Hoe, or the Church of the Virgin, was also built in the 1100s in the Irish Romanesque style, and it too has some very stylish ornamentation.

The majority of the cathedral building, however, dates from the mid-1200s. By far its most distinctive feature is the way the east end of the church is lit, with three particularly tall windows in the end wall and a row of nine slender 'trefoil-headed' lancet windows in the side wall.

The church had an aisle on the south side of the nave and a single long transept, also on the south side. The latter has been roofed over and now houses an exhibition on the history of the cathedral.

In Ardfert, Co Kerry. In the centre of the village.

The ruined Ardfert Cathedral, dating largely from the 1200s, has recently undergone a major restoration.

The little Romanesque church of Temple na Hoe, its chancel now gone, has some fine stonecarving.

Ardfert Friary

Dúchas • Free • Open access during usual hours

Standing in a grassy field rather than a graveyard, this is a more pleasant place to visit than the Cathedral. It has a number of rather interesting features, too.

The most striking thing about it is how much the design of the church owes to the nearby cathedral: its east end is lit by rows of tall lancet windows in just the same way as the east end of the cathedral. In fact, the friary church was built in the late 1200s, not long after the cathedral. It is noticeably more elaborate than most Franciscan friaries in Ireland, but then it belonged to a different order of Franciscans, followers of the Conventual Rule. It joined the majority Observantine Rule in 1518.

The church is mostly intact, along with a tower at its west end and substantial parts of the cloister, both of which were added in the 1400s. The tower was converted into a barracks in Elizabethan times, and a flight of steps leads up the outside to end tantalisingly at a door on the first floor, but unfortunately this is kept locked up, so you can't get in.

The best-preserved part of the cloister is the dormitory wing, and from the top of the steps that lead up to the first floor you can see a most unusual style of roofing, with block-like stone tiles, which helped rainwater to drain from the roof.

In Ardfert, Co Kerry. To the east of the village, beside the minor road to Abbeydorney.

Left: In the east end of the church at Ardfert Friary, certain similarities to the cathedral are obvious...

Ballynahow Castle

*Dúchas • Free • Open access at reasonable
times only*

It's not big, and it's not elegant, but this is
one of the most enjoyable tower houses to
visit in Ireland. Built by the Purcell family
in the late 1500s, it's a very rare example
of a round tower house, and it stands in

Not only is it a rare example of a round tower house, Ballynahow is also a highly enjoyable place to visit.

the farmyard of a farm which offers B&B.
The farm's owners unlock the place every
day, so you can just wander in and show
yourself around.

Inside, the rooms are mostly square.
Those on the lower floors were for storage,
but the upper rooms are grander, with

toilets, side-chambers, large fireplaces,
and elegant windows. Eventually the stair
leads out to a wall-walk at rooftop level,
which is precarious, but great fun.

*Near Thurles, Co Tipperary. Signposted from
the R503 west of Thurles, east of Ballycahill.*

Bunratty Castle

Privately owned by Shannon Heritage • ££££ •
Open daily all year round

This huge, brutal-looking and thoroughly impressive tower house is an enjoyable one to visit. The size and the interesting layout of the tower make it great fun to explore, and some of the later decorative detail inside is very attractive.

It's just a shame that the ticket price is so high, artificially inflated by the so-called Folk Park in the grounds – a whole village of reconstructed homes, shops, farms, churches and other buildings from roughly 100 years ago. There's even a working pub. You can sort of see the point, but it's all a bit – well, *soulless*, really.

However… back to the tower. It was built in the early 1400s, on the site of an earlier castle once owned by the De Clares, by Maccon MacSioda Macconmara, but from 1500 onwards it was a stronghold of the O'Briens. It consists of a big rectangular main block – in which there are two halls, one on top of the other, over a basement – and four towers on the corners, each of which has five storeys.

The basement is not terribly interesting, and nor is the lower hall, kitted out with tables and benches for the 'medieval' banquets that are held here. Move on up, though, and it all gets more entertaining. The large upper hall is a very grand space, decorated with some fine (but restored) plasterwork of the 1600s.

From the upper hall, spiral stairs lead up all four corner towers, visiting a series of chambers along the way. It's good fun to explore each of the towers: in most cases, the stair eventually leads out on the roof, with fine views all round.

The enormous tower at Bunratty is the most impressive fortified residence of its type in the whole of Ireland.

At either end of the castle, two corner towers are linked by an arch with a room built on top of it. At one end, this room is a later library; at the other, it is a grand solar or private living room, fitted out with some rather splendid wood panelling.

In Bunratty, near Shannon, Co Clare. Off the N18 north-west of Limerick.

Desmond Hall, Newcastle West

Dúchas • ££ • Open mid-June to mid-September

The castle after which the town is named is far from new, having been built in the early 1200s as the main stronghold of the Fitzgeralds, the principal Anglo-Norman landowning family of the region.

There doesn't appear to be much of the castle left, but in fact a major programme of restoration is currently uncovering more of it from under a mass of derelict later buildings and trying to get it into a fit state to be opened to the public. In the meantime, a good job has been done of cleaning up the castle's only notable surviving building: this hall of the 1400s, with a turret at one end.

The wooden roof of the hall has been beautifully recreated, and the room has been furnished with a table and benches, with a scattering of tableware, to give a taste of its original appearance. You can climb a spiral stair to the roof of the turret, but the views are restricted.

The external wall of the hall formed part of the circuit of curtain walls which were the castle's main defence. It didn't have a keep or great tower. Within the walls there were a number of freestanding buildings, including another much larger hall, which is now the focus of the restoration work.

In 1569, when the castle was surrendered to the English, it is said to have consisted of a square of walls with a round tower at each corner, two halls, and a tower house, parts of which also survive.

In Newcastle West, Co Limerick.

The hall of the Desmond castle at Newcastle West occupied the entire first floor of this building.

Dysert O'Dea Castle

*Local archeological trust • £££ • Open May
to September daily*

Not only is this a fine example of a typical
medium-sized Irish tower house, standing
in a pleasant rural setting, it's also at the
centre of a fascinating archeological trail,
which gives visitors a unique opportunity
to look in detail at a patch of countryside
and discover a scattering of ruins and
minor monuments dating from the iron age
through to Victorian times.

The tower was built between 1470 and
1490 by local lord Diarmuid O'Dea. It was

The battlements of the tower at Dysert O'Dea were wrecked to make it indefensible, but have been restored.

eventually put out of action in 1651 by
Cromwellian forces who broke down the
battlements and the spiral stair so that the
castle could no longer be defended.

The tower was rebuilt in the 1980s, and
now houses a local archeological museum.
What its displays lack in polish, they more
than make up for in enthusiasm. The
building itself is not especially interesting,
but you can get out on to a wall-walk at
roof level, which is fun, and this is a good
place from which to get your first glimpse
of the bare limestone hills of The Burren.

At the teashop in the basement of the
tower, you can buy a guide-map which
describes the Dysert O'Dea History Trail.
At the very least, you must make the short
walk to St Tola's Church, the decorative
Romanesque door of which is reproduced
in the Dublin museum. On the way you'll
pass St Tola's Cross, carved with a
crucifixion scene: the head of Jesus used
to be removable and was used by local
people as a cure for toothache.

North of Ennis, south of Corrofin, Co Clare.

Grange stone circle

Dúchas, on private land • £ (honesty box) •
Open access at reasonable times only

This is often said to be the largest and finest stone circle in Ireland, but that's not the whole truth. It's certainly a grand and atmospheric monument, but it's not really a stone circle at all. Rather, it's what's known as an embanked enclosure.

The enclosure consists of a large bank of earth in the shape of a ring, with stones set in the inside of the bank. There's a distinct entrance on the north-east side, between two of the larger boulders, and this has been interpreted as showing an interest in the midsummer sunrise.

The embanked enclosure is a type of monument very similar to the neolithic henges of Britain, which are seen as being ritual sites or meeting places. Excavations here uncovered pottery of late neolithic and early bronze age types, suggesting a date of 2000BC to 1500BC for its use.

Although it's not immediately obvious, the circle stands just a couple of fields away from the shore of *Lough Gur (see page 117)* and is part of the diverse group of monuments clustered around the lake. In the field to the left, there is a small

Below: The embanked enclosure at Grange is an elegant monument, similar to a henge in character.

stone circle; and back on the other side of the road, to the right of the farm, are some standing stones thought to be the remnants of a neolithic tomb.

The farmer who owns the field in which the monument stands has put up a wooden fence to keep the cows out – except for a couple of calves who act as lawnmowers. He has also put up an honesty box for access fees and delights in popping up to introduce himself to visitors.

By the R512 north of Holycross, Co Limerick.

The Lough Gur wedge tomb is a good example of this unusual variety of burial monument.

See also… **Lough Gur wedge tomb**

Dúchas, free, open access at any reasonable time. Beside the minor road on the south side of Lough Gur; from the R512 at Grange, follow the signs for Lough Gur Visitor Centre.

Of the many monuments scattered all around Lough Gur, this is the only other notable one. It's a decent example of this early bronze age type of tomb, though it has a crumbling look about it, its dark stone curiously weathered.

Kilmallock Friary

Dúchas • Free • Open access in usual hours only

It's hard to imagine a less touristy place than the small town of Kilmallock, and yet, in its humble and slightly run-down way, this agricultural backwater has masses of historical interest to offer the visitor.

The church of Kilmallock Friary, built in the early 1300s, has lots of fine decorative stonework of that period.

An early monastery was founded here in the 600s by St Mocheallóg, but the town itself was established by the powerful Anglo-Norman Fitzgeralds. The large collegiate church that superseded the monastery, built in the 1200s and modified in the 1400s, survives as a shell, and its exterior can be visited. It played an important role in the history of the region, too; inside it, in 1600, the Earl of Desmond surrendered to the Queen's representatives.

The Fitzgeralds fortified the town in 1375, and one of the original town gates, called the Blossom Gate, survives intact. There is also a tower house of the 1400s standing at one end of the main street, and this looks like a gate, too, because it has an arch in the middle through which the road seems to have run – but apparently this is just one of many alterations that have been made to it over the years. It is known, for no very good reason, as King John's Castle.

Left: The five-light lancet window in the east end of the church is said to be one of the best in Ireland.

Currently, only the exterior of these buildings can be visited.

Easily the most impressive historic building in the town, however, is the ruin of the Dominican friary founded in 1291. It stands on the far side of the river, and is reached by a path which turns off the main street by the side of the King's Castle.

The friary church is in good condition, topped off as usual by a slender tower. The graceful five-light lancet window at the east end is said to be the finest in the whole of Ireland, and certainly it's a candidate. Actually, the window at the west end isn't bad either, and there are some very fine details in the stonework throughout the church.

The buildings of the cloister are in less good condition. The range on the north side, opposite the church, which probably housed the kitchen and refectory, is pretty much intact, but sadly it is kept locked up, so you can't explore and find out more.

In Kilmallock, Co Limerick. Reached by a path from the high street near the King's Castle.

King John's Castle, Limerick

Privately owned by Shannon Heritage • ££££ •
Open daily all year round

This was one of Ireland's largest and most important medieval fortresses, the equal of *Trim Castle* in Co Meath (*see page 160*) or *Carrickfergus*, near Belfast (see *page 172*). Unfortunately it is now not much more than a shell, having had the heart ripped out of it by many successive phases of rebuilding: it was adapted as a barracks in about 1750, and remained in military use well into the 1920s.

It is unique amongst Irish castles named after King John in that it actually had something to do with the king: it was built during his reign, in the early 1200s, and was the only royal castle in Ireland. It was positioned here both to suppress the native Irish north-west of the Shannon and to put a limit on the expansion of the Anglo-Norman lords to the south and east.

The castle's basic structure is still mostly intact, and its circuit of high walls defended by round towers still looks thoroughly impressive – particularly on the west side, near the bridge over the river, where there's a gatehouse made up of two more large round towers.

It's just a shame that there is not more of the original interiors of the towers left, and there is practically nothing of any of the buildings that stood in the courtyard. Instead, a large visitor centre tries to make up for the lack of inherent interest by offering a series of spectacular (but not always informative) audio-visual displays on the history of the region.

However, a series of archeological digs has made some interesting discoveries within the walls, including a number of houses from the Viking town which was here long before the Normans arrived.

In the city of Limerick. On Nicholas Street near Thomond Bridge, off the N7 (Galway road).

Knappogue Castle

Privately owned by Shannon Heritage • £££ •
Open April to early October daily

A medieval tower house said to date from 1467 (though many authorities argue that it is more likely to have been built in the 1500s) with many later additions, mostly of the 1800s and in a rather plain, square Gothic-revival style, so that it's more of a stately home than a castle.

The tower was owned by the MacNamaras for most of its early career, but it was sold to the Scott family in 1800, who started its modernisation, and then to Lord Dunboyne in 1855, who finished the job with the help of architect James Paine, designer of the full-scale Gothic-revival extravaganza of nearby Dromoland Castle (now a very smart hotel).

With its odd mix of genuine medieval stonework and Victorian interior design, the castle is of interest mainly for its role in the founding of the Irish Free State, when it was used as a secret meeting place of the Clare County Council, a body that was staunchly in favour of the Republic.

Beside the R469 just south of Quin, Co Clare.

Knappogue Castle, rebuilt in the 1800s in a mock Gothic style, is now a venue for medieval banquets.

Below: King John's Castle at Limerick was one of the most important medieval fortresses of Ireland.

Loughmoe Castle

On private land • Free • Open access at reasonable times only

Ireland's countryside is dotted with ruined towers standing in fields, but all too often public access is positively discouraged by the landowner, so it's gratifying to find one that is signposted and accessible, thanks in part to a European initiative. Mind you, I had to hop over an electric fence.

It's an interesting castle, too, consisting of a thick-walled tower house of the 1400s with a later, less heavily fortified mansion built on the side, generously equipped with large fireplaces and mullioned windows. It's just a shell, and cows shelter in the vaulted basement of the old tower; but it's good to come across an old-fashioned neglected ruin from time to time.

The castle is also called Purcell Castle, after the family who owned it. The last of the line, Colonel Nicholas Purcell, who had fought at the Battle of the Boyne, died here in 1722.

Signposted from the N62 south of Templemore, north of Thurles, Co Tipperary.

Nenagh Castle

Dúchas • Free • Access to view exterior only

Although its dignity has been compromised by a silly set of pseudo-gothic arches built around its top in the 1800s, making it look more like a folly than the genuine article, the tower here is in fact a large and powerful cylindrical keep which formed part of a very compact and unusual castle

Loughmoe Castle started off as a tower house (on the right) and was later turned into a grand mansion.

built in the early 1200s by Theobald Walter, ancestor of the Butlers, Earls of Ormond.

Originally, there were two smaller round towers and a twin-towered gatehouse here too, but only part of the latter and some of a hall behind it now survives.

Currently the tower is closed while it undergoes restoration, but it will reopen in the near future, and visitors should then be able to climb to the top. Up close, it's a very impressive structure; the walls are almost 5m (16ft) thick at the bottom, but the tower tapers as it climbs, and they are only 3.6m (12ft) thick at the top.

In Nenagh, Co Tipperary.

Newtown Castle

Privately owned • ££ • Open daily for guided tours from May to September

This is a charming round tower house of the 1500s, its spurred base and pointed roof making it look a bit like a space rocket. The tower has recently been restored with a great deal of care, and is well worth seeing. There is also a cafe, and guided walks in the neighbourhood are offered.

By the N18 south of Ballyvaghan, Co Clare.

Below: Newtown Castle, at the heart of The Burren, has been beautifully restored in recent years.

The enormous round tower at Nenagh Castle was decorated with battlements and arches in the 1800s.

Mooghaun hillfort

Dúchas • Free • Open access at any time

This is a rare and very interesting example of a large hillfort of the late bronze age, constructed in about 950BC. What makes it a particularly instructive place to visit is that the site has recently been excavated, and at the same time archeologists also carried out an extensive study of bronze age remains in the surrounding area, building up a fascinating picture of what life was like here at that time.

Usefully, the results are summed up in a guidebook to Mooghaun published by The Discovery Programme. It's a good idea to get hold of a copy, but you don't necessarily have to bring it with you, since a walking route has been laid out which visits all the major features of the site, with explanatory signboards in place to fill in some of the detail. If nothing else, it's a pleasant walk in the woods; to complete the whole circuit won't take an hour.

The hillfort consists of three massive stone ramparts, the outer one enclosing an area of some 30 acres. It is estimated that the population of the region at the time

Right: One of two cashels – farmsteads defended by a stone wall – built on the hill in about 700AD.

The stone ramparts of Mooghaun hillfort don't always look impressive, but it's a fascinating site all the same.

would have been about 9,000 people, of whom maybe 3,500 could have been spared for building work, which would mean the fort could have been completed in a very reasonable 16 years.

Besides the bronze age walls and traces of round huts, there are also two cashels on the hillside. These enclosed farmsteads, protected by a stone wall, were built in the the 700s or 800s AD using stone from the ramparts of the fort.

South of Quin, Co Clare. Signposted on minor roads off the N18 near Newmarket on Fergus.

Quin Friary

Dúchas • Free • Open access during usual hours

This elegant Franciscan friary is probably the best-preserved in Ireland. The domestic buildings around its cloister are more or less complete and, uniquely, the upstairs rooms are all carpeted with a thick layer of lush green grass, which gives them a rather attractive appearance (though it can be a little squelchy underfoot if there's been a lot of rain).

The only slight disappointment is that many guidebooks say that visitors can climb a spiral stair to the top of the tower, from where there are supposed to be superb views in all directions, but sadly it seems this is no longer the case. It would certainly be worth asking, if there's anyone around to ask: apparently the friary has a caretaker of some sort, since it is unlocked every morning and locked up again in the evening.

Most unusually, the friary was built on top of, and presumably recycled a certain amount of stone from, the remains of a castle which previously stood on the site.

Probably the best-preserved of Ireland's Franciscan friaries, Quin is an extremely interesting place to visit.

The castle was a substantial enclosure of walls with round towers at the corners, built in a classic Norman style. It was erected by the De Clares in about 1280, but destroyed by the Macnamaras in the early 1300s. Round the back of the friary, the base of one of the castle's round corner-towers is still in place; it can be seen easily from the upstairs rooms on the east side of the cloister. Parts of two other towers also survive; and it is said that you can look down from the top of the tower and clearly see the plan of the castle walls all around you.

The friary was founded in 1433 by Síoda Cam Macnamara, a relative of the builder of *Bunratty Castle* (*see page 105*). Its church is on the usual Franciscan pattern, with a transept on the south side only and a narrow tower supported on arches. It is quite a plain one, however, so the main interest here is in exploring the superbly well-preserved buildings of the cloister.

In Quin, Co Clare.

Franciscan friaries in western Ireland

From about 1400 until the 1530s, Irish nobles enjoyed great freedom from interference by the English crown, and one consequence was that they were free to spend money on rebuilding old abbeys and founding new ones.

The big beneficiaries were the Franciscans, whose friaries from the early and mid-1400s are a distinctive feature of the western counties in particular. The best examples, though ruined, still have many of the domestic buildings from around the cloister. These are the ones to visit…

Moyne Friary, *Co Mayo* – Complete cloisters in an interesting layout with a library, chapter-room and scriptorium on the west side.

Rosserk Friary, *Co Mayo* – Smaller version of nearby Moyne, intended for married members of the Franciscan 'Third Order'.

Ross Errily, *Co Galway* – Upstairs rooms are not well preserved, but there's an extensive and unusual layout of domestic buildings.

Muckross Friary, *Co Kerry* – More or less complete cloisters, with intact arcades in the slightly heavy Franciscan style.

Roscrea Castle

Dúchas • £££ • Open June to September daily

Appearances can be deceptive. Although it scarcely looks it, this is in fact a fairly heavyweight Anglo-Norman castle built in the 1280s, consisting of a walled enclosure defended by two D-shaped corner towers and one very large gatehouse-tower. Despite a series of later alterations, the walls and corner towers are still intact, but you can't currently get into the interiors of the towers, so the main focus of interest is the keep-like gatehouse.

The idea of having the gate defended by the strongest tower and also putting all the most important accommodation into it was a popular one at the time, but didn't last very long – perhaps because a keep with an archway running right through it was simply too exposed. Here, as elsewhere, the gateway was later blocked up; but the original drawbridge has been reconstructed on the outside, facing the street.

The interior of the tower is interesting, and good fun to explore. There's a large and rather grand hall on the first floor, with large windows and elegant vaulting. The winding mechanism for the portcullis is exposed, looking a little out of place in the tower's main reception room. The floor above is said to have been a kitchen, but it seems an odd place for it. There's a very good model of the castle on display here.

The topmost level was rebuilt in the early 1300s, and you can make out traces of the earlier parapet on the wall. There are several intriguing little corridors off to one side, but they don't really go anywhere.

Roscrea was acquired by Edward I and then given away by Edward II in 1315, after which it was owned by the Butler Earls of Ormond for several centuries.

The immense gatehouse-tower of Roscrea Castle is a fine example of the sort of keep built in the late 1200s.

In 1722, however, it was bought by a gentleman called John Damer, who built a Queen Anne-style house in its courtyard. The house now contains an eccentric local history museum, confusingly displayed, but it's worth popping in, if only to admire the very impressive staircase. The formal gardens of the period behind the house have also been restored.

Elsewhere in the town are a church doorway and a round tower from the early monastic site of St Cronan's Abbey.

In the town of Roscrea, Co Tipperary.

▢ *See also...* **Monaincha early monastic site**

Dúchas, free, open access at any reasonable time. South-east of Roscrea, signposted on a minor road from a roundabout on the N7 south-east of the town. You can drive up the track to the site.

Not far from Roscrea you'll find this intriguing early monastic site, consisting of a small ruined church with a high cross in front of it, standing on what used to be an island in a marsh. The name translates as 'The Monastery of the Island of the Living', and there's an extraordinary legend attached which says that no woman or female animal could ever come to the island without instantly dying.

The monastery, founded in the 700s, adopted the Augustinian rule in the 1100s, when the present nave-and-chancel church was built. The carved west doorway and chancel arch are particularly elegant.

Left: The small early monastery of Monaincha was built on an island in the middle of a bog.

Poulnabrone dolmen is a very attractive monument in the dramatic setting of a field of limestone.

The Burren

Catch a distant glimpse of this upland part of north Clare and you'll notice that the hills are not green or a misty blue, but a startling pale grey. The Burren is an area of remarkable landscape, most of which has recently been made into a national park; its distinctive feature is bare rocky terrain of a type known as limestone pavement. This is not a barren place, however: in fact, it provides the perfect habitat for a number of rare varieties of plants and animals, including pine martens.

The coast near here, overlooking Galway Bay, is also rather beautiful, and as a result the area receives many visitors. It's something of a disgrace, then, that access to many of the historic monuments in the area is poor. A concerted effort to improve public access to some of the smaller monuments on the page opposite would be very welcome.

Corcomroe Abbey

Dúchas • Free • Open access at any time

The Cistercians were fond of setting up abbeys in wild country, so this area – described as recently as 1815 as 'a wild, barren and unreclaimable waste' – was a perfect location for them. But in fact, the sheltered valley which they chose was far from unpromising, as the name given to the abbey church – 'Saint Mary of the Fertile Rock' – would suggest. It's a very pleasant, surprisingly grassy spot.

Not much of the abbey survives apart from the church, which is modest in scale but on the typical Cistercian pattern, with two transepts, and more richly ornamented than you might expect. In particular, the choir at the east end of the church has some really nice ornamental stonework, with plant motifs such as opium poppies and lily of the valley decorating the capitals at the tops of the columns. Part of the vaulted roof of the choir is still in place.

The abbey is thought to have been founded in 1194 by Dónal Mór O'Brien, King of Thomond. A signboard explains the layout of the abbey compound.

Signposted down a minor road off the N18 at Bealaclugga, north-east of Ballyvaghan.

Poulnabrone portal dolmen

Dúchas • Free • Open access at any time

This is the most famous ancient monument in Ireland, and it's pretty easy to see why. Its sculptural qualities are immense, the thin slabs of limestone balanced together in an extremely satisfying composition. One of the stones is a modern replacement, mind.

Hopping out of their cars and picking their way across the field of bare limestone to stand next to the monument is probably the only time most visitors to The Burren will get to see this extraordinary landscape at close quarters, so make the most of it. Take care, though – it's surprisingly easy to stick your foot down a crack in the rock, and you could do yourself a mischief.

You can still discern traces of a low mound of stones that once surrounded the monument, but probably never covered it. Excavations discovered the disarticulated bones of 16 individuals, both adults and children and both male and female. Also found were a polished miniature axehead of the sort which is usually interpreted as a pendant, and a number of flint tools. Incidentally, the name translates as 'The hole of the sorrows'.

In a field by the Corrofin to Ballyvaghan road.

☐ See also…

Cahermacnaghten stone fort

Dúchas, free, open access at any reasonable time. Signposted on a minor road south of the N18 between Lisdoonvarna and Ballyvaghan.

This small 'cashel', a round, stone-walled enclosure, probably started life as a defended homestead in the early Christian period, but was home in the late 1600s to a famous school of law, when a large house 'with its own kitchen' (presumably this was a rarity at the time) stood here. Hard to believe now that the place was ever of great importance. The low wall is mostly intact, but not all that impressive.

Gleninagh Castle

Dúchas, free, open access to exterior only at any reasonable time. Signposted from the coast road to west from Ballyvaghan to Black Head.

A very handsome little tower house standing right on the shore, but there is no access to its interior – a great shame. The castle shows Scottish influence, with the stair in a side-tower, giving the building an L-plan, and corbelled-out round turrets at the top. It was built by the O'Loughlins in about 1500 and was lived in as late as 1840.

Leamaneh Castle

On private land, no access permitted. Where the Ballyvaghan road leaves the road to Kilfenora, north of Corrofin.

Largest and finest of The Burren's ruined castles, consisting of a slender tower house built in about 1480 and a grand mansion added in the 1640s. Tragically, no access is permitted. There are many stories about its legendary female owner at the time of the rebuilding, Máire Rua – learn more by visiting the museum at *Dysert O'Dea Castle (see page 106).*

☐ And…

Cahercommaun stone fort

On private land, no regular access. On minor road to the north of the Corrofin-to-Kilfenora road, just north of Killinaboy.

A dramatic hillfort of the 800s or earlier, with three stone ramparts, set on the edge of a steep cliff. It is theoretically possible to visit – indeed, the landowner sometimes charges a fee – but there is no signposting and the place is very difficult to find.

Kilfenora high crosses

In churchyard, free, open access at any reasonable time. In the centre of Kilfenora.

A noted collection of high crosses of the 1100s, the grandest of which is the Doorty Cross, which depicts three bishops and a double-headed bird that looks as if it's devouring skulls. They stand next to a cathedral of the 1100s, part of which is still used: its bishop is the Pope.

Poulawack cairn

Dúchas, free, open access at any reasonable time. Signposted on a minor road to the west of the Ballyvaghan to Corrofin road at Caherconnell, not far south of Poulnabrone dolmen.

Deserves a mention simply because it's that rare thing in The Burren – an ancient monument that is clearly signposted. A footpath leads from the road up to the top of a ridge, where a large cairn stands with views in all directions. The pillar on the top is probably not original, and what appears to be an 'entrance' on one side is more likely to be a fairly modern disturbance of some sort, such as a lime kiln. The main reason to come here is because it's another excuse to get out for a quick walk (about 10 minutes to the monument) in this unique environment.

An elegant L-plan tower house in a Scottish style, Gleninagh Castle was still lived in as late as 1840.

Below: The remains of Corcomroe Abbey stand in a sheltered setting at the head of a small valley.

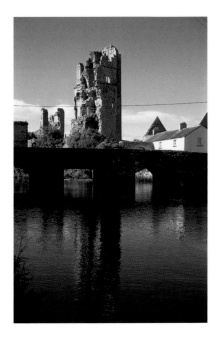

Above: Askeaton Castle.

Below: Ardpatrick early monastic site.

See also…

Ardpatrick early Christian settlement

Dúchas and church authorities, free, open access at any reasonable time. Signposted up a steep track from the R512 at Ardpatrick, Co Limerick.

It's a very steep walk up to this hilltop burial ground, which contains the ruin of a church said to date from the 1100s. Its *antae* (projecting side-walls) and the enormous stone blocks from which it is built make it look even more ancient. Just outside the broad stone wall that encloses the burial ground is the stump of a round tower.

The monuments are not too spectacular, but the views out over the flat, fertile farmland of Limerick's 'Golden Vale' are superb.

Askeaton Castle

No access permitted. In the centre of the town of Askeaton, Co Limerick.

This is an extensive ruin and looks like an extremely interesting one to visit, but sadly it is currently kept locked up and cannot be visited. The castle stands on an island in the River Deel, right by the bridge over the river. It consists of a circuit of walls around the island; a banqueting hall of the 1400s alongside the river; and an inner circuit of walls, inside which stands a tower house of the 1400s built from the remnants of an earlier keep. Most of the buildings are in poor condition, but there would be plenty of interesting details to see if you could get in.

The castle was founded shortly before 1200 by William de Burgo, but later became a stronghold of local ruling family the Desmonds.

Ballyportry Castle

Privately owned, opening times and prices to be confirmed. Beside the R352 (Gort road), just to the north-east of Corrofin, Co Clare.

A very charming little tower house of the mid-1500s with a lot of its bawn wall surviving. It was restored in 2000 and is due to open to the public for the first time in 2001.

Beal Boru (Brian Boru's fort)

Dúchas, free, open access at any reasonable time. The footpath to the monument is signposted from the R463 just north of Killaloe, Co Clare.

This is one of the best examples of a ringwork – a defended farmstead fortified by a circular earthen bank which would originally have been topped with a wooden palisade. It's not thrilling, because it's just a small earthwork, but it is easy to get to and in a pleasant, woodland location. Gaps in the trees give glimpses of Lough Derg; the fort is ideally placed to guard the River Shannon, on a hill overlooking the river as it runs out of the lake.

No proof has been found to confirm the traditional association of the fort with Brian Boru, High King of Ireland between 1002 and 1014, but coins found during excavations show that a house here was occupied in the 11th century. The fort was slightly remodelled by the Normans shortly after 1200.

Carrigafoyle Castle

Dúchas, free, open access to view exterior only at any time. On the coast near Ballylongford, Co Kerry.

This five-storey tower house of the late 1400s or early 1500s is in a very scenic spot and makes a most attractive ruin. Worth seeing.

Castle Matrix

Privately owned, £££, informal opening during usual hours. Signposted on the west side of Rathkeale, Co Limerick; the castle's drive turns off the N21 opposite the Rathkeale turning.

This elegant tower house, built in the mid-1400s by the Desmonds, was the home of the Elizabethan poet Edmund Spenser in the 1580s. The castle was restored as a home in the 1970s, and the owners are happy to show visitors around on an informal basis.

Cloghan Castle

Privately owned, ££, open June to August daily except Monday, afternoons only. Near Banagher, Co Offaly, signposted from the village.

A rather fine tower house of the 1400s which has remained in use, adapted to a house by the addition of a more comfortable later wing and now suitably Gothic in a Victorian kind of way. It is still lived in, and admission is by guided tour. The grounds are very elegant, and are home to Ireland's largest flock of Jacobs sheep.

Craggaunowen

Privately owned by Shannon Heritage, £££, open mid-March to October daily. Near Quin, Co Clare, signposted on the R469 between Kilmurry and Quin.

In the grounds of a small tower house, built in the mid-1500s and restored in the early 1800s, stands a collection of reconstructed Celtic buildings, including a crannog (a defended farmstead on an artificial island) and a cashel complete with souterrain. The castle is not terribly interesting, and the reconstrutions lack a feel of authenticity, making it a little disappointing. Also here, kept in a modern building, is the modern version of St Brendan's boat in which Tim Severin crossed the Atlantic.

Ennis Friary

Dúchas, £, open late May to late September daily. In the centre of Ennis, Co Clare

The large church of this Franciscan friary founded in the 1240s is pretty much complete, though now a roofless shell. Apart from its flamboyant battlemented tower, it is notable mainly for a number of very appealing stone sculptures that adorn its walls.

Holycross Abbey

Church authorities, free (voluntary donation appreciated), open daily during usual hours. In the town of Holycross, south of Thurles, Co Tipperary.

The church of this large Cistercian abbey, founded in 1169 as a Benedictine friary, was re-roofed and restored in the 1970s and is now in full use again. What makes it well worth visiting is a very rare medieval wall-painting in the north transept, which shows three hunters and a dog, with deer hiding behind trees nearby.

Iniscealtra early monastic site

Dúchas, free, open access at any time. On the island of Iniscealtra, also called Holy Island, in Lough Derg; can be reached by boat from Mountshannon, north of Scarriff, Co Clare.

A monastery was founded on this island as early as the 600s, and Brian Boru is said to have built a church here. There's still a considerable number of ruined churches and chapels dating mostly from the 1100s and 1200s, as well as a ruinous round tower. The East Clare Heritage Centre at Tuamgraney can provide information on boat trips to the island.

Killaloe Cathedral and Oratory

Dúchas and church authorities, free, access via church during usual hours only. In Killaloe.

A monastery was established here in about 600 by Saint Fachnan. The present cathedral was started in 1189 and completed not long after, but the most interesting part is an elaborate Romanesque doorway surviving from an earlier building. In the churchyard is a fine stone-roofed oratory of the 1100s, but sadly you're not allowed inside it.

Lorrha Priory and early churches

All sites Dúchas, free, open access at any reasonable time. In the village of Lorrha, Co Tipperary, off the R489 between Portumna and Birr.

The large and handsome ruined church of a priory founded in 1269 by Walter de Burgo, Earl of Ulster, stands in a churchyard on the edge of the village. Back in the village is a ruined church of the 1400s and, best of the lot, an earlier church with *antae* and interesting carvings, a part of which is still in use.

Lough Gur visitor centre

Privately owned by Shannon Heritage, ££, open May to September daily. South-east of Limerick, signposted from the R512 Kilmallock road.

The lake, presumably because it offered an excellent food resource, attracted people to live here from neolithic times onwards, and as a result is the focus for a vast number of small archeological sites, as well as two larger ones – *Grange stone circle* and *Lough Gur wedge tomb* – both of which have been covered in the preceding chapter (*see page 107*).

The visitor centre, built to look like a group of bronze age thatched huts, is intended to explain the archeology of the area. A visit involves watching a slide show and then looking at a few worthy but poorly presented displays; it's a bit disappointing. However, this is the start point for a pleasant walk around the edge of the lake, taking in several small and unspectacular archeological sites along the way, and passing two tower houses: Bourchier's Castle, which is lived in, and the badly ruined Black Castle.

Old Court Castle, Terryglass

On farmland, free, open access at any reasonable time. Near Terryglass, Co Tipperary.

Not far from the shores of Lough Derg is this interesting ruin of a large keep-like tower thought to date from the early 1200s. The tower is rectangular with a round tower on each corner; originally it probably stood three or four storeys high, but there's now not much more than one storey left. It was owned by the Butler family.

Scattery Island early monastic site

Island site: free, open access at any reasonable time. Visitor centre: Dúchas, free, open from mid-June to mid-September daily. Near Kilrush, Co Clare.

Besides having exhibitions that will introduce you to the history of the site and the fascinating legends associated with it, the visitor centre is also the place to catch a ferry to the island. The monastic settlement here was founded in the early 500s by Saint Senan, but the remains date mostly from the 1100s and 1200s. They are amongst the most substantial on a site of this type, but the most spectacular building is the round tower, standing some 37m (120ft) tall and with its door, very unusually, at ground level.

Left and above: Craggaunowen.

And...

Ballingarry Castle *(in a farm, no access), Ballingarry, Co Limerick* – Ruin of a tall L-plan tower house on the site of a Norman motte; used as a farm outbuilding. Sadly it is in poor condition and there is no access.

Bauraglanna stone circle *(on farmland, free, open access at any reasonable time) on Keeper Hill, Bauraglanna, 4km (2.5 miles) south of Silvermines, Co Tipperary* – Very modest stone circle of eleven stones (one is a tall pillar, the rest are a lot smaller; some are broken) in attractive hillside setting. It's not spectacular, but it's a rarity in this area.

Birr Castle Demesne *(privately owned, £££, open daily all year), near Birr, Co Offaly* – The castle here is private and cannot be visited, but its famous gardens are open to visitors. Attractions include a Science Centre and a telescope built in the 1840s, which for many years was the largest in the world. The original castle was demolished in 1778, and a house was built shortly afterwards, incorporating the original medieval gateway.

Caheraphuca wedge tomb *(on private land, free, open access at reasonable times only), footpath to the monument is signposted from the Burren to Killinaboy road in the Burren area, Co Clare* – Decent but not especially impressive example of this early bronze age variety of chambered tomb.

Carrigogunnel Castle *(on farmland, no formal access arrangements), by a minor road north-west of the N69 near Mungret, west of Limerick* – This is a fine-looking ivy-covered ruin on a long, low hill overlooking the Shannon, but unfortunately it is crumbling, and access is discouraged. The remains include a very early round stone tower, and a later tower house of the O'Briens.

Clonkeen Church *(Dúchas, free, open access at any reasonable time), signposted from the N24 between Limerick and Tipperary* – Ruin of a simple little Romanesque church of the 1100s with *antae* and fine decorative detail around the doorway.

Dromore Wood *(Dúchas, free, open mid-June to mid-September daily), signposted off the N18 north of Ennis, Co Clare* – This large woodland nature reserve contains the ruin of an O'Brien tower house of the early 1600s. It's picturesque, but the interior is unsafe to visit.

Farney Castle *(privately owned, limited access), signposted from the R498 north-west of Thurles, Co Tipperary* – Built in about 1495 and heavily remodelled in the 1800s with a rather appealing Gothic flavour, this castle-turned-house can be admired externally by visitors to its craft shop.

Glin Castle *(privately owned, £££, open daily in May and June), at Glin, Co Limerick* – A grand Georgian mansion built in the 1780s, which only started being called a castle after it had gothicky battlements added in 1825.

Lackeen Castle *(on farmland, no formal access arrangements), off the R438 south-west of Pike, north of Borrisokane, Co Tipperary* – Good ruin of a four-storey tower house of the mid-1500s, standing in a pretty much intact bawn. The basement is used for storage by the farm.

Above: Ballingarry Castle.

Leap Castle *(Privately owned, £££, open all year), south-east of Birr, Co Offaly; signposted on the R421 north of Roscrea* – As a gaunt ruin, this medieval tower house with later Gothic alterations was famous as Ireland's most haunted castle; but now it has been restored, is lived in, and is open for tours.

Lislaughtin Abbey *(Dúchas, free, open access at any reasonable time), signposted on a minor road north of Ballylongford, Co Kerry* – Ruined church of a Franciscan friary founded in 1438, plus parts of the cloister, including the dormitory and refectory.

Magh Adair *(in a field, free, open access at any reasonable time), north-east of Quin, Co Clare, signposted from the village* – A small mound in a field was the traditional inauguration place of the Kings of Thomond, amongst them the famous Irish High King Brian Boru, but not much to look at. Stories attached to the place are far more interesting than the site itself.

Mungret Church *(in churchyard, free, open access at any reasonable time), by the R510, off the N69 west of Limerick* – Remains of two clearly very ancient churches, but in an extremely decrepit state.

Rathkeale Abbey *(Dúchas, free, open access at any reasonable time), in Rathkeale, Co Limerick* – Just a part of this small abbey church survives.

Rattoo round tower *(Dúchas, free, open access to view exterior only at any reasonable time), off the R551 south of Ballyduff, Co Kerry* – Well-preserved round tower with a nicely carved doorway. The church nearby was built by Augustinian monks in the 1400s.

Redwood Castle *(Privately owned, ££, open May to September daily), near Lorrha, Co Tipperary* – This tower house, dating largely from the late 1500s but based on much earlier work, has recently been restored and is now lived in and open to the public.

Shanid Castle *(on farmland), between Ardagh and Foynes, Co Limerick* – Interesting round tower, but in very ruinous condition and there's no easy access.

*Leamaneh Castle in The Burren
(see page 115).*

West

Galway, Mayo and Roscommon

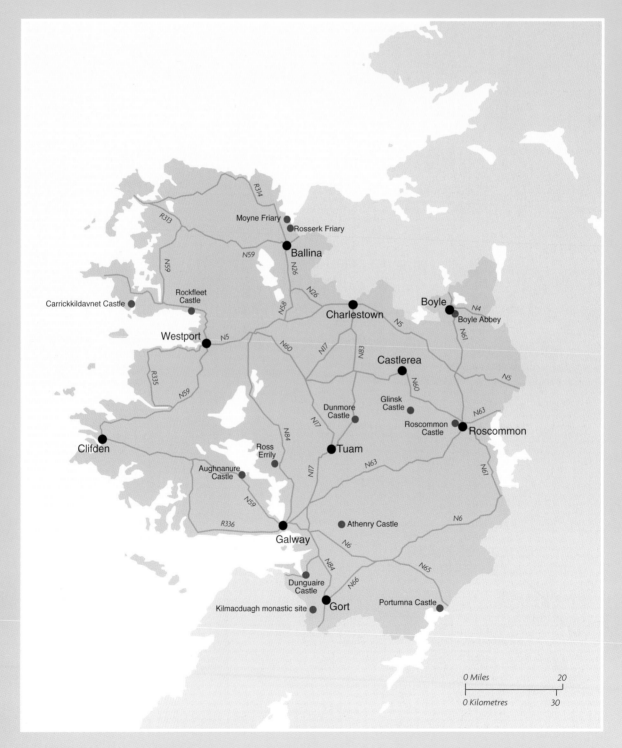

Moyne Friary
Rosserk Friary
Ballina
Boyle
Boyle Abbey
Carrickkildavnet Castle
Rockfleet Castle
Charlestown
Westport
Castlerea
Glinsk Castle
Clifden
Dunmore Castle
Roscommon Castle
Roscommon
Ross Errily
Tuam
Aughnanure Castle
Athenry Castle
Galway
Dunguaire Castle
Kilmacduagh monastic site
Gort
Portumna Castle

0 Miles 20
0 Kilometres 30

Athenry Castle

Dúchas • ££ • Open daily from mid-June to mid-September

This is an interesting and unusual type of Anglo-Norman tower, of much earlier date than the tower houses that are so common all over Ireland. It was in a healthy state even before a recent restoration gave it back its roof, but a slight drawback is that later modifications to the tower have made it impossible to restore it to anything like its original form, so that the interior is now an unconvincing and mildly disappointing mish-mash of styles.

The tower is typical of a kind of castle built in this area by Anglo-Norman lords after they overran Connacht in 1235, more than 50 years after the first Norman settlements in the east of Ireland. There was probably already a town here at Athenry, at the crossing point of the Clareen River, and the site was chosen by Meiler de Bermingham, who had been granted a large proportion of Connacht, as the ideal place for his castle.

The castle consisted of a circuit of walls with several round towers, quite a lot of which still survives, safeguarding a long, low, rectangular tower very reminiscent of the hall-houses being built in Scotland at about the same time. The tower had a wide splayed base, to make the walls more difficult to break down, and the only entrance was on the first floor, reached by a wooden stair. The whole first floor was occupied by a single big hall. The basement, reached only by a ladder from above, would have been used just for storage.

Meiler's son Piers modified the tower not long after it was built, raising the walls to make the first-floor hall more spacious, and adding the arched doorway, with its attractively carved pillars, and several elegant, narrow windows with trefoil heads, which are most unusual for a castle. There were still no fireplaces: the hall would have been heated by a central hearth or by braziers, with an opening in the roof to let the smoke out, covered by a louvre. Piers also built a banqueting hall on the east side of the castle courtyard, up against the curtain wall.

Some time in the 1400s the tower was raised again, with extra floors added, turning it into a bleakly functional accommodation block. The basement was fitted with stone vaults and given its own ground-floor entrance. It's these later changes that make it totally impossible for Dúchas to put the tower back to its original state. Instead, the first floor is presented in its original role as a grand hall, which is by far the most satisfying part of the interior, while the floor above it is now

Athenry Castle is a uniquely well-preserved example of an Anglo-Norman hall-tower from the early 1200s.

used for an over-dramatised, fact-light audio-visual display.

The castle was attacked by the native Irish led by the O'Conors in 1316, by which time work was already under way on the large circuit of walls that enclosed the town. Parts of these walls still survive, along with one of the five town gates and a market cross of the 1400s.

The large ruined church of the Dominican friary founded by Meiler de Bermingham in 1241 stands just a short walk from the castle; it has some attractive details, but it's normally kept locked up, and has a rather neglected air.

Nearby Athenry Friary was founded by the man who built the castle, Meiler de Bermingham, in a cooperative venture with native Irish townspeople.

In the town of Athenry, Co Galway. On the east side of the town centre, beside the R347, across the river from the ruined priory.

Aughnanure Castle

Dúchas • ££ • Open mid-June to mid-September daily

The eccentric appearance of this splendid tower house of the 1600s is immediately endearing, but it's also a particularly large and well-preserved example, and it has a number of unusual features.

One of its most appealing peculiarities is that the tiny nooks and crannies of its interior are home to a large number of bats of several different species, whose droppings fleck the whitewashed walls. There's a display in the basement of the tower which explains a bit about the bats, but if you're keen to find out more, they hold early-morning bat-watches here from time to time, so it would be worth phoning to get the details. There's no danger that you'll come across any bats during the day, incidentally, though some people may occasionally be able to hear them.

Equally appealing is the castle's secluded setting. You reach it by a short walk from the car park alongside a peat-darkened stream, with the tower partly hidden by trees on the far bank. The stream is actually the continuation of an underground river, and you approach the castle gate over a natural rock bridge. The field to the right of the gatehouse used to contain further castle buildings, but these were destroyed when the land collapsed into the underground river.

Still in place, though greatly restored, is the majority of an outer circuit of walls which guarded the castle, equipped with several small towers. There's no wall by the river, where the land slopes down to a sort of jetty. The tower house was also protected by an inner circuit of walls built much closer to it, of which one round tower survives, converted into a dovecot in later times, with a funny little conical corbelled roof. It's quirkily elegant, but you can't get into it.

Don't miss the remaining piece of the banqueting hall, immediately to the right as you enter the castle courtyard. Most of the building disappeared when the ground under it subsided, but if you go through the door in the surviving wall, you can admire the beautiful carved decorations that surround the windows.

The tower itself is an interesting one to explore. It's of the type where the main rooms are stacked one on top of the other, while one end of the tower is almost like a separate stair-tower: this 'extension' contains both the spiral stair in the corner and a series of small chambers across the width of the tower, usually with two floors of these little chambers squeezed in for each one floor in the main part of the tower. One of these little end-chambers gives

The funny little round tower was part of an inner circuit of walls protecting Aughnanure's tower house.

access to the murder hole over the ground-floor door, while from another chamber it is possible to gain access to one of the large machicolations that protect all four corners of the tower.

The vaulted basement would have been used for storage. There's another fireproof stone vault between the first floor and the second, and it's on the upper of these two floors, where the windows and fireplace are bigger, that the main reception room would have been. Along a passage that leads to a garderobe toilet there's also a trapdoor giving access to a secret chamber built inside the thickest part of the vaulted floor below; this might have been a prison, but was more likely a strongroom for hiding the lord's money and valuables.

The castle was the stronghold of the O'Flaherties, one of the principal native Irish dynasties of the region, into which the pirate queen Grace O'Malley married in the mid-1500s.

In 1564 an O'Flaherty known colourfully as Murrough of the Battleaxes won a battle against an English force at Trabane, near Galway, but he was later pardoned for his offences and made ruler of this part of Connacht by Queen Elizabeth. He aided the English President of the province, Sir Edward Fitton, in capturing Aughnanure Castle from the non-sympathising members of his clan, and as a reward in 1572 he was given the castle, which he then strengthened and made into his principal residence.

Near Oughterard, Co Galway. Signposted from the N59 Galway-to-Oughterard main road about 2km (1.2 miles) south of the town.

Boyle Abbey

Dúchas • £ • Open April to October daily

High walls and a gatehouse guard the elegant church at Boyle Abbey, a legacy of its later military role.

If Boyle doesn't look like you'd expect a ruined abbey to, that's because it was later converted into a well-defended barracks. As a result, it is now surrounded by a formidably high wall and entered through a funny little gatehouse. With military efficiency, this restructuring has destroyed most of the monastic buildings that once surrounded the cloister garth, but the majority of the rather beautiful abbey church has been left intact.

And beautiful it undoubtedly is. Like most of the finest monastic buildings in Ireland, it's the work of the Cistercians, who seem to have believed in creating hymns in stone to the glory of God, on a grander scale and with more elaborate detail than the worthy, practical friaries produced in later centuries by the Franciscans (several of which have survived in much better condition in this part of Ireland).

In particular, two sets of arches help to give the church such appeal: the four high, soaring arches that make up the crossing, and the bounding row of more down-to-earth rounded arches that runs along the south side of the nave. The easternmost

five of this row of arches are thought to make up the oldest part of the church, dating from about 1180. There's also an interesting row of arches on the north side of the nave: these are pointed rather than rounded, and therefore slightly later in date (about 1190–1200), demonstrating the transition from the earlier Romanesque style to the later Gothic. The only slight drawback is that this side of the church has started to subside heavily and lean over at an alarming angle, and at some stage has been propped up by heavy stone buttresses.

There are lots of very pleasing little carved details to look out for in the stonework of the church, notably on the capitals at the tops of the columns that support the arches on the south of the nave. One has several little figures standing between trees, while another depicts dogs apparently fighting over a bird. There's a display in the upstairs room of the gatehouse describing these carvings; and there are some interesting carved stones, including an

elaborate early sundial, on display here too. The gatehouse was built some time after 1589, when the military occupation of the abbey, then known as Boyle Castle, began. It was besieged by Hugh O'Neill in 1595 and again by Cromwellian forces in the mid-1600s, and remained in use by the army until the late 1700s. As for the history of the abbey itself, it was founded in 1162 by Cistercian monks from *Mellifont*, Co Louth (*see page 164*), but it was sacked by William de Burgo in 1202, which delayed the completion of the west end of the church.

After 1227, when there was a split between the Anglo-Norman and Irish abbeys in Ireland, Boyle was affiliated to Clairvaux in France rather than to Mellifont. By the 1400s it was already in decline, but it may have staggered on until after the dissolution, before the buildings were leased to William Usher in 1589 and began their military career.

In the town of Boyle, Co Roscommon. Signposted on the east side of the town centre, beside the N4 main road.

The tiny thin tower of Carrickkildavnet Castle is in an extremely scenic setting on the shore of Achill Island.

Carrickkildavnet Castle

Dúchas • Free • Open access to exterior only at any reasonable time

This tiny little tower house of the 1400s on the shore of Achill Island, just next to a little harbour, is notable mainly for its picturesque setting and its romantic associations with the pirate queen Grace O'Malley, to whom the castle is said to have belonged.

It's really surprisingly small – so small, in fact, that there is no room for a stair: presumably access to the upper floors was via a ladder, as at Grace O'Malley's other castle at *Rockfleet*, just down the coast towards Newport (*see page 129*).

The stonework of the building is in good condition, and you can get inside the interior, but it's just a shell: you look upwards to a barrel vault about two floors up, where you can see a hole for a trapdoor, which was presumably where the stair-ladder went.

By the coast road south from Achill Sound, on the south-east side of Achill Island, Co Mayo.

Dunmore Castle

Dúchas, on private land • Free • Open access at any reasonable time

Not one you'd go out of your way to find, but worth seeing because of its similarity to nearby *Athenry Castle* (*see page 121*). Standing on a rocky outcrop beside the romantically named Sinking River, this is another stout tower of the distinctive type that the Anglo-Normans built in these parts in the early 1200s. In its ruinous state, it looks much as Athenry must have done before its recent restoration.

The structure is thought to date largely from a rebuilding of about 1325 and like Athenry it was owned by local Norman bigwigs the De Berminghams (it's also known as De Bermingham Castle). Again it started as a simple two-storey building but was later increased in height. It was further remodelled in the late 1500s, when lots of large, ornate windows were added to make it more habitable, and it was lived in until the 1800s. There are the tumbledown remains of an outer wall hidden amongst the trees.

Dunmore Castle is an early Anglo-Norman tower similar to Athenry, with a few later alterations.

It's now just a shell: all four walls are intact right up to the gables, and you can get inside, but there are no floors and there is no access to upper levels.

Near Dunmore, Co Galway. Signposted beside the R328 (Claremorris road) 2km (1.2 miles) west of the town.

Dunguaire Castle

*Privately owned by Shannon Heritage • £££ •
Open May to October daily*

Dunguaire is one of the most picturesque of Ireland's many smaller tower houses, standing in a very attractive coastal setting, on a small island in Kinvara Bay, an inlet of Galway Bay. When the tide is in, the castle is practically surrounded by water; and when it's out, the muddy rocks and seaweed are still just as photogenic.

The tower was built in 1520 on the site of a far older stronghold, and it was lived in right into modern times. It has the slightly over-tidy look of an early 1900s restoration about it, and indeed it was bought in 1924 by a friend of WB Yeats (who himself lived in a small tower house not far from here) and modernised so that it could be lived in – though in the event the new owner never moved in.

The tower was bought in the 1950s and its restoration was completed, and indeed it was used as a house for a while, before its sale in the 1970s to the present owners, who operate several castles in the region – including *Bunratty* and *Knappogue* in Co Clare (*see pages 105 and 109*) – both as tourist attractions and as venues for 'medieval' banquets.

The legacy of these recent alterations is still evident in the castle. For example, the various outbuildings in the small courtyard – none of them open to visitors – include a modern kitchen for the banquets and a garage for the former owner's car. But it's nice that the bawn wall survives more or less intact, complete with a tower in the corner nearest the gate.

Inside the tower, too, the modifications are obvious – particularly on the top floor, where a large, airy room open to the rafters is designed and furnished as a 1960s living room. It's rather nice, actually. Equally, the room that in medieval times might have been the main hall, on the first floor, is now crammed full of benches and tables for the banquets.

But in fact, all three lower storeys – including the first-floor hall, the basement on the ground floor (with traces of wickerwork in its vaulted ceiling) and the chamber on the second floor – have been kept very plain, giving a good idea of the building in its original state. It's quite surprisingly primitive, considering that the place was lived in quite recently: lots of bare stonework is exposed, and the rooms are dark, lit only by tiny windows.

Best of all, you can get out on the narrow wall-walk around the battlements, with fine views in all directions. There's a slightly nerve-jangling view down through the box machicolations at the top of all four walls.

The castle is named after an earlier stronghold which belonged to Guaire, King of Connacht, who died in 662AD. The king was noted for his generosity and his hospitality – so much so, that it is said his right arm grew longer than his left – and he plays a key role in the Irish legend of *Bothar na Mias*, The Road of the Dishes. The story tells how dishes laden with food magically danced from Guaire's table to the hermit St Colman MacDuagh at his home on a mountain in The Burren. The road which the dishes are said to have followed is certainly a reality – it was probably a traditional pilgrimage route.

The present castle was built by the O'Hynes, descendants of Guaire, but in the early 1600s it passed into the hands of the Martyns of Galways, who were its owners right up until the derelict tower was sold in the 1920s.

Near Kinvara, Co Galway. Right by the N18 (Galway road) north of the town.

Below: Dunguaire Castle is a good example of a smaller tower house, in a scenic coastal setting.

Glinsk Castle is an especially elegant example of a fortified manor house of the early 1600s.

Below: The round tower at Kilmacduagh is not only a particularly fine one, it also leans over!

Glinsk Castle

Dúchas, on private land • Free • Open access at any reasonable time

Not really a castle at all, but a fortified manor house built in the 1630s by the Burke family. Its only obvious defensive elements are box machicolations up at gutter level at the front corners of the house and above the door, from which missiles could have been dropped, and small gun loops by the door, for firing pistols through. There would have been a parapet walkway round the roof, too.

It's a simple and attractive building, with fine mullioned windows and a row of impressive chimneystacks on each side; but as is usually the case with ruined houses of this era, all that remains is a shell. It stands in a field beside the road, near a farmhouse: access into the field is easy, thanks to a stone stile, but the doors and windows of the castle are barred, so you can't get in. Shame. It's said to have fine fireplaces to go with those big chimneys, but you won't get to see them.

Near Ballymoe, Co Galway. Just east of the village of Glinsk: the village is signposted from the R360 (Williamstown road) south of Ballymoe. Follow the minor road through the village and carry straight on until you see the castle.

Kilmacduagh monastic site

Dúchas & church authorities • Free • Open access to exteriors at any reasonable time; key for interiors in usual hours only (deposit required)

There's a collection of interesting buildings in this out-of-the-way location not far from the dramatic limestone hills of The Burren. The most striking is a very fine round tower which leans 60cm (2ft) out of the vertical. Unsurprisingly, you can't get inside it. Nearby, standing in a graveyard that is still used, is a cathedral as small as a parish church, built in the 1200s to replace an earlier church, the blocked west door of which it incorporates. Again you can't get inside, but it's not all that attractive in any case. Just over the road is another small church thought to have been exclusively for women.

More interesting is the Glebe, or abbot's house, by the car park, a building of much later date which has recently been restored and re-roofed. The key, available from a nearby house, will also get you in to the best building of the lot: the roofless ruin of O'Heyne's Church, built in the early 1200s, which has some really beautifully carved details in its ornate stonework.

Kilmacduagh, Co Galway. Signposted from the R353 (Corrofin road) just south of Gort.

Moyne Friary

Built in the 1460s, Moyne is a very handsome and well-preserved example of a large Franciscan friary.

Dúchas • Free • Open access at any reasonable time

Although it has been ruined for many years, this large Franciscan friary is still in remarkably complete condition, give or take a few small modifications. Indeed, it's a rival for *Ross Errily* in nearby Co Galway (*see page 131*), which is said to be the best-preserved abbey in Ireland.

Like smaller, more modest *Rosserk*, just a couple of miles down the estuary of the River Moy from here (*see page 130*), Moyne was built fairly recently in comparison with most abbeys. Possibly that's why the buildings are still in such good condition today. Founded in 1460, it was still occupied by friars long after the dissolution (and even after it was burned by Sir Richard Bingham in 1590). In 1617 an unnamed widow who lived here allowed six friars to remain.

Access is very good, provided you park your car carefully (without blocking any gates belonging to the farm on whose land the ruin stands) and you don't mind meeting a few cows as you cross the field to reach the abbey. The church is in good condition – though as usual with Franciscan friaries, it's very plain, and as usual with ruined churches in Ireland, it's full of later tombs – and the cloister arcades are pretty much complete.

The church is laid out in a classic Franciscan pattern, with a large chapel opening from the nave on your right as you enter, and a single transept to the south. An unusual addition, though, is the long Lady Chapel, which opens off to the right at the east end of the church. Another door also at the east end of the church, this time to the left, leads to the sacristy, where the treasures of the friary – the robes and vessels used in services – were kept.

The tall, narrow tower is supported on arches that bridge the church – another classic Franciscan feature – and although many guidebooks refer to the excellent views from the top, unfortunately the spiral stair that climbs it is now locked up. Which is a great shame. Apparently, the beam from which the church bell hung is still in place.

The largish cloister is, on the usual Irish pattern, to the north of the church. The buildings on all three sides (the fourth side being the church) are in good condition, and you can get up to the upper floors. The rooms on the west side include the chapter room (upstairs, with a big fireplace), which was a kind of common room cum meeting room, and near it the scriptorium, where books were read and copied.

The upstairs door is said to have been the only entrance to the friary after curfew, reached by a wooden ladder which could be lowered to let people in.

The refectory was in a kind of extension, next to the chapter house on the north-east corner; at the back, on the right, you can see the large window lighting the pulpitum, where the reader sat and read from the bible while the monks ate.

Between the refectory and the dormitory (over the chapter house) are the toilets: until recently, a drainage stream still flowed under the kitchen and the toilets. Beyond the toilets are the remains of a house built on in the mid-1700s, when members of the Knox family were still actually living in the abbey buildings – probably still in the company of a few remaining friars.

Near Killala, Co Mayo. Signposted on a minor road to the east of the R314 just south of Killala, north of Ballina. It's just a short walk, across two fields and two stiles, to the friary.

Portumna Castle

Dúchas • ££ • Open May to September daily (but closed Mondays in May and June)

Considering that it's basically just the shell of a big, old house, Portumna Castle is a surprisingly interesting and enjoyable place to visit. The house was built shortly before 1618 as the principle Irish residence of Richard Burke, 4th Earl of Clanricarde, a man of great wealth and influence both in England and in Ireland; but it was gutted by fire in 1826, and until recently it stood neglected, an eerie, crumbling ruin.

Work started to conserve the castle in 1968, and looks likely to continue for a number of years yet. One of the things that makes it such an interesting site is that a decision has been made not to restore the house completely, but to preserve it as a well-kept shell. The roof has been replaced, the chimneys have been put back, the stonework has been renewed, the windows have been re-glazed; but the walls will not be plastered and the rooms

Below: Portumna Castle was once the grandest fortified mansion in Ireland, and its gardens are being restored.

will not be furnished. It's a good decision, because the bare interior has a kind of simple grandeur that might otherwise be lost. And after all, the ornate exterior is starting to look much as it must have done in the castle's heyday.

As things stand, the only access to the interior is to part of the ground floor at the front of the building, where there's a series of interesting exhibition panels explaining the structure of the castle and the history of its owners.

The castle takes the form of a large rectangular block with a tower at each of its four corners, and the front half is divided from the back by two parallel walls across the width of the building. The stairs originally went up in the space between these two walls; before long, a staircase of some sort will be put back in so that there's access to the upstairs, though the floors will only ever be partially restored. The basement level, where the kitchens were, was reached by a separate entrance at the side of the house.

Ornate though it is, the exterior of the castle does have its defensive features: there are gun loops on either side of the grand front door and a machicolation

above it, and the battlements and gun loops of the turrets would have done a good job of defending the walls.

Besides the extra protection of its outer walls and gates, the castle was also surrounded by formal gardens, which again have been restored. Their graceful formality contributes an air of tranquillity to the place which certainly adds a great deal to its charm. To one side is the walled kitchen garden, filled with fruit and vegetables, herbs and flowers, which could probably keep gardening enthusiasts occupied for hours.

Outside the garden walls, you can walk down the side of the castle and stroll across the grounds at the back of it – this area is like a public park, openly accessible at all times – to the marina at the north end of Lough Derg. If you turn left along the road, back towards the town, you soon come across the ruin of a Dominican friary dating mainly from the 1400s. Immediately to the west of the castle is Portumna Forest Park, with a series of walks and trails to explore.

In Portumna, Co Galway. Signposted on the south-west side of the town, in parkland.

Rockfleet Castle

Dúchas, on private land • Free • Key from a neighbouring house during usual hours only

This little tower house is one of the best-preserved in Ireland, and it stands in an attractive setting on the shore of an inlet of Clew Bay, with water lapping right up to its walls.

You are free to get the key from the neighbouring house and let yourself in to look around at your leisure. Details of how to get the key are on a sign at the site, but you must respect the owner's wishes and visit between 10am and 6pm only.

Also known as Carrickahowley Castle, the tower was the home of clan leader Grace O'Malley, otherwise known by her Irish name of Granuaile, who led her people in sea-going raids.

Grace had several strongholds along this part of the coast, but she was here at Rockfleet in 1574 when the British sent a force from Galway to try to put a stop to her activities. She repulsed the attack, and later came to an agreement with the Crown. When she went to London to meet Queen Elizabeth, Grace refused to bow.

She came to live here after the death of her second husband, Sir Richard Burke,

Rockfleet Castle is a well-preserved little tower in a scenic location with a romantic story attached…

in 1583. Her wealth was described as '1,000 head of cows and mares'. The four-storey tower is far from a grand residence, though: it's very dark inside, lit by arrow slits rather than proper windows (it would be worth bringing a good torch). There's not even a stair from the ground floor to the first floor, which is reached by a ladder.

On the coast north-west of Newport, Co Mayo. Signposted as Carrickahowley Castle off the N59 about 8km (5 miles) north-west of Newport.

Roscommon Castle

Dúchas, on farmland • Free • Open access at any reasonable time

The facade of this once-important castle still looks mighty impressive when you see it across the meadows from the main road to Castlerea. It started life as a major-league fortification of the late 1300s, its fat round towers representing the cutting edge of military design, but it was later converted into a grand Elizabethan mansion with lots of large windows.

Work on the first castle here was begun by Robert de Ufford, Lord Justice of Ireland, in the 1260s, with the idea of suppressing the O'Conors, descendants of the kings of Connacht. However, that castle was captured by Hugh O'Conor even before it was finished. What happened next makes Roscommon a puzzle for castle experts: it was rebuilt on an identical pattern to Harlech Castle in Wales, which is thought to have been an innovative new design dreamed up by Edward I's chief castle-builder, Master James of St George – except that Roscommon was built a couple of years before Harlech.

The castle changed hands regularly over the years, until in 1341 it was captured by the O'Conors and held for many years. The modernisation to a well-lit Elizabethan mansion took place in more peaceful times, after 1578, when it was owned by the Governor of Connacht, Sir Nicholas Malby.

The remains are still impressive and are kept in decent condition, but there's no access to any of the towers, which somewhat limits the interest for visitors.

In Roscommon, signposted on the north-west of the town centre, off the road to Castlerea.

Tiny but very well preserved, Rosserk Friary was set aside for married members of the Franciscan orders.

Rosserk Friary

Dúchas • Free • Open access at any reasonable time

A nice little ruin of a small Franciscan friary, in remarkably complete condition, standing in a pleasant setting by the banks of the River Moy. The wading birds on the mudbanks of the river are almost as interesting as the ruin, and it's a good spot for a picnic.

Very like a smaller version of nearby *Moyne Friary* (*see page 127*) in design, Rosserk was founded in about 1460 by a member of the Joyce family. Interestingly,

it was intended for the 'Third Order' of Franciscans: married couples, who were excluded from the First Order (men) and the Second Order (nuns).

The friary went out of use after it was burned down in 1590 by Sir Richard Bingham, Governor of Connacht, though the fire doesn't seem to have done the stonework much harm.

It's a humble place, with little in the way of fancy detail. The most notable ornamentation in the church is the piscina – two shallow, scalloped basins for washing sacramental vessels, with an interestingly carved surround – at the east end of the church on the right. There is a transept on the south side of the church, and the funny little room in the transept is a secretarium, where books were kept.

The cloister buildings, which in typical Franciscan style are to the north of the church, are still almost completely intact. There are no fancy cloister arcades, however – just a yard surrounded by plain walls, with a few doors opening from it.

As usual, the dormitory was upstairs on the east side of the cloister – note the toilets at the far end – and the refectory and kitchens were on the north side, while on the west is a chapter room very like the one at Moyne, with a scriptorium and a library next to it.

North of Ballina, Co Mayo. Signposted on a minor road off the R314 Ballina to Killala road.

Left: the round towers of Roscommon Castle were fitted with large windows in the Elizabethan era.

Ross Errily

Dúchas • Free • Open access at any reasonable time

Standing in graceful isolation in acres of river meadows is the impressive ruin of the largest Franciscan friary in Ireland. It's also said to be the best-preserved, but *Moyne* (*see page 127*) and *Rosserk* (*opposite*) in nearby Co Mayo, as well as *Quin Friary* in Co Clare (*see page 112*), would run it a close contest for this honour. Access, incidentally, is excellent: a long track passes through a gate and leads to a small car park, and then all you have to do is hop over a stile and explore.

The basic layout at Ross Errily (Ross Abbey) will hold no surprises for anyone who has visited any of the other great friaries, but it does have its own peculiar features, too. Not least of these is the unique double cloister – or rather, one proper cloister, with most of its arcading intact, and next to it a slightly smaller yard. Most of the usual buildings of the cloister are in pretty good condition: as ever, look out for the refectory, with the well-lit balcony for the reader to sit in.

Right: Ross has two open yards, one of which has these heavy cloister arcades running around it.

Ross Errily is the most impressive of Ireland's Franciscan friaries, with fine buildings around its two cloisters.

The church has the typical slender Franciscan tower supported on cross-arches, and as usual a locked gate prevents access to the spiral stair that climbs up it. The church is distinguished mainly by its double transept on the south, which is reflected on the exterior by a distinctive pair of pointed gables.

Ross seems to have had a very large range of rooms used for food preparation, with what was probably a bakery – it has a round oven – opening on to the yard, and a larger kitchen behind, its vast fireplace sharing a chimney with the bakery. In the big kitchen is another of the friary's unique features: a large tank which would have been filled with water to keep live fish in, good and fresh for the pot.

Perhaps one reason why the place is so well preserved is that it wasn't founded until 1498, making it one of the last to be built before the Reformation. Even after the monasteries were dissolved, the friars at Ross were protected by the Earls of Clanricarde, but in 1596 English soldiers occupied the buildings, and in 1656 Cromwellians took off the roof and stripped the place of any useful materials they could find.

Near Headford, Co Galway. Take the minor road west from the crossroads in the middle of the village (off the N84), and Ross Errily is signposted at a turn after about 2km (1.2 miles).

See also…

Abbeyknockmoy Abbey

*Dúchas, free, open access at any reasonable time.
In fields north of Abbeyknockmoy village, off the N63
south-east of Tuam, Co Galway.*

A fair bit survives, standing in a field, of a Cistercian
abbey founded in 1190 by the King of Connacht.
There's a lot left of both church and cloisters, but
best preserved are the east range of the cloister and
the east end of the church. There's a grand chapter
house, spoiled by being divided in three in the 1400s:
it stands to its full height, but sadly is kept locked up.

The abbey's highlight, however, is an extremely
rare medieval wall painting on the wall of the chancel.
The east end of the church has been re-roofed to
help protect it from the elements, and fenced off to
protect it from vandals: tragically, it too is kept
locked up, so you can't even see the painting.

Ballintober Castle

*Dúchas, free, open access at any reasonable time.
In Ballintober, south-east of Castlerea, Co Roscommon.*

Ruin of an impressively large castle that was the main
stronghold of the O'Conors, rulers of Connacht.
There's a very large, rectangular walled enclosure;
at one end of it, there are large polygonal towers on
either corner which provided the main accommodation.
The castle may have been built as early as 1300,
perhaps influenced by Roscommon Castle, which
the O'Conors knew intimately from capturing it, but
it was altered at various times in its career, and was
lived in in the 1800s.

Above: Cong Abbey.

Below: Ballintober Castle.

Breastagh ogham stone

*Dúchas, free, open access at any reasonable time.
Signposted from the R314 west of Killala.*

A rare example of a free-standing ogham stone in its
original location, this tall pillar stands in the middle
of a field. its inscription makes no sense at all when
translated. Also nearby are the very badly ruined
Rathfran dolmen and, down by the shore, the
remains of the church of **Rathfran Friary**, a small
Dominican abbey founded in 1274.

Céide Fields neolithic landscape

Dúchas, ££, open mid-March to November daily.
On the R314 west of Ballycastle, Co Mayo.

Peat, which is basically rotted-down plants, builds up over thousands of years, and when it is cut away it often reveals items of interest to archeologists. Here, uniquely, neolithic fields and houses some 5,000 years old have been uncovered by peat-cutting.

It doesn't look like much, however, so there's a posh visitor centre to explain it all, with lots of extra information on local geology. The excellent coastal views and the tea and cakes in the cafe are just as interesting as the fields themselves – which, for all that they're from 3000BC, are, after all, just fields.

Cong Abbey

Dúchas, free, open access during usual hours only.
In the middle of the small town of Cong, Co Mayo.

There's not much left of the abbey: half the walls of the church, traces of the buildings on the north side of the cloister, and a short section of cloister arcade (and even that is partly reconstructed). But the abbey is certainly worth a look, if you find yourself in the town made famous by the film *The Quiet Man*.

You can tell that it was an important and wealthy establishment from the size of the cloister garth, which is probably the biggest in Ireland, and from the richness of the decorative detail on the two doors that lead off the cloister. The door with windows on either side led to the chapter house.

In fact, the Augustinian abbey was founded in 1135 by no less a person than the high king of Ireland, Turlough O'Conor, on the site of an earlier monastery. It was built largely by his son, Rory, and rebuilt after an attack on the town by William de Burgo in 1203.

From the abbey cloister you can stroll down to the woods, where the river is crossed by an interesting old stone bridge. Beside the bridge stands a small house, also of stone, built right over the river and with a hole in the floor so that it could be used for fishing. The job of supplying the abbey with fresh fish would have been an important one. There are still plenty of fish in the river, too, as you will no doubt see for yourself.

Above: The fisherman's house at Cong Abbey.

See also… The Aran Islands

These three islands in Galway Bay are all inhabited and are not at all difficult to get to, with regular services by boat and plane. It is perfectly possible to go just for a day trip, though it would be more rewarding to stay on the islands for a while: they are a popular holiday destination in summer, famous both for their rocky scenery and for their preservation of the Irish language and a traditional way of life.

The three islands, in descending order of size, are Inis Mór ('Big Island'), Inis Meáin ('Middle Island') and Inis Oírr ('East Island'). The names are anglicised to Inishmore, Inishmaan and Inisheer.

It tends to be easier to get to any of the islands from the mainland than it is to get there from one of the other islands, however, and that is a factor which may affect your planning.

Inishmore

Dun Aengus fort

Dúchas • £ • Open daily all year round

This spectacular monument is the largest and finest of the many stone forts that dot the rocky landscape of these islands. These forts are notoriously difficult to give an exact date to, but they are probably from late in the iron age, after about 100AD.

Like many of the others, Dun Aengus was built on the edge of a cliff so that one side of it has the natural defence of a sheer drop. It consists of a massive stone wall that curves round to enclose a roughly semicircular area. Steps on the inside of the wall make it easier to defend, and there is a narrow entrance passage through it.

Two things make this fort especially impressive: a series of large stone ramparts in front of the fort, and a defensive feature known as a *chevaux de frise*, where an area is filled with stones set on end to make it more or less impossible to walk on. Perhaps more than anything else, though, it's the extraordinary scenery that makes the place really special to visit.

About 7km (4.4 miles) west of the port of Kilronan, Inishmore.

Also on Inishmore

There are several other forts on the island, the two most worthwhile being **Dun Onaght**, not far from Dun Angus, and the **Black Fort** (like Dun Angus, it's on the cliffs on the south side of the island, but back nearer the port), which is a fine variant of the Dun Angus style, cutting off a small promontory.

Other monuments include a vast number of small churches scattered across the island, and the Cromwellian fort of **Arkin's Castle** near the port.

Inishmaan

Dun Conor fort

On farmland • Free • Open access at any reasonable time

Inishmaan is the least-visited of the three islands, and as far as monuments are concerned is notable mainly for this fine oval fort, which is one of the best in the islands. Again it is very difficult to date, but it was probably built after 100AD. Steps on the inside of the wall lead to a platform near the top, and there's a large outer wall too. Its position gives the fort fine views over the whole island.

There is also a smaller fort, known as Dun Fearbhai or Dun Moher, near the village of Baile an Mhothair.

Easily found in the middle of the island.

Inisheer

O'Brien's Castle

On farmland • Free • Open access at any reasonable time

The smallest of the Aran islands doesn't have the wealth of archeological sites offered by Inishmore, but it is easy to get here on a day trip from Doolin, Co Clare. The island is dominated by a rocky hill with a ringfort on top, and with this small ruined tower of the 1400s inside.

On the highest point of the island.

Glebe stone circle

On farmland, free, open access at any reasonable time. In a field beside the R345 north-east of Cong, Co Mayo.

This small stone circle is one of several that lie in the fields on either side of the road; there is another in the next field, just beyond this one. Perhaps the most interesting of them is **Nymphsfield stone circle**, on the other side of the road, which is a neat little circle of low stones set in a bank.

Rathcroghan earthworks (Crúachain Connacht)

Visitor centre: privately owned by a charitable trust, £££, open daily all year round (but closed Sunday and Monday from October to May). Visitor centre is in Tulsk, Co Roscommon; the field monuments are on either side of the N5 at Rathcrogan Crossroads, west of the village.

This fascinating site, consisting of an extensive group of earthworks spread over a wide area of farmland, is another of the major ritual sites of Celtic Ireland, similar to *Tara* in Co Meath (*see page 159*) or *Navan 'fort'* (often called by its legendary name of Emain Macha), near Armagh in Northern Ireland (*see page 182*).

It's worth starting by taking a look at some of the earthworks, which include ringforts, ring barrows and large mounds of no obvious purpose; but they don't make a lot of sense without the visitor centre in the village of Tulsk, which provides some of the context you need. It also has a souterrain on display.

Thoor Ballylee (Ballylee Castle)

Privately owned by charitable trust, £££, open from May to September daily. Signposted from the N18 or N66 north of Gort, Co Galway.

This small tower house of the 1500s was restored in the early 1900s as the home of WB Yeats. It is a very appealing building in a lovely setting beside a stream, but it is currently a most unsatisfactory place to visit; a short audio-visual display is followed by a silly tour, with commentary narrated at the press of a button in each room. All the interiors are bare, with no sense of this being a home. The most enjoyable bit is the roof.

And...

Ashford Castle (*privately owned and run as a hotel), near Cong, Co Mayo* – This massive, rather splendid neo-Gothic creation was built in about 1870 by the Guinness family, and is now a luxury hotel.

Claregalway Castle (*on private land, access to view exterior only), by the N17 north of Claregalway, Co Galway* – This four-storey tower house of the 1400s is pretty much complete, but it is in a sorry state and there is no access to its interior.

Clonfert Cathedral (*church authorities, free, open access during usual hours only), off the R356 in Clonfert, Co Galway* – St Brendan is buried here on the site of a monastery he founded. The main attraction of this still-used, much-modernised church is a superb ornamental doorway of the 1100s.

Coole visitor centre (*Dúchas, ££, open mid-April to September daily, but closed Mondays until mid-June), signposted on the N18 north of Gort, Co Galway* – The stately home of Coole Park burned down in the 1920s, but its grounds are now a nature reserve, open all year round for walks in the woods. A visitor centre offers several audio-visual displays.

Derryhivenny Castle (*on farmland, no formal access arrangements), off the R355 north of Portumna, Co Galway* – An attractive-looking tower house, dated 1643 but probably built earlier, has large parts of its bawn wall left, with round towers on two corners. Sadly there is no easy way to get to the castle.

Dunmore Friary (*Dúchas, free, open access at any reasonable time), by the supermarket in the middle of Dunmore, Co Galway* – Smallish ruined church of an Augustinian friary founded in 1245 by Sir Walter de Bermingham. It's not much to look at, but it has an attractive west door from the 1400s.

Elphin windmill (*privately owned by local trust, £, open daily all year round), signposted from the N4 or the N5 west of Boyle, Co Roscommon* – Nice little mill of the early 1800s, recently restored.

Fiddaun Castle (*on private land, no access), off the R353 south-west of Gort, Co Galway* – This is a fine-looking tower house with a well-preserved bawn wall, standing in farmland near a lake. Unfortunately, public access is prevented.

Inishbofin Island: Cromwell's Barracks and Coleman's Abbey (*monuments are free, open access at any reasonable time), ferry trips from Cleggan on the N59 west of Clifden, Co Galway* – This island off the Connemara coast has several enjoyable monuments, including a ruined abbey in a lakeside setting, and a fort of the mid-1600s.

King House (*local council, £££, open daily from April to mid-October), in Boyle, Co Roscommon* – Imposing mansion built in about 1730 by Sir Henry King, later used as a barracks and now restored as a modern museum with an emphasis on local history.

Kylemore Abbey (*privately owned, £££, open daily all year round, all proceeds to restoration fund), off the N59 near Letterfrack, Connemara, Co Galway* – This enormous and thoroughly mad neo-Gothic castle-style house, built in 1868, is now an abbey for Benedictine nuns. Access is limited to an exhibition in the reception hall and the ornate restored church, plus the grounds and Victorian walled garden.

Rinndoun Castle (*on private land, free, open access at any reasonable time*) – At Warren Point, off the N61 south-east of Roscommon – On a peninsula in Lough Ree stand the crumbling and overgrown remains of a large Norman castle built in the early 1200s and developed in the 1270s and 1290s.

Roscommon Friary (*Dúchas, free, open access at any reasonable time), by the N63 on the south side of Roscommon* – Rather disappointing ruined church from a Dominican friary founded in 1253, but with a couple of interestingly carved tombs.

Turoe carved stone (*on private land, free, open access at any reasonable time), in the grounds of Turoe House, near Bullaun village, Co Galway* – This unusual iron age monument is a small stone pillar decorated in the swirling patterns of the Celtic 'La Tène' style.

Left: Glebe stone circle, Cong.

Opposite page: Thoor Ballylee.

North West

Donegal, Sligo, Leitrim, Monaghan and Cavan

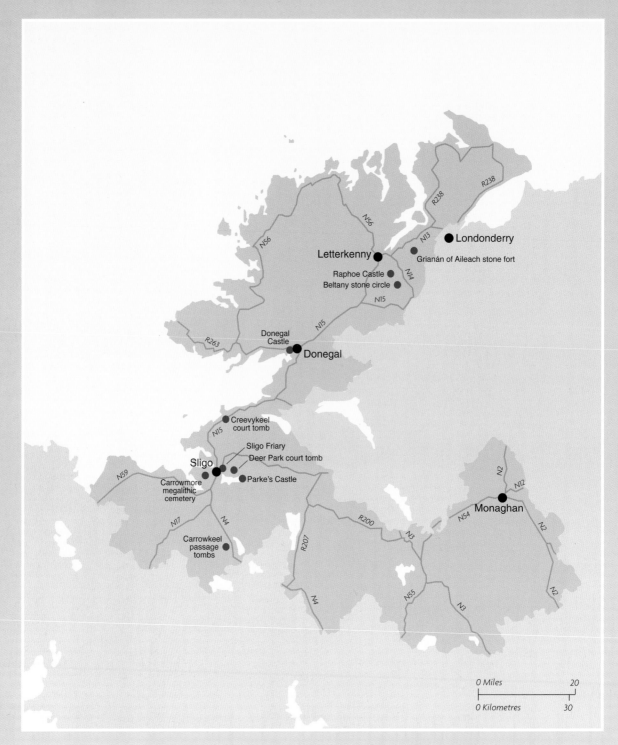

Beltany stone circle

Dúchas, on farmland • Free • Open access at any reasonable time

The large stone circle of Beltany stands in a splendid setting in a field on top of a hill, with superb views.

Far and away the most impressive stone circle in Ireland, and also the most enjoyable to visit, thanks to its superb hillside setting and easy access. A well-made track leads uphill from beside the farm entrance, and a short walk – steep, but not dauntingly so – brings you to the field in which the monument stands, from where there are extensive views of the surrounding countryside, with hills and mountains marching off into the distance.

This is not actually the largest stone circle in the country – that honour belongs to *Grange stone circle*, near Lough Gur in Co Limerick (*see page 107*) – but it's certainly one of the largest, consisting of more than 60 closely spaced stones set in a true circle roughly 44 metres (165ft) in diameter. Originally there would have been no gaps, so there would have been about 80 stones in total. Most of the stones aren't particularly large; they average just over a metre (3ft 6in) in height, though one of the larger slabs on the south-west side (which is possibly significant) is 2.75m (9ft) high. There's a single outlying pillar to the south-east.

One very obvious difference between Grange stone circle and Beltany is that the stones in the former are set into the inner face of a bank that surrounds the circle, whereas here the ground inside the circle is raised, and the stones are set around this

central raised area. There seem to be lots of humps and bumps in the central area, along with large quantities of loose stone. In fact, it is thought that this is all that's left of a huge stone cairn, which may have had a passage grave or some similar kind of chambered tomb at the centre of it.

This combination of stone circle and cairn makes Beltany unique in Ireland, though it is thought that a ruined site in north Antrim might have been a similar kind of monument, and there are comparable sites in Scotland.

A signboard near the entrance to the field describes an interesting carved stone head which was found here, but that is thought to be from the iron age and therefore of much later date than the

monument itself, which is presumed to be from the early bronze age, about 2000BC.

That apart, little is known about the site, though the name 'Beltany' suggests that local people have long associated it with Beltane, the Celtic festival of fertility at the beginning of summer, echoes of which survive in modern times in the celebrations of May Day.

Near Raphoe, Co Donegal. On Tops Hill, 4km (2.5 miles) south of Raphoe; clearly signposted from the minor road between Convoy and Ballindrait, which passes south of Raphoe; or take the Clady road in the centre of Raphoe, and then the second turning to the right. The track to the monument leads uphill to the right of the farm gateway.

Left: The largest stones in the circle are all on the south-western side, but it's not clear if the monument was deliberately aligned in that direction.

Cairn G will probably be the first tomb you come to, and it has a superb chamber which is easily accessible.

Cairn K, a little higher up the ridge, also has an excellent chamber, but the entrance is harder to get through.

Carrowkeel passage tombs stand on the Bricklieve Mountains south of Castlebaldwin, Co Sligo. The site is well signposted from the N4 Boyle-to-Sligo main road at Castlebaldwin, but look out for the final turning near the top of the hill, which has only a handwritten sign (the turn is also signposted for the donkey sanctuary). Just a short way up this lane, the road to the monuments turns to the right (the donkey sanctuary is straight on). After passing through a gate, park at the bottom of a track that turns off to the right just as the road bends sharply to the left. It's a walk of about 20 minutes, with some fairly gentle uphill stretches, from here to the monuments.

Carrowkeel passage tombs

Dúchas, on high moorland • Free • Open access at any reasonable time

Ireland's four great neolithic cemeteries stand in a curving line that runs from coast to coast across the northern part of the centre of the country, from *Brú na Boinne* (*see page 152*) near Drogheda in the east, to *Carrowmore* (*see overleaf*) near Sligo in the west. The sites at either end are near the coast and fairly low-lying, but the two in the middle of the country – *Loughcrew*, Co Meath (*see page 157*) and this one at Carrowkeel – are both in splendid hilltop locations with extensive views.

The limestone ridges on which the Carrowkeel tombs stand are particularly dramatic when seen from a distance, but it's a slightly eerie landscape when you get up here. There are 14 cairns here on several ridges, each cairn now identified by a different letter. Many are passage tombs, but some do not appear to have had any kind of structure under the heaped

stones of the cairn. One, Cairn E, is a long cairn built over a passage tomb, with a 'blind court' – a facade that looks like an entrance, but has no opening – at one end.

Most of the cairns aren't too interesting and don't get many visitors, and there's no obvious path up the heather-covered hillside to reach them, so it's best to concentrate on the four most exciting and most visited cairns, to which there is a well-defined path. Two of them are classic cruciform-chambered passage tombs in excellent condition, with the corbelled roofs of their beautifully constructed chambers still intact.

Access to the chambers is not difficult, provided you don't mind going on hands and knees over a rocky surface at the entrance, but it's a good idea to bring a decent torch. What you won't find, however, is elaborate decoration like that at Loughcrew and Brú na Boinne.

It's best to park your car shortly after passing through the gate across the road, at the point where a track leads off to the

right and the road bends sharply to the left. From here, walk on round the bend, up the road and over the shoulder of the ridge. It's a steady amble of about 20 minutes to the monuments. There are a couple of small parking places further up the road if you really don't fancy walking that far, and people can be dropped at the turning circle below the cairns, but don't park there.

A short and not too steep scramble up the ridge brings you to the first two cairns: Cairn G, with an excellent intact chamber that's fairly easy to get into; and just beyond it Cairn H, which appears to have a way in, but either the passage has collapsed or it's a false entrance. A little further up the ridge you come to Cairn K, which again has a very splendid chamber; and the badly ruined Cairn L.

From up here, you can really appreciate the superb views to the north and west, with the extraordinary mountains around Sligo visible in the distance. In the foreground is Lough Arrow, the fertile shores of which may have been the reason

From the ridge on which the pale stone cairns stand, there are superb views to the mountains around Sligo.

the tomb-builders settled in this area in the first place. To your right as you look this way, though not visible from here, is another ridge, on the lower parts of which stand about 80 hut-circles. This might possibly have been the village in which the people who built the tombs lived, but the round houses are undated, so they could just as easily be from a later period.

Dating evidence suggests that the tombs were built between 3800 and 3300BC, but artefacts from the bronze age (after 2000BC) were also found here. In a rapid investigation of all 14 tombs in 1911, large quantities of cremated human bone were found, along with personal ornaments typical of passage tombs – beads, pins and pendants – and pieces of pottery in a style that became known as Carrowkeel ware, also typical of passage tombs.

Directions to the site are given opposite.

Queen Maeve's cairn

The site at Carrowmore is dominated by the towering ridge of Knocknarea to the west, with an enormous cairn silhouetted on the skyline (*see picture on opposite page*). This is *Miosgán Meadhbha*, or Queen Maeve's Grave, a truly immense pile of stones which is said to be the burial place of the legendary Celtic queen of Connacht.

Opinions vary on whether or not the cairn conceals a passage grave: the official guide booklet for Carrowmore suggests that it probably does, but the archeologists on hand in the visitor centre reckon it probably doesn't, their argument being that the weight of the stones in the cairn is such that any structure underneath would be crushed. Of course, it may depend on whether or not the mound is a solid pile of stones. Certainly it is not likely to be excavated in the near future, since the task of shifting all those stones would be daunting.

You can certainly walk up and take a closer look at the cairn. A path leads from a car park on this side of the hill: it's probably best to ask for directions at the Carrowmore visitor centre. The views are spectacular.

There's also a passage tomb with a cruciform central chamber on the ridge to the north of the cairn, and what might be the remains of three others to the south.

Below: Tomb No 7 is just about the perfect example of Carrowmore's distinctive type of neolithic tomb.

Carrowmore
megalithic cemetery

Dúchas, partly on private land • Visitor centre: ££, open May to September daily • Field monuments: free, open access at any reasonable time

The fourth of Ireland's great neolithic cemeteries is the least dramatic, but in many ways it's the most curious. It may also be the oldest, though the dating evidence is ambiguous.

The hummocky, bumpy ground on which it stands is not only good farmland, but also turned out to be rich in deposits of useful sand and gravel, which was extensively quarried in the last century. The result is a slightly odd rural landscape in which farmhouses huddle up against stone circles and fields suddenly give way to disused quarries.

Even so, you only have to look around (provided it's not raining) to see that this is a pretty special place. There's some spectacular and unusual scenery around here, particularly the mountains on the far side of Sligo, their pale limestone cliffs shining in even the faintest glimmer of sunlight; and, in the opposite direction, the single great ridge of Knocknarea, topped by a truly immense mound of stones known as Queen Maeve's Cairn (*see left*). In addition, the nearby coast provides a

wealth of natural resources: on the shores of Ballysadare Bay near Cullenamore Strand, to the west of here, there are large prehistoric middens – piles of shells discarded after the oysters, winkles and mussels they contained had been eaten – and just offshore is the Great Seal Bank, home to one of Ireland's largest populations of seals.

There's a large number of tombs at Carrowmore (at least 30 remain of more than 60 originally identified in the early 1800s) spread over a wide area (seven or eight fields). Most are of a similar type, rather different from the passage graves of the other great cemeteries, consisting of a simple chamber (a fat capstone supported by typically five uprights) surrounded by a circle of boulders. In some cases there are scattered stones remaining from what might be a passage leading from the opening of a chamber towards the edge of the monument. An obvious assumption is that the chamber would have been covered by a mound, the surrounding stone circle acting as a kerb, but it ain't necessarily so.

Thanks to arrangements with local farmers, the fields in which the monuments stand can easily be accessed via stiles or gates, and in fact you can come here and visit them at any time, even when the visitor centre is not open. During its opening times, however, you are

encouraged to drop in at the visitor centre first: it's well worth doing so, because even a very brief look at the small exhibition and a chat with the guides will give you a better idea of what to look out for, and you can buy a leaflet that features a useful map of the site.

The field next to the visitor centre is owned by Dúchas, and contains what is thought to be the most important of the monuments – a large mound known as Listoghil (or alternatively No 51). This has fairly recently been excavated to reveal a chamber quite different from the others, carefully constructed of square slabs of stone (rather than the boulders of the other tombs), its massive roof-slab delicately balanced on small chock-stones and decorated with incised markings (which aren't very obvious, but you can just about discern them in the right light).

As the only decorated monument in the cemetery, and possibly the only one to have originally been covered by a cairn, Listoghil seems to have been of particular importance, and may have been a focal point for the cemetery in a similar way to the great mound at *Knowth* (one of the Brú na Boinne sites – *see page 152*) or the highly decorated Cairn T at *Loughcrew* (*see page 157*).

On the other hand, the focus of the monuments might be more general. If you look at a map of the tombs here at Carrowmore, they seem to form a rough oval around an open area in the centre, and indeed all the entrances of the chambers face inwards towards this central area. Again this compares with Knowth, where it is thought a number of small, inward-facing tombs surrounded an empty patch of ground before the great mound in the middle was built.

When you've seen the tombs in the Dúchas-owned field by the visitor centre, walk across the field and hop over a low stone stile to emerge on the road. (If you're a little confused about your bearings, stand with your back to the visitor centre, and the stile is to your left.)

There are more tombs in both directions: you can turn right and walk down the smaller road, where the tombs are mostly in fields to your right; or you can turn left, where the smaller road meets the larger one at a T-junction. Here the main group of tombs is in the fields on the far side of the junction. The gate to these fields is reached by turning left at the junction and walking back towards the visitor centre, with the gate on the right of the road opposite the car park.

Carrowmore is overlooked by Queen Maeve's Cairn on the ridge of Knocknarea to the west.

The two most complete and most picturesque tombs to visit are No 7, which is through the field opposite the car park and on into the next field; and No 27, down the smaller road, where the chamber in the middle has a cruciform shape which makes it rather more like a passage tomb.

Excavations were carried out at several tombs in the 1970s and have been conducted at others since, and these have uncovered deposits identical to those usually found in passage graves: cremated human remains, pottery of the sort known as 'Carrowkeel ware', tools of flint or stone, large round-headed pins made of antler or bone, and balls made of chalk or stone.

Dating evidence in the form of burnt bone or wood has also been found, but this has produced controversial radio-carbon dates long before 4000BC. This would be far earlier than most neolithic tombs: indeed, it would be before some people think neolithic farmers were settling and growing corn. The dates might apply to middle stone age activity on the site.

Near Sligo, Co Sligo. Signposted on minor roads to the west of the town.

Court tombs

This interesting type of neolithic burial monument is unique to Ireland, and by chance the two biggest and best examples in the country happen to lie quite close to each other, not far from the town of Sligo.

A court tomb is a variety of chambered tomb in which the burial chamber is entered from a large enclosed area known as the court, as in courtyard, where it is presumed some sort of ritual might have taken place. The court prompts comparison with certain long barrows and long cairns in England and Scotland, where a facade or forecourt at one end of the monument suggests a similar ceremonial purpose. It is not thought that the court would have been roofed over.

Creevykeel court tomb

Dúchas • Free • Open access at any reasonable time

This is by far the more accessible of the two court tombs, standing in a field beside a main road with a large lay-by to park in, though this accessibility has its drawbacks; you may find yourself swamped by a coach party or two when you visit. It's an appealing monument, though, especially with its surprisingly pale stones glowing in the evening sun. The field in which it stands is higher than the road, so from up here you can better appreciate the setting of the monument, very near the coast and in the shadow of the mountains.

Here the monument takes the form of a long, wedge-shaped stone cairn, with an entrance in the wider end leading into the

A view of the court at Deer Park, with a single chamber on the right, and a pair on the far side.

oval court. Directly opposite, on the far side of the court, is the entrance to a burial chamber of two compartments. The lintel stone was found fallen, inside the chamber, and has been re-erected.

Excavations in 1935 discovered cremated human remains, neolithic pottery, leaf-shaped flint arrowheads, scrapers, polished stone axes and a chalk ball. They also revealed an iron-smelting furnace of the early Christian period which had been built inside the court.

By the N15 Sligo to Bundoran road, just north of Cliffony, Co Sligo.

Deer Park court tomb

Dúchas, on forestry land • Free • Open access at any reasonable time

This one is a fair bit more difficult to get to, reached by a steepish walk of 20 minutes uphill through forestry. The monument, also known as The Giant's Grave, stands in a clearing in the trees, the views that it apparently used to boast now obscured; but the extraordinary scenery nearby suggests that the builders of the tomb chose their hilltop site carefully.

This is a different variety of court tomb, known as a central court tomb. The large court in the middle has its entrance at one side, with burial chambers opening off either end: there are two smaller chambers to the right of the court, and a single large one to the left. All the burial chambers have two compartments. Two of the lintels fell in the 1920s and lie across the entrances they once spanned; the third is broken in the middle and looks ready to collapse.

There's not much trace of a covering mound or cairn – only big upright slabs defining the outline of the monument remain – but there are traces of a passage leading from the court to a kerb around the outside of the monument. Excavations in the 1800s found human bones and the bones of animals, mostly deer.

In Deerpark Forest, east of Sligo, Co Sligo. From Parke's Castle, follow the R286 towards Sligo and take the second turn to the right; turn left at crossroads; turn left to forestry car park (signposted 'Giant's Grave'). From the car park, walk up the track and look for the footpath to the right after about 35m (40yds); take the right-hand branch of the footpath, following a sign reading, somewhat inaccurately, 'Stone circle'.

The pale stones of Creevykeel, with the court in the background, beyond the entrance to the burial chamber.

Donegal Castle

Dúchas • ££ • Open from mid-March to the end of October daily

A powerful and impressive tower house was built on a rocky outcrop in a bend of the River Eask, not far from the sea, some time in the late 1400s by a member of the O'Donnell clan, rulers of Tyrconnell. However, in about 1600, when the tide of political fortunes turned against Hugh Roe O'Donnell, last of the O'Donnell chiefs, and he was forced to flee to Spain, he ordered that his castle should be destroyed, and it was set on fire.

In 1611 the partially ruined castle was given to Captain Basil Brooke, an Englishman who had come to Ireland in 1598 with the English army. He built a new manor house alongside the tower, in a style fit for a wealthy Jacobean gentleman, and had the old tower rebuilt to match.

To bring the story right up to date, the tower has been restored, with the grand bay window in its front rebuilt, and it has been given a new roof.

It's a thoroughly pleasant place to visit, sheltered by its partly rebuilt curtain wall and entered through a gatehouse added in the early 1600s. The corner-turrets, gables and mullioned windows of the tall tower, eccentrically half-matching the elegant manor house wing next to it, give an appealing look to the exterior. The manor house wing has been left as a shell. Its grand main entrance is on the first floor, but the steps that led up to it have disappeared. The ground floor housed the kitchens, and there's a large fireplace with an oven.

You can enter the tower either by a doorway into the basement, added as part of the remodelling, or by modern external steps to the first floor. The basement is dark and cavernous, giving a good impression of the size and strength of the original tower house, even though it's divided by a modern supporting wall and its vaulted roof has partially collapsed. The original entrance was at the front end, where the bay window now is, and the spiral stair is still in place, leading up to the first floor.

The first floor would still have been the main reception room of the castle after it was remodelled in the early 1600s, and it is indeed a grand room, light and airy, well lit by the restored bay window. It is ornamented by a large, elaborately carved fireplace (said to be a rare example of secular sculpture from the first half of the 17th century) in which the arms of the Brooke family are combined with those of his wife's family, the Leicesters.

Upstairs from here, the second floor has now been left as one large room open to the roof, though originally there would probably have been partition walls to divide the room, and there would certainly have been a floor above to create an attic storey. The new wooden roof, its beams pegged together with wooden dowels in the customary Dúchas manner to avoid metal nails or bolts, is a very handsome piece of work. This upper room houses a series of well-presented and interesting displays on the history of the O'Donnells and the region they once ruled.

In the centre of Donegal, Co Donegal. Just off the town square (The Diamond), in a turning from the N56 Killybegs road.

The extravagantly remodelled tower at Donegal, and (below) the doorway to the Jacobean manor that was built alongside the tower in the early 1600s.

Grianán of Aileach stone fort

Dúchas, on moorland • Free • Open access at any reasonable time

This is an interesting monument, but what makes it really special to visit is the superb views from its ramparts, particularly to the north-west, out over the long, thin finger of sea known as Lough Swilly. It really does feel like the top of the world up here. Fortunately, you don't have to climb all the way up on foot: the road leads up to a car park that's just a short walk from the monument – and not a steep one, either.

Grianán of Aileach is a very pleasing example of a stone fort of the late iron age or the early Christian period: evidence of

Steps lead up the inside of the wall to a broad wall-walk at the top, but this aspect of the fort may not be original.

What this exterior view of Grianán of Aileach doesn't show is the stunning views from the top of the walls.

exactly when it was built is sadly lacking, but it is thought that its career spanned some 600 years from about 500AD.

From the outside, the fort has a satisfyingly stout, bulging appearance, which it owes to the dry-stone building techniques used in its construction: basically, the walls have to be thicker at the bottom than at the top to support the weight of stone, so the outer wall curves gently inwards as it rises.

A well-made entrance tunnel, roofed over with fine lintel slabs, leads to the interior, where a series of steps climbs to several lower walkways before leading out on a broad walkway at the top of the ramparts. However, the experts point out that the fort was extensively reconstructed in 1879 by Dr Bernard, Bishop of Derry, with more enthusiasm than skill, so that the internal arrangements as they appear today probably don't closely reflect their original state.

Typically for a later iron age dry-stone fortification (like the brochs and duns of Scotland, for example) the fort has a couple of storage chambers built into the thickness of the wall, though here they are long passage-like affairs rather than simple corbelled-over rooms like the ones at the Irish mainland's other great stone fort, *Staigue* in Co Kerry (*see page 89*).

It's definitely worth bringing a torch and taking a look in one of these long chambers; the one to the right of the entrance is rather easier to get into because the roof is higher.

The walls of the fort are as much as 4m (13ft) thick and enclose an area 24m (78ft) in diameter, slightly smaller than Staigue's 28m (90ft). You can just make out the remains of three concentric outer walls which once helped defend the fort.

The name Grianán means sunny place or palace, and indeed this was the royal stronghold of the north-western branch of the Uí Néill (the O'Neills), the great ruling dynasty of early Christian Ireland. It was eventually destroyed in 1101 by Murtagh O'Brien, King of Munster, in revenge for the destruction of his own royal stronghold at Kincora, near Killaloe, Co Clare. Murtagh is said to have ordered his men to bring away one stone each so that the fort could not easily be rebuilt.

There is, incidentally, a visitor centre on the main road below the fort, near Burt, which explains the history and archeology of the fort in greater detail.

Clearly signposted on the N13 (Letterkenny to Derry) road near Burt, Co Donegal. Look for a right turn and then, after about 5km (3 miles), a left turn up the minor road to the fort.

Parke's Castle

Dúchas • ££ • Open April to October daily (but closed on Mondays in April and May, unless it's a bank holiday Monday)

For all the formidable appearance its high walls present, this is not really a castle at all, but a fortified manor house of the early 1600s. It's a very picturesque place, standing on the shores of the immensely scenic Lough Gill, which WB Yeats immortalised in his poetry, so the castle can perhaps be forgiven if it's not quite as interesting to look round as might be hoped. It does have a teashop, however, which is always a redeeming feature.

There was once a 'proper' castle on this site, in fact: a big tower house of the 1500s which is thought to have belonged to the local ruling family, the O'Rorkes. It is thought that this may have been the castle in which Sir Brian O'Rorke sheltered a shipwrecked officer of the Spanish Armada, Francisco de Cuellar, in 1588, and that the tower was then destroyed by the English as a reprisal. O'Rorke was executed for high treason in London in 1591. The foundations of his tower house were uncovered during recent excavations, hidden under the cobblestones of the courtyard. It seems likely that the ruined tower house was pulled down so that its stone could be used for the construction of the fortified manor house that we see today.

The present castle was probably built by, and named after, Captain Robert Parke, who settled here when Leitrim was 'planted' with English landowners in the 1620s. A village known as Newtown was also established nearby: it was abandoned a long time ago, but its ruined church can still be seen.

Parke was arrested in 1642 on suspicion of disloyalty to the Commonwealth, and his castle was captured by an Irish lord and held until 1652, when it was surrendered to the Parliamentarians. After the Restoration, however, Captain Parke's fortunes recovered, and in 1661 he became MP for Leitrim.

Captain Parke's castle was built inside the large curtain wall, or bawn, of the original tower house. To start with, the fairly modest main accommodation was in the gatehouse-tower; but after the Cromwellian wars were over, Parke built the manor house in between the gatehouse and a largish round tower surviving from the original walls. The stonework of these buildings has been fully restored, and new floors, roof and panelling of native Irish oak have been put in.

The manor house is three stories in height, with a large hall on the first floor and kitchens below. There's an audio-visual display downstairs, to introduce you to the history of the place, if you go in for that sort of thing. The hall houses an exhibition on the archaeology of Leitrim, while the upper rooms of the gatehouse have reconstructions to show how it might have looked when it was used as living accommodation in the early 1600s. Visitors can also walk round the wall-walk and pop their heads in at the dovecote, converted from a small round tower on the wall; and there are stables and a reconstructed (and fully operational) forge ranged around the edge of the courtyard.

Near Fivemilebourne, Co Leitrim. Clearly signposted on the R286 on the shore of Loch Gill, east of Sligo and north-west of Dromahair.

Below: its high walls look formidable enough, but Captain Parke's 'castle' was really a fortified manor.

Sligo Friary

Dúchas • ££ • Open June to September daily

This Dominican friary was founded in about 1253 by Maurice Fitzgerald, 2nd Baron of Offaly, who also founded the town of Sligo. The oldest remaining part is the choir of the church, lit by a row of tall lancet windows. The sacristy and chapter house are nearly as old.

The friary was accidentally burned down in 1414 and was rebuilt two years later, and most of the rest of it is from this period, including the cloister and the majority of the buildings around it. Some of the older and newer bits don't quite seem to fit together.

Two sides of the cloister arcade are well preserved, along with a substantial part of the third side. It's in the slightly heavy style, with overhanging buildings supported on the arches that you find in Ireland's Franciscan friaries.

The most interesting survival is the first-floor refectory, opposite the church, with a balcony-like bay window in which a friar would sit to read aloud from the bible while his brothers ate.

There are several unusual features inside the ruined church, the most striking being the stone arches of a rood screen, dating from the 1400s and partially reconstructed, which separated the public part of the church from the important eastern end. The altar, carved with a rose and a bunch of grapes, is probably also from the 1400s, and is one of only a few medieval altars to survive in this country.

There are two striking later tombs: the O'Conor Sligo monument of 1624, near the rood screen, and the O'Crean tomb of 1506, high on the wall in the far corner of the church, which shows the crucifixion and a number of saints.

Sligo, Co Sligo. On the south-east corner of the town centre, off Castle Street near its junction with Thomas Street (the main road to Dublin).

Sligo Friary's cloister arcades are intact on two sides, but its real highlight is the carvings inside the church.

See also... Raphoe Castle

On private land, free, open access at any reasonable time. On the south-east side of the small town of Raphoe, Co Donegal.

It looks splendid from a distance, but the ruin of this grand fortified manor of the 1630s is, as is usually the case with large ruined houses of this era, nothing more than a shell, so it's not hugely interesting to look at close-up. It's very similar to *Rathfarnham Castle*, Dublin (*see page 168*) in design, consisting of a rectangular block divided lengthways by a central wall, with a tower at each of its four corners. A crucial detail is that the corner-towers are of a slightly pointed shape that reflects the 'angle bastions' used in artillery forts of this period.

Also known as Raphoe Palace, the castle was built by Bishop Leslie. In a brief but dramatic career it was besieged in 1641, captured by Cromwellian forces in 1650, restored, sacked by supporters of James II in 1689, and then restored again. Many of the grand mullioned windows were added in the 1700s.

See also...

Ballinafad Castle

Dúchas, on farmland, free, open access at any reasonable time. Beside the N4 Boyle to Sligo main road at Ballinafad, Co Sligo.

The interesting thing about this picturesque ruin is that it's a castle of the 1600s built in a very much earlier style, consisting of a square central block with a small round tower on each corner. The castle is easily spotted from the main road between Boyle and Sligo, and will only occupy you for five minutes if you care to take a look round, since it's now little more than a shell.

It is also known as the Castle of the Curlews, from its setting near the Curlew Pass – the road through the pass was an important route from Sligo to Roscommon in earlier times. The castle was built between 1590 and 1610 by Captain John St Barbe. Its old-style design must have been effective, since its English garrison was able to hold out against Irish attackers led by the Burkes in 1641, though it was forced to surrender following a siege in 1642, having run out of water.

Ballymote Castle

Dúchas, free, open access to view exterior only at any reasonable time. In Ballymote, Co Sligo, just across the road from the railway station.

The ruin of a large and important medieval castle, which would be interesting to visit if the effort were made to do something to its interior and open it up to the public on a regular basis. There has recently been some restoration work, and the area around it has been tidied up, which is a step in the right direction.

An enclosure-type castle, consisting of a fairly compact circuit of walls strengthened by impressively large round towers, it was built in about 1300 by Richard de Burgo, the 'Red Earl' of Ulster. At the time, it was the most powerful fortress in Connacht. Later it was owned by a series of prominent local families, and in 1498 it was sold to Red Hugh O'Donnell for £400 in cash and 300 cows. It was from here that a later O'Donnell set out in 1601 to join the ill-fated Irish and Spanish forces which were defeated at the Battle of Kinsale.

Above: Ballinafad Castle.

Below: Ballymote Castle.

Clogher cashel

Dúchas, free, open access at any reasonable time. Signposted for pedestrian access from the Lough Gara Cultural Resource Office, south-west of Monasteraden, Co Sligo, on the Ballaghaderreen road.

There are many cashels – round stone enclosures of the early Christian period, most of which protected a fortified farmstead – scattered around the Irish countryside, but this example, partly rebuilt in the 1800s, is one of the few that is easily accessible to visitors and is both large enough and sufficiently well preserved to be worth seeing. There are four souterrains inside the cashel, two of which run under the walls for considerable distances.

Cohaw court tomb

Dúchas, free, open access at any reasonable time. Signposted from the R192 south-west of Cootehill.

Interesting if rather wrecked example of a 'double' court tomb, with two of these neolithic burial monuments standing back to back.

Creevelea Franciscan friary

Dúchas, in churchyard, free, open access at any reasonable time. Best reached on foot via a riverside path signposted on the west side of Dromahair, Co Leitrim.

One of the smaller and less spectacular examples of a ruined Franciscan friary, reached by a pleasant walk along the river. The best part is the cloister, where there are two carvings of St Francis which are very difficult to find (though it's fun to try).

Doe Castle

Dúchas, opening arrangements to be confirmed.
Off the R245 north of Letterkenny, Co Donegal.

This smashing tower house of the early 1500s in a
picturesque setting on the shore of Sheep Haven Bay
still has most of its bawn wall, with fat round towers
at the corners. Lived in until 1843, the castle has just
been restored, and seems sure to open to visitors
during the summer months (May to September).

Above: Doe Castle.

Below: Heapstown cairn.

Glencolumbkille

*Monuments are on publicly accessible land. In the
village of Glencolumbkille, Co Donegal.*

There's a variety of ancient monuments in the area,
including several megalithic tombs and a host of
early Christian crosses. The fascinating thing,
however, is that it is still used as a ritual landscape,
in a way that echoes pre-Christian traditions.

The site is dedicated to St Columba, also known
as Colmcille, founder of the influential monastery
on the Scottish island of Iona. It is the venue for an
annual *turas* or day-pilgrimage on June 9th, the
saint's feast day, when a procession visits various
sites around the valley. Similar day-pilgrimages are
common in Ireland, with some of the more famous
ones involving an arduous trek to a hilltop.

Greencastle

On farmland. Near Greencastle, Co Donegal.

An attractive ivy-covered ruin in a scenic location
near the mouth of Lough Foyle. The castle was built
in about 1300 by Richard de Burgo, Earl of Chester.

Heapstown cairn

*On private land, free, open access permitted at any
reasonable time. Signposted from Castlebaldwin,
Co Sligo; in a garden near the crossroads by a pub
called the Bow and Arrow.*

This HUGE cairn of heaped stones, with a kerb of
limestone slabs, is an awesome sight, and was much
bigger before cartloads of stone were hauled away
to build roads and walls in the 1800s. It may conceal
a passage grave, but it has not been excavated.

Innismurray early monastic site

Dúchas, no formal access arrangements. On an island off the Sligo coast; can be reached by hired boat from Mullaghmore or Rosses Point.

A remarkably well-preserved monastic complex with a number of small churches and other buildings surrounded by a large stone wall or cashel. It would be a 'must see', except that there is no proper landing place on the island, making visiting difficult.

Moygara Castle

On farmland, access with permission of landowner at any reasonable time.

This substantial ruin looks impressive from outside, but there isn't much to see inside. It seems like a proper medieval fortress, but in fact it's really just a tower house (and not a particularly big one, either) accompanied by an unusually large bawn wall. There are flanking turrets on the corners of the bawn, and the relatively low walls would have been topped off with timber parapets.

The three-storey tower house in one corner is in pretty decent condition, but the floors are missing, and there is no access to any upper levels. Look out for weathered carvings of two figures near the gate on the western side of the castle.

The whole ensemble as it appears today dates from the 1500s, as is evidenced by the gun-loops in the walls; but inside the courtyard there are also traces of a much earlier keep, thought to have been built in the 1300s. The castle was the principal stronghold of the O'Gara family until 1581, when a troop of Scottish mercenaries under English command burned the castle and killed many of its occupants.

And...

Burt Castle *(on farmland), in a field beside the N18 north-east of Newtown, Co Donegal* – There's little more than one wall left of what was originally a Scottish-style tower house built to a Z-plan, with round towers on diagonally opposite corners of a main block. However, it stands in a fine spot on a hill with good views, and it makes quite a landmark. It was an important English garrison for some time after being captured in 1608.

Cashel Bir *(on farmland, free, open access at any reasonable time), signposted from the R287 Sligo to Dromahair road to the north-west of Ballintogher* – This nice little stone-walled enclosure represents a good chance to see a typical smaller cashel, since access is very well arranged.

Clones round tower and high cross *(in churchyard, free, open access at any reasonable time), in the town of Clones, Co Monaghan* – A group of modest monuments from a monastery founded in the 500s. The round tower lacks its top; nearby is an odd shrine in the shape of a house. The carved cross, now in the town square, is made up of parts from two crosses.

Donagh high cross and pillars *(free, open access at any time), just outside Carndonagh, Co Donegal, beside the road to Buncrana* – Unusual and very early carved cross, almost 2.8m (12ft) high, in a naive style with incised decoration. It may be as old as the 700s. Beside it are two smaller pillars, also displaying interesting carvings.

Drumcliff *(in churchyard, free, open access at any reasonable time), in Drumcliff, Co Sligo* – This early monastic site has a high cross of about 900 and the stump of a round tower, but it is famous mainly as the place where the poet WB Yeats is buried.

Glebe House and Gallery *(Dúchas, ££, open from mid-May to September daily except Friday), at Churchill, near Letterkenny, Co Donegal* – Regency house in a glorious stretch of countryside, notable for its Victorian Arts & Crafts interiors, and for the paintings by 20th-century artists on show here.

Glenveagh national park *(Dúchas; park and castle open separately from mid-March to early November, castle by guided tour only; each ££), near Letterkenny, Co Donegal* – A rather fine Victorian mock-castle, with famous gardens, surrounded by a vast and very picturesque estate, which is now a national park.

Knocklane promontory fort *(on farmland, free, open access at any reasonable time), on the coast west of Drumcliff, Co Sligo* – Rather splendid example of an iron age promontory fort, consisting of two large banks and ditches cutting off a headland.

Newmills corn and flax mills *(Dúchas, ££, open from mid-June to September daily), at Letterkenny, Co Donegal* – Fascinating complex of restored industrial buildings, with several water-powered mills used for grinding corn and in producing linen, which was a major local industry.

Below: Moygara Castle.

Midlands East

Wicklow, Kildare, Laois, north Offaly, Westmeath, Longford, Meath and Louth

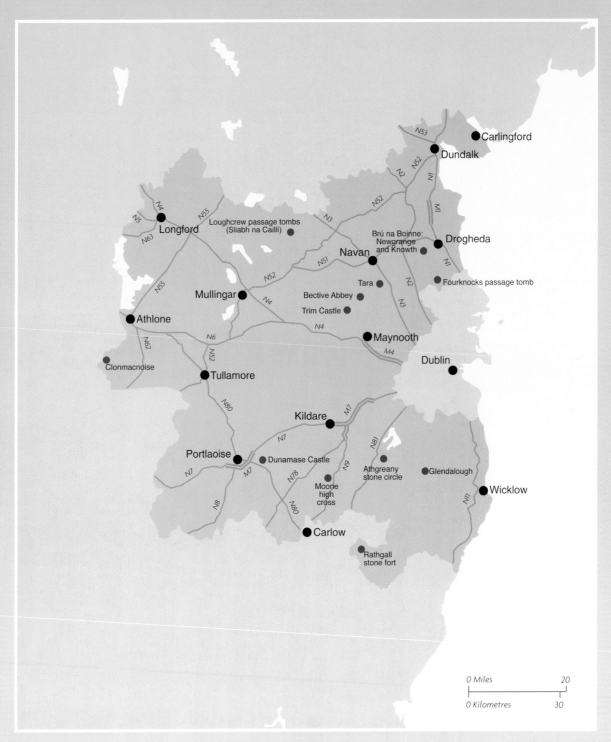

Carlingford

N53

Dundalk

N52

N2

N52

N1

M1

N52

Longford

N4

N55

N5

N63

Loughcrew passage tombs
(Sliabh na Cailli)

N3

Brú na Boinne:
Newgrange
and Knowth

Drogheda

N1

Navan

N51

Fourknocks passage tomb

N52

Mullingar

N4

Tara

N2

Bective Abbey

Athlone

N55

Trim Castle

N3

N6

N4

Maynooth

N62

N52

Clonmacnoise

Tullamore

M4

Dublin

N80

Kildare

M7

N81

Portlaoise

N7

Dunamase Castle

N9

Athgreany
stone circle

Glendalough

N7

M7

N78

Moone
high
cross

N11

Wicklow

N8

N80

Carlow

Rathgall
stone fort

0 Miles   20

0 Kilometres   30

150

The stone circle at Athgreany is rather an atmospheric spot, even though the monument itself is incomplete.

Athgreany stone circle ('The Piper's Stones')

Dúchas, on farmland • Free • Open access at any reasonable time

Even though it is no longer complete, there's something quite intriguing about this medium-sized circle of plump, squarish boulders. As is so often the case, the quality that ultimately gives the monument its appeal is the way it is placed in relation to the surrounding country, and it makes you wonder why the builders of the circle chose this spot.

There are 12 stones left, but only five are in their original positions. It is thought that the circle would originally have been about 23m (75ft) in diameter. There is no obvious entrance or alignment; stone circles in this region are rare, and this one doesn't fall into any particular type. It has been suggested that there was an avenue or an alignment of stones leading up to the monument, but this seems unlikely. Rather, one particularly notable boulder off to the north-east of the circle is thought to be a 'glacial erratic' – a stone of unusual appearance deposited here by the glacial ice that once covered the region.

The monument is also known as The Piper's Stones, and there is a legend that fairies can sometimes be heard playing the bagpipes here. Quite a few stone circles in south-western England have similar names, with folk tales attached that say the stones are people who were turned to stone for making music or dancing on a Sunday. Perhaps these legends reflect a pagan tradition of celebrations at the stones which was frowned upon in the Christian era.

Access is not too bad, provided you don't mind a few cows coming over to say hello. Note that to reach the monument, you should follow the right-hand fence up the hill as the field opens out.

Beside the N81 (Baltinglass to Blessington) main road, south of Hollywood, Co Wicklow.

Bective Abbey

Dúchas • Free • Open access at any reasonable time

One of the first Cistercian abbeys in Ireland, founded in 1147, long before the Norman invasion, by Murchad O Maeil-Sheachlainn, King of Meath. Some traces survive of the original stonework from this first abbey – a plan on the site will help you work out which piece is which – but most of what you see dates from the 1400s, when the buildings were fortified and a new cloister was added.

At first sight, it looks as if the abbey was converted into a fortified house at the end of its career; but in fact the castle-like tower with its formidable battlements is part of the 1400s remodelling. This was a time when local lords maintained large private armies and were frequently engaged in feuds, and many abbeys were inclined to protect their wealth with fortifications. The most dramatic example is the walled enclosure at *Kells Priory* in Co Kilkenny *(see page 66)*, but similar works were also carried out at several abbeys in Meath and Westmeath.

Unfortunately, you can't get into the tower – actually, it would be a good thing if the stairs and upper floors were restored – and so the main points of interest are the large hall alongside it, and the cloisters, where you should try to find a carving of a cleric carrying a crozier.

Near Trim, Co Meath. Signposted from the R161 north of Trim, west of the village of Bective.

Strongly fortified in the 1400s, Bective Abbey looks almost more like a castle than a religious establishment.

The white quartz facade of Newgrange, studded with black, was reconstructed using material found at the site.

Brú na Boinne: Newgrange and Knowth

Dúchas • Newgrange ££, Knowth ££ • Open daily all year round

The Boyne Valley, now normally referred to by the Irish version of its name, is a quiet, tucked-away piece of countryside on the banks of the river of the same name. It is also a remarkable ritual landscape of the neolithic era, featuring not only three major monuments – the enormous burial mounds of Newgrange, Knowth and Dowth – but also a wealth of smaller monuments which look set to keep archeologists happily occupied for years to come.

The star attraction, of course, is Ireland's most famous passage tomb, Newgrange. In an attempt to relieve the pressure of visitor numbers on this fragile monument, a new visitor centre has been built. It scoops up all visitor traffic, keeping it on the south side of the river and away from the little lanes to the north of the river where all the monuments are located.

The visitor centre houses a good exhibition that sketches in the archeology of the neolithic era, with a particularly fine display on the designs used in passage grave art. There's also an audio-visual display, and there's a good cafe downstairs. Essentially, though, the centre exists primarily to allocate visitors to timed tours which depart from here on buses.

As you arrive, you will be asked which of the two tours – Newgrange or Knowth – you wish to take. Each tour lasts about an hour: if you would like to do both, allowing for waiting time before and between your tours, you are unlikely to be here for anything less than three hours. You will be given a sticker (or two stickers, if you are doing both tours) that acts as your ticket to the tour. Printed on the front of the sticker is the time your tour departs. At the appointed hour, you make your way out of the front of the visitor centre and cross the river on a footbridge, then hop on a bus which will deposit you at the site. A tour guide will collect you and lead you to the monument.

Numbers on each tour are limited, and in busy periods tours get fully booked up early in the day. Widely repeated advice for visitors in the summer season is to come here early in the morning, expecting to get booked on a tour for late afternoon, and then zip off somewhere else in the car to fill in the time.

Inevitably, there is an extent to which everyone wants to see Newgrange, but some will be disappointed and will be 'fobbed off' with Knowth as a poor second best. Unquestionably, this is not fair to Knowth, which is a fascinating site in its own right. But frankly there is no point coming here and not seeing the incomparable Newgrange, which is the finest neolithic tomb in Europe.

Signposted from the N2 south of Slane, Co Meath, or from Drogheda town centre.

Newgrange

Dúchas • ££ • Access via visitor centre only

You have to remember that its exterior was reconstructed following painstaking excavation in the 1960s; but even bearing in mind the possibility that it might never have looked exactly like this, the shining, quartz-covered facade of Newgrange is extraordinarily impressive. This is truly a neolithic cathedral, a monumental place of awesome size and presence.

It's a well-known fact that the passage is aligned with the midwinter solstice, so

The huge central mound at Knowth (in this view, at the back on the left) was surrounded by a number of smaller tombs. It is kerbed all round with inscribed stones.

that at sunrise on the shortest day of the year (and on a couple of days either side) the sun shines along the passage. This is not all that remarkable in itself, but the way it has been arranged here is very clever. Because the chamber is at the very top of the hill on which the tomb stands, the passage runs uphill to it: as a consequence, the sun's rays have to be let in through a box-like opening high above the entrance to the passage. It's neatly engineered.

There are many more examples of the unusual care and precision used by the builders of this tomb – including a system of grooves in the upper surfaces of the stones from which the roof is built that helps water drain off. Along with a clay-like mortar packed into all the gaps, this has kept the chamber dry for 5,000 years.

Just as impressive as the engineering, though, is the artistry. Many of the slabs inside the tomb are decorated with the swirling patterns of 'passage grave art'. The single most famous design is a triple spiral that appears on a large kerbstone that blocks the entrance.

There are traces of all sorts of later monuments around the tomb, including the remnants of a vast bronze age stone circle.

Knowth

Dúchas • ££ • Access via visitor centre only

This enormous mound is still the subject of extensive archeological investigation. It has not one but two passages leading to chambers, on opposite sides of the mound, aligned with the equinoxes at spring and autumn – one passage faces the sunrise, the other the sunset. Both are unsafe, so there is no access to the interior.

The guided tour is something of an outdoors experience, therefore, with lots to talk about, but not all that much to see. The immense main mound at Knowth was surrounded by a number of smaller tombs, most of them also passage graves. In the course of time, earth slid down and turned this collection of tombs into one big hill, which became the site of an early Christian village, and later a Norman castle.

Excavations are uncovering houses and souterrains from this historic phase, as well as all sorts of bronze age structures, including a 'wood henge'. By far the most remarkable thing about Knowth, though, is the vast array of 'passage grave art' designs engraved on the stones that form a kerb all round the large mound.

The entrance to the tomb at Newgrange: above the doorway is the 'light box' that allows in the sun.

Clonmacnoise

Dúchas • £££ • Open daily all year

The most notable feature of this important early monastic site is the air of serenity about the place. It's a pleasant spot, in a very gentle, open piece of countryside. The monastic enclosure stands on a low ridge beside the River Shannon, and the low-lying fields nearby are often flooded by the river. Originally, most of the low ground here was marshland.

Peaceful though it is now, this must have been a bustling place in earlier times. The monastery stood at something of a crossroads of major routes in Ireland, where traffic heading from north to south on the River Shannon met the roads that ran east to west along a series of low gravel ridges. Its central location helped Clonmacnoise become a great centre of learning, craftsmanship and trade, and it was also an important place for pilgrimages since St Ciarán, who founded the monastery in about 548, was buried here.

Another significant aspect of the location was that it was on the borders of two of the great kingdoms of ancient Ireland,

Below: Clonmacnoise is a peaceful spot by the River Shannon, scattered with ruined churches.

Meath to the east and Connacht to the west. Royal patronage played a major role in the development of the monastery, but its allegiances fluctuated. Its links with Connacht were stronger until the 800s; after that, Meath became more influential; and then in the early 1100s, Connacht again gained precedence.

The remains on the site are not as striking as either the atmosphere of the place or its history, but some of the details are quite interesting. There are several churches ranging in date from the 900s to the 1600s and in varying degrees of ruination. The best is Temple Finghin, a small Romanesque church thought to date from about 1170, which has a belfry in the style of a short round tower.

There's also a rather good round tower on this site, plus several fine high crosses. Replicas of the crosses have been set up where the real ones previously stood, and the originals are now housed in the rather good visitor centre, where well-designed lighting brings out the dramatic qualities of the carvings on their surfaces. There are also excellent displays on the natural history of the area and on illustrated manuscripts.

Near Shannonbridge, Co Offaly. Signposted on the R444 (Athlone road).

Dunamase Castle

Dúchas • Free • Open access at any reasonable time

This is the most splendidly situated castle in Ireland, standing on a rocky hill with superb views over the surrounding countryside. Unfortunately there's not really much of the castle left, and what little there is is mostly inaccessible.

Archeological excavations have been 'in progress' on the hill here for a number of years, but there is not the faintest sign that they are getting anywhere. Most of the site has been fenced off to prevent the delicate archeological evidence from being disturbed, but the fences are broken down and clearly ignored by many visitors. If the digs were completed, and some effort was made to tidy up the remains and present them for the public, you can't help but feel that the results would be interesting.

Even as it stands, there are enough walls left to sketch a picture of a surprisingly large and powerful castle for such a relatively inaccessible hilltop site. You enter through a small lower 'ward', or courtyard, then between the round-fronted towers of a formidable gate-tower, beyond which is a roughly triangular

The great tower which once dominated the castle of Dunamase is badly ruined, but it's a fine setting.

circuit of walls enclosing the summit of the hill. There are places where the thick walls are slipping down the slope in most dramatic style.

Inside the enclosure is a very large keep-like tower, much of which has been destroyed. The northern part, to the right as you approach, was converted into a sort of tower house in the late 1600s, and the walls here are slightly better preserved. It would be nice to have signs explaining the layout of the tower, perhaps telling us what the excavations have found inside. Still, in the mean time, the views are worth coming for.

The Rock of Dunamase was originally home to a hillfort of the early Christian era, and later to a stronghold of the Kings of Leinster. With the arrival of the Normans, it passed to Strongbow by marriage and on to his daughter's husband, William Marshal, who probably started work on the walls of the enclosure and the great tower some time in the early 1200s, though they were developed further not very long afterwards. The efficient destruction of the place can, as usual, be credited to Cromwell's army.

Near Port Laoise, Co Laois. On a minor road off the N80 (Stradbally road) east of the town.

Fourknocks passage tomb

Dúchas • Free • Open access at any reasonable time

This is a very interesting passage tomb. It's in a classic location, on a ridge with wide views, and has a typical cruciform layout, with a short passage leading to a chamber and three niches. The difference is that the chamber is much, much larger than usual: far too large to be covered by capstones or a corbelled stone roof.

Instead, it almost certainly had a roof made of timber, probably carried on a ridge pole, rather than supported by an upright post in the middle of the chamber. No post-holes were uncovered in

excavation, but more than 60 burials were found in the passage and side-niches.

The tomb has now been covered by a concrete dome, with small grilles allowing a few fitful patches of light to filter through into the interior. As your eyes adjust, you can make out some rather good carvings in key spots, like the lintel-stones over the alcoves; and on one large surface on the left-hand side is an angular, criss-crossing design which is said to be the best representation of a face in prehistoric Irish art – though you'll have to decide for yourself if that's really what it is.

Near Clonalvy, Co Meath. Signposted from the R108 north of Naul, Co Dublin.

Left: The modern mound and doorway of Fourknocks conceal an interesting and unusual passage tomb.

One of the best-preserved buildings at Glendalough is St Kevin's Church, with its unusual round belfry.

Below: Two streams meet in front of the monastic enclosure at Glendalough. It's a very pretty spot.

Glendalough

Dúchas • Visitor Centre: ££, open daily all year • Site: free, open access at any reasonable time

Along with *Clonmacnoise* in Co Offaly (*see page 154*), this is one of Ireland's two most famous early monastic sites. Just as at Clonmacnoise, there is a lingering air of calm and sanctity at Glendalough which makes it a pleasant place to visit.

The interest is supplied by a scattering of small ruined churches, a larger church known as the cathedral, a rather elegant round tower, and several high crosses. Most of the buildings date from between the 900s and the 1100s. In truth, though, the remains are nowhere near as spectacular as the splendid scenery in this high valley, with mountains all around, and the reason to come here is to stretch your legs and breathe the clean air.

The monastery was founded in the late 500s by St Kevin (in Irish Cóemhghein, meaning 'fair-begotten'), a son of the ruling family of Leinster, who as a boy is said to have studied in this spot under the tutelage of three holy men, living in the hollow of a tree.

Kevin's monastery flourished until the early 1200s, but its importance declined after the dioceses of Glendalough and Dublin were united. It was left in ruins after a raid by English troops in 1398, but it was still a significant place of pilgrimage, and fairs were still held here on the feast of St Kevin, June 3rd, right into the 1800s.

According to the earliest version of his life, Kevin chose to place his monastery at a place where two clear rivers flowed together; and indeed, the fast-flowing streams are still there, with the monastery standing on a neck of land between them. A pleasant way to approach is by crossing a bridge over the stream to the left of the visitor centre, and turning right to walk up beside the stream; after a short distance, there's another bridge that takes you into the monastic enclosure near the church with a round-tower-style belfry, known as St Kevin's Church.

If instead you continue on up the same path alongside the stream, it leads up the valley to the Upper Lake, where there is a smaller group of monuments, including a church that now stands on an island.

But the walk no visitor to the site should miss is the 15-minute stroll the other way down the same path to the ruin of St Saviour's Church, the last to be built, which has some superb carved details.

At Glendalough, Co Wicklow.

Loughcrew passage tombs (Sliabh na Caillí)

The fascinating Cairn T on the top of Carnbane East, with a smaller satellite tomb in the foreground.

Dúchas • Tours: £, mid-June to mid-September • Otherwise free, access only with key

This group of passage tombs is in many ways the finest of the four great neolithic cemeteries of Ireland. Like the cairns of *Carrowkeel*, Co Sligo (*see page 138*), the tombs stand in a superb hilltop location, but like *Newgrange* and *Knowth* (*page 152*) they are decorated with the loops, swirls and zig-zags of 'passage grave art'.

There's a group of four hills here, known as *Sliabh na Caillí*, or The Hills of the Witch. The minor road that leads to the car park for the monuments crosses the ridge between two of the four peaks, Carnbane West and Carnbane East, and to the east is Patrickstown Hill which, like the other two, has cairns on top. The witch is said to have fallen and died while trying to jump to the fourth hill.

The focus of interest for visitors is the summit of Carnbane East, reached by a footpath that starts from a set of stone steps next to the car park. It's a fairly steep walk to the top, but it takes less than 15 minutes, and the views alone make it worthwhile. It's said that you can see half the counties of Ireland from up here.

The hill is crowned by the large mound of Cairn T, the most impressive of the Loughcrew tombs. This is the one that's explained by guides in the summer months – but you must buy a ticket from the ticket office in the car park before you walk up. It's undoubtedly worth the small fee, not least because you won't be able to get inside the tomb otherwise.

The interior of the tomb is fascinating. The passage faces east and is aligned towards the sunrise at the equinoxes in spring and summer, halfway between the shortest and longest days. The chamber has three niches, in classic cruciform shape. By far the most impressive feature is the decoration incised in many of the stones. Some of the symbols are, tantalisingly, almost decipherable: circles with rays around them almost *have* to be sun symbols, while the guides suggest highly plausible interpretations for some of the others.

It's worth taking a stroll around the outside of the mound of Cairn T, too, not only to note its kerbstones, but also to see the other smaller tombs – all now roofless – gathered around it. Cairn U, near where the path comes up, is also extensively decorated with passage grave art.

You can also stroll over the fields to the top of Carnbane West, collecting a key from the ticket office first if you wish to see inside the still-roofed Cairn L, another large cairn which, like Cairn T, has smaller graves grouped around it. Cairn L has seven, not three, recesses opening off its passage, and two of these contain 'basin stones' in which cremated remains were placed, as at Newgrange and Knowth. An unusual feature is an upright pillar stone that stands inside the chamber.

There's also a second large mound on this hill, but it contains no passage tomb. There's a theory that it was built purely to look impressive from below, Cairn L being hidden from view in some directions. All the tombs on Carnbane West face towards Cairn T on the neighbouring summit.

Outside the summer months it is possible to obtain from a nearby house a key that opens both Cairn T and Cairn L, but you must first arrange to do so by telephoning the keyholder. The telephone number is available from the Brú na Boinne visitor centre.

Near Oldcastle, Co Meath. Signposted from the R154 from Athboy and the R163 from Kells.

The tall, slender high cross at Moone is the most spectacular example of this type of monument.

Below: The stone ramparts of the inner enclosure at Rathgall, which is defended by two outer walls.

Moone high cross

Dúchas, on farmland • Free • Open access at any reasonable time

This is far and away the most spectacular high cross in Ireland, notable for the quality of the scenes carved on all its faces as well as for its height (it's 5.25m, or 17ft, tall) and its unique shape.

The cross has been moved to the shelter of the interior of a ruined church, around the walls of which are fixed a number of clear and very useful display panels which explain the detail of the scenes on the cross. These scenes include Daniel and seven lions; Adam and Eve; the crucifixion; the miracle of the loaves and fishes; and (a bit of an epic, this) the flight into Egypt.

It would be a more pleasant place to visit if more care had been taken over making the interior of the old church feel more like a historic monument and less like a derelict building, but you can't have everything. There are fragments of several other crosses on display here too, and the display panels refer to other high crosses that can be visited in the locality at Castledermot, Old Kilcullen and Nurney.

Signposted from the N9 (Carlow to Dublin road) at Moone, south of Timolin, Co Kildare.

Rathgall stone fort

Dúchas, on farmland • Free • Open access at any reasonable time

The name means either 'The Bright Fort' or 'The Fort of the Foreigners'. It's a large, interesting hillfort of an unusual kind, and it's easy to get to, since it's not actually on a hill but on the edge of a ridge; all you have to do to find it is stroll across a field.

The fort has three concentric walls, roughly circular in shape. The outer two are thought to be older, though their age is not certain. They are banks of earth faced by stone. The small inner ring is constructed entirely of stone, and is said to be of much later date. It may have been built or modified as recently as medieval times.

Overall, the fort is thought to date from the early Christian period, perhaps about 500 or 600AD, and it may have been a stronghold of the kings of South Leinster. However, the most important discoveries made during excavations were all from the late bronze age, about 700BC; they included several cremated burials, and about 400 moulds used by a smith for casting bronze spearheads and swords.

Near Kilquiggin, Co Wicklow. Signposted from the R725 east of Tullow, Co Carlow.

Tara

*Dúchas • Visitor Centre; ££, open daily all year
• Monuments; free, open access at any time*

The earthworks of Tara are steeped in legends of the early Christian era, but their real story is far older…

The trouble with Tara is that it is a place of legends. If you come here expecting to see the feasting hall of kings described in the stories, you'll be disappointed. If you come expecting a modest set of earthworks – not impressive, but intriguing – and a splendid view, you should enjoy it.

The legendary Tara seems to have been created in the 600s, when the kings of the Uí Néill (the O'Neills) from the northern regions of Ireland were trying to legitimise their claims to be the foremost among the rulers of Ireland. By bolstering a tradition that the King of Tara had primacy over the whole island, the Uí Néill could reinforce their claims. In about 680 Tara was said by St Patrick's biographer to be 'the capital of the Irish'. King Mael Sechnaill I, who died in 862, was the first King of Tara to actually control other provinces.

It suited subsequent rulers to build up the tradition and boost their own claims.

Many of the stories attached to the visible remains at Tara come from a book called *Dinnshenchas Érenn*, 'The Place-lore of Ireland', thought to have been written by the court poet of Mael Sechnaill II in the early 1000s, when the king was contending with the King of Munster, Brian Ború, for the position of high king.

The idea of Tara as the symbolic heart of Ireland continued into modern times: in August 1843 it was the venue for a protest calling for Irish independence that is said to have drawn a million people.

However, underneath all the layers of meaning built up over the years, it is certain that Tara was an important place, and it's not hard to believe that it might have been of national significance. The archeological truth of Tara is that it was in use for thousands of years as a burial place and ritual site. It started as a neolithic enclosure very similar to ones in England that seem to have been used for ceremonies involving feasting and the deposit of offerings in pits

or ditches. A neolithic passage grave, now known as The Mound of the Hostages, was placed here too, and in bronze age times many barrows were constructed.

Most of the interest, however, focuses on the iron age, when Tara was a major ritual site along the same lines as Crúachain in Connacht, Emain Macha in Ulster, and Dún Ailinne in Leinster.

The most prominent remains today are the double circular earthworks known as The Forrad and Tech Cormac, which are thought to be defended habitations, but the most important originally was the mess of bumps known as the Rath of the Synods, which was once the site of a series of circular enclosures ringed by timber palisades, similar to ones found at both Dún Ailinne and Emain Macha. Later, it was made into a type of ringfort with four sets of ramparts, marking it out as one of a special class of ritual monuments.

South of Navan, Co Meath. Signposted off the N3.

Trim Castle

Dúchas • ££ • Open daily from May to September

This is the largest and most impressive Anglo-Norman castle in Ireland – a true medieval fortress. It has a substantial set of curtain walls fortified by towers, but easily its dominant feature is the huge keep, which again is the most impressive structure of its type in Ireland.

It's a considerable surprise, therefore, to discover that until recently the keep was unsafe and was kept locked up, and the courtyard of the castle was used as a pitch-and-putt golf course. Luckily, the keep has now been restored, and opened to visitors in 2000. The remainder of the castle is now fenced off and has been given back its dignity as a historic ruin.

Access to the keep is currently by guided tour only, though that may change once all the major rebuilding work has been completed. A guided tour is not the ideal arrangement for a building like this, which has plenty of space to soak up a large number of visitors and has lots of

With its stout curtain wall and its fascinating keep, Trim is the most impressive Norman castle in Ireland.

interesting corners to explore, some of which are omitted altogether on the tour for lack of time. There are no fragile items lying about the place that need to be protected (like the period furniture in some castles) and there are no particularly dangerous places, so it seems odd that tours are considered necessary.

The keep with curtain walls is the classic form of castle in England and Wales, but it's a rarity in Ireland. The only other major Norman keep is at *Carrickfergus* in Northern Ireland (*see page 172*), which was built in about 1200 by John de Courcy, an Anglo-Norman lord who was trying to carve out his own little kingdom in Ulster.

Not only is Trim's keep the only major Norman keep in Ireland, it is also of an unusual and interesting design. It consists of a roughly square block in the centre, with small turrets at each corner at the top, and with a tower right in the middle of each side – so from above, it looks like a cross with a smaller square imposed on it.

Towers at the corners would be a far more obvious arrangement. It's not known what the thinking behind the design was, but one useful side-effect is that the entrance – which is on the first floor, reached by a set of stairs – does not need to be protected by a separate forebuilding, since it is located in one of the side-towers.

When it was built in the 1170s, the keep had just one tall storey above the basement. Inside, the main block is divided in two by a cross-wall, and had a public hall on one side of the wall and the lord's private rooms on the other. There are cellars below. In 1196 two more floors were added to the top of the keep. The whole top floor was given over to a single great hall, but this was later divided into smaller rooms.

There's a variety of rooms in the four towers around the keep, including a chapel on the second floor over the entrance and a series of private rooms (some with their own toilet in the corner) in which the more important members of the garrison lived.

Recently restored, the keep has been left as a shell, with modern walkways giving access to the upper levels.

The courtyard of the castle is roughly triangular, with the River Boyne flowing along the long north-western side, which has barely anything of its walls remaining. The south side faced open country, and the wall was protected by a moat and a series of round-fronted towers. Also on this side is a barbican gate, with a forework on the far side of the moat, crossed by a drawbridge.

The third side faced the town, as indeed it still does. The largest and most important towers were on this side, including the primary gatehouse, which is still in use as the main entrance. The polygonal shape of its upper floors is a later adaptation, intended to make missiles glance off it, as well as to give a wider field of fire.

Alongside the river are the foundations of the strongest tower of all, which after 1250 was remodelled as the lord's day-room. Next to it was the hall, and beyond that was a dock for landing supplies from the river.

In the town of Trim, Co Meath.

The history of Trim Castle

It's something of a surprise to find that the most impressive early Norman castle in Ireland was not a royal castle, but it did come into existence as a result of royal policy, and it had plenty of royal involvement in its later career.

In 1172 King Henry II gave the lands known as the Liberty of Meath to Hugh de Lacy as part of a plan to limit the expansion of Strongbow, who seemed to be making a fair bid to establish a kingdom of his own in south-east Ireland.

De Lacy built an earthwork-and-timber castle here, but it was abandoned and burned by one of his men, whom Hugh had left in charge, when it came under attack from the King of Connacht.

By 1176 De Lacy had built the first phase of the large keep, which was raised in height in 1196 by his son, Walter de Lacy. After Walter's death in 1241, the castle passed by marriage to Geoffrey de Geneville. In 1306 his granddaughter Joanna married Roger Mortimer, the first Earl of March, and their descendants held the castle until 1425.

The large, well-lit Great Hall alongside the river was built in the late 1200s to replace the hall on the top floor of the keep. It was rebuilt in 1367 on the orders of King Edward III, because the then owner of the castle, Edmund Mortimer, had just married the king's granddaughter, Phillipa.

When Richard II visited Ireland in 1399, he also arranged for improvements so that his two wards – the sons of Henry Bolingbroke – could live here. One of them was the future King Henry V.

In 1649 the already neglected castle surrendered to Cromwell's forces. It was never occupied again.

See also...

Aghowle church

Dúchas, in churchyard, free, open access at any reasonable time. Signposted on minor roads south of Boley, Co Wicklow, to the south of the R725 between Tullow and Shillelagh.

In a lovely, peaceful spot in a secluded valley stands a big old ruined church, its tiny, ancient-looking arched windows (two in the east end, one in the north wall) and huge, flat-lintelled west door suggesting that it is of great antiquity. In front of the church is a very plain stone cross, which somehow looks as if it might originally have had a design painted on it, with a large stone trough nearby.

The church is thought to date to the 1100s, but nothing is known of its history, except that the monastery here is believed to have been founded in the early 500s by St Finian of Clonard.

Athlone Castle

Local council, varying access arrangements. By the River Shannon in Athlone, Co Westmeath.

The walls of the castle have been remodelled as the ramparts of an artillery fort, and can be visited free of charge during opening hours. Inside the castle is a new visitor centre, while the unusual ten-sided keep – which, despite its odd appearance, is basically the original Norman structure, built in the early 1200s on the orders of King John – houses an eccentric museum of local history on its two floors. Both the museum and visitor centre are open daily all year, with a charge for admission.

Above: Athlone Castle.

Below: Carlingford Castle.

Baltinglass Abbey

Dúchas, in churchyard, free, open access at any reasonable time. In Baltinglass, Co Wicklow; from the N81, turn for Hacketstown, then take the first lane on the left after crossing the river.

Not terrifically interesting remnant of a major Cistercian abbey founded by local big cheese Dermot MacMurrough in 1148. Surviving pieces of the abbey church include a nice series of pointed Gothic arches on the south side of the nave and soaring, curved arches at the crossing, with traces of Romanesque decorative detail. A tower in the middle was built in the 1800s.

In its prime, Baltinglass was the mother house of *Jerpoint Abbey*, Co Kilkenny (*see page 64*). When it was made subject to Furness in Cumbria, England, the monks kicked out their abbot as a protest, and he was obliged to return with troops and take back his abbey by force.

Carlingford Castle

Dúchas, free, open access to view exterior only at any reasonable time. In Carlingford, Co Louth, overlooking the harbour.

The castle is probably the least interesting thing about Carlingford, a little town steeped in history which is now a picturesque coastal resort.

The place has quite a few historic buildings, including two small, stoutly fortified tower-house-like fortified mansions. One, called **Taafe's Castle**, is currently being restored as self-catering accommodation; the other, known as **The Mint**, is just a shell, but is worth taking a look at for its elaborately decorated facade.

Carlingford Castle itself, frequently referred to as King John's Castle, stands on a rocky outcrop by the shore, overlooking the harbour. It consists of a D-shaped circuit of thick walls with a large tower; unfortunately there is no access to its interior.

Castledermot monastic remains

In churchyard, free, open access at any reasonable time. In the centre of Castledermot, Co Kildare.

An assortment of remains from an early monastery stands in the churchyard of a Victorian church which uses a ruined round tower as its bell-tower. The most unusual sight is a pair of church doorways, one from the 900s and one of the 1100s, which have been restored and set up to stand on their own, like ceremonial arches.

There are two carved high crosses of the 800s, with an unusual hump-backed grave slab nearby. Scenes on the South Cross include the crucifixion, Daniel in the lion's den, and Adam and Eve; while the North Cross shows, among other things, the miracle of the loaves and fishes on its south face.

The monastery here, which is known to have been attacked by Vikings in 841 and 867, was the burial place of Cormac MacCuilleannáin, a king of Leinster who was also Bishop of Cashel, whose head was cut off in battle in 908.

Clonony Castle

On farmland, free, open access at any time. Next to the R357 west of Cloghan, Co Offaly.

A tall, solid and rather splendidly decrepit-looking four-storey tower of the 1500s, with substantial parts of its bawn intact, including a gate. It stands right by the road and is easily accessible, so it's disappointing to find that the place is badly neglected, with a great deal of vandalism evident inside. The spiral stair has been broken down at the bottom, so there is no access to the upper floors.

Corlea trackway visitor centre

Dúchas, £££, open April to September daily. Signposted from the R392 south of Ballyclare, near the village of Corlea, Co Longford.

This excellent visitor centre tells the fascinating story of an iron age trackway, made of planks of oak laid on top of brushwood, which was built here in 148BC. The well-preserved remains of it came to light during peat digging operations. The visitor centre also does a superb job of explaining the ecology of the peat bog, which is an important economic resource for Ireland, as well as being a rare and fragile wildlife habitat.

The full visit involves watching a short film and getting some background information from a series of displays, then being given a guided tour of the room where a section of the trackway is kept in a controlled climate. Why it was built is a mystery, but the effort involved must have been immense; and yet the track seems hardly to have been used.

Dunmoe Castle

On farmland, no formal access arrangements. On a minor road off the N51 west of Slane, Co Meath.

Only one side-wall remains, with a rounded tower at either end, of a very large 'great tower' or keep. The tower was built in the 1400s, but is in the style of keeps built in the 1200s. It's still quite a sight, looming over the River Boyne.

Granard motte

On farmland, free, open access at any time. By the N55 south of Granard, Co Longford.

Said to be the most impressive motte in Ireland, and certainly one of the largest examples of this early type of Norman earthwork castle. It was built in the late 1200s, with stone buildings added later.

Above: Clonony Castle.

Below: Killeshin church doorway.

Killeshin Romanesque church

Dúchas, free, open access ay any reasonable time. In Co Laois, by the R430 west of Carlow.

This small ruined church of the 1100s has a west door that is probably the most impressive example in Ireland of the ornate Irish Romanesque style. Decoration around the door includes geometric and organic patterns, heads, Celtic beasts, and even a written inscription. It leaves you wondering how splendid and beautiful the church must have been in its original state, perhaps painted in rich colours.

The inscription is thought to read 'A prayer for Diarmit, King of Leinster' and might refer to a king of that name who died in 1117, though it is thought the church was built a few decades later.

The monastery is said to have been founded by St Comdhan in the 400s, and was burned in 1077.

Lea Castle

In fields, no formal access arrangements. Near the R420 south-east of Portarlington, Co Laois.

This was one of the largest Norman castles in Ireland, and though it is now a crumbling, ivy-covered ruin, it still looks mighty impressive. The huge keep was rectangular with a round tower at each corner, and stood inside a small inner bailey; beyond was a far larger outer bailey with a large gatehouse.

The keep was built in 1250 by Maurice Fitzgerald, Lord of Offaly, on a motte built by William Marshal. The castle was destroyed by Cromwellian forces.

Maynooth Castle

Dúchas, new access arrangements to be confirmed. In Maynooth, Co Kildare.

A thoroughly impressive castle consisting of a large keep-like tower surrounded by a curtain wall, with a substantial and imposing gatehouse, plus another substantial tower just beyond. The castle has recently undergone an extensive restoration, which should make it rather an interesting place to visit.

The lower part of the main tower was built not long after 1200 by Gerald FitzGerald, Lord of Offaly, at which time it was basically a very big hall-tower, not dissimilar to *Athenry Castle*, Co Galway (*see page 121*). It was later raised in height, and had a number of other modifications made to it.

In 1535, when its owner was involved in a rebellion against the English, the castle was taken from the Fitzgeralds, and for a while became the home of the Lord Deputy; but in 1552 it was given back to Gerald, Earl of Kildare. The castle was restored in the 1630s, which explains some of its present appearance; but it was finally abandoned only about 30 years later.

Monasterboice

Dúchas, in churchyard, free, open access at any reasonable time. In Monasterboice, Co Louth.

This early monastic site, with a ruined round tower, is notable mainly for two very fine high crosses, both of which probably date from the 800s. One is called The Cross of Muiredach after an inscription naming the man who erected it; it depicts many biblical episodes, but it also has a good deal of attractive interlaced decoration. Nearby is the Tall Cross, on which the carved scenes are not so clear. There is a record of the round tower being burned during an attack in 1097, with the monastery's library and all its other treasures inside.

Old Mellifont Abbey

Dúchas, ££, open from May to mid-October daily. North-west of Tullyallen, near Drogheda, Co Louth.

This was Ireland's first Cistercian abbey, founded in 1142 by monks from Clairvaux in France on land granted by the Prince of Uriel. Besides being the most important abbey in the land, it was also just about the grandest – as can clearly be seen from the remains even though nothing of the church and very little of the cloisters survives above knee height.

The only substantial parts that remain are the chapter house, with its fine vaulted roof, which is more or less intact, and an unusual octagonal lavabo dating from about 1210. It stood in the cloister and was used for washing of all sorts.

There's a visitor centre, with an exhibition covering the history of the abbey and various pieces of fallen ornamental stonework recovered from around the site, and it's this to which the opening times quoted above apply. Presumably the ruin itself is accessible free of charge in the winter months.

Proleek dolmen

On private land, free, open access at any time. On a golf course in the grounds of Ballymascanlon Hotel, north of Dundalk, Co Louth. Take the first road on the left after the hotel and look out for the footpath.

A decent portal dolmen, a little comical in appearance, with a fat capstone said to weigh 40 tonnes resting on the tips of rather pointy supporting stones. There's a local tradition that anyone who can throw a small stone so that it lands on top of the capstone and stays there will be granted a wish.

St Columb's House, Kells

Dúchas, free, access with key from nearby house during usual hours only. In Kells, Co Meath.

In the town made famous by the Book Of Kells, there is very little left of the monastery at which the historic manuscript was produced. In a churchyard at the top of the hill, there's a decent round tower, with some high crosses next to it; but the highlight is this small, primitive-looking stone oratory standing incongruously in a modern housing estate. The oldest parts may date from the 800s.

Timahoe round tower

In churchyard, free, open access to view exterior only at any reasonable time. In Timahoe, Co Laois.

This elegant round tower of the 1100s has a fair claim to be the finest in Ireland, since it is not only tall and well-built, but also has a unique double doorway in the Romanesque style which is carved with superb ornamentation. Bring binoculars to get the full benefit: the door is very high up.

Below: Maynooth Castle.

And…

Ardee Castle *(local council, opening arrangements to be confirmed) on the main street in Ardee, Co Louth* – A castle was founded here in 1207, but the present building is a large tower house from the late 1400s. It has just been restored as a museum.

Athlumney Castle *(in the grounds of Loreto Convent, free, access with key from convent during usual hours only), signposted from the centre of Navan, Co Meath* – An excellent four-storey tower house of the 1400s, plus the shell of a Tudor manor house built on the side in about 1600.

Ballaghmore Castle *(privately owned, £££, open by arrangement), off the N7 west of Borris-in-Ossory, Co Laois* – This largish tower house, built in 1480, has recently been restored and is open to the public by arrangement. It is also rented out as holiday accommodation and for weddings or parties.

Castleroche Castle *(on farmland, no formal access arrangements), north-west of Dundalk, Co Louth* – Ruin of a major castle of the 1200s which still looks thoroughly impressive from a distance, though it is not quite so interesting up close. Built in about 1260, it consists of a roughly triangular circuit of walls, with a large gate-tower and a two-storey hall.

Castleruddery stone circle *(Dúchas, free, open access at any reasonable time), signposted from the N81 north-east of Baltinglass, Co Wicklow* – Actually, this is not really a stone circle at all, but a type of monument known as an embanked enclosure. It consists of a wide bank of earth, faced on either side with upright slabs of stone, forming a ring around an area roughly 31m (100ft) in diameter. Two huge quartz boulders form an entrance on the eastern side of the enclosure.

Castletown *(Dúchas, £££, open daily from June to September and on Sunday afternoons only in April, May and October), near Celbridge, Co Kildare* – If you only ever visit one Irish stately home, make it this splendid Palladian mansion built in 1722.

Drogheda historic remains *Drogheda, Co Louth* – The town has a number of monuments, including a Norman motte and big gateway (St Laurence's Gate) which survives from the barbican of a former castle.

Dunsany Castle *(privately owned, ££££, open July and August daily, mornings or afternoons only – please check locally), off the N3 north of Dunshaughlin, Co Meath* – This enormous and very grand stately home has its origins in a tower house of the 1500s, now greatly modernised, and has been lived in by the Plunkett family for over 400 years. The house is open to visitors on a regular basis, but with arrangements that alter from year to year, and is worth seeing, though very expensive.

Fore Abbey *(Dúchas, free, open access at any reasonable time), at Fore, Co Westmeath, off the R195 south of Oldcastle, Co Meath* – There is a collection of decent ecclesiastical remains here, not least a large early church, with *antae* and a huge

Above: Old Mellifont Abbey.

rectangular lintel-stone over its west door. The chancel was added in the 1200s. The most striking item is the ruined abbey (actually a Benedictine priory founded in about 1200) which was converted into a fortified residence in the 1400s. It is of limited interest, but there's a good dovecot next to it.

Slane Friary *(Dúchas, in churchyard, free, open access at any reasonable time), on the Hill of Slane, off the N2 north of the town, Co Meath* – The hill itself is an attraction, because this is the place where St Patrick is said to have lit a fire at Easter in 433 as a challenge to the druidic traditions of nearby Tara. The large ruined church is from a Franciscan friary founded in 1512, and at the time of writing it was still possible to climb the 60-odd steps of the spiral stair leading to the top of the tower, for superb views.

Termonfeckin Castle *(Dúchas, free, access with key from nearby house during usual hours only), Termonfeckin, near Drogheda, Co Louth* – A small tower house of the early 1500s with an interesting corbelled roof. It was partially rebuilt in 1641. Nearby, in the churchyard of St Fechin's Church, is a good carved high cross – and look out too for a re-used stone built into the porch of the church with an inscription which reads: 'A prayer for Ultan and Dubthach who built this stone fort'.

Tullynally Castle *(privately owned, £££, open from mid-June to end July and in first two weeks of September, afternoons only), near Castlepollard, Co Westmeath* – An older house converted into a pleasingly bonkers Gothic revival castle in the early 1800s and featuring fine Victorian kitchens and laundries packed with the latest gadgets of the time. Admission includes access to the splendid gardens.

Wicklow Abbey *(Dúchas, free, open access at any reasonable time), in Wicklow* – Fragments of a Franciscan friary founded in 1279, too ruined to be of tremendous interest. The town also has a rather fine restored gaol built in the 1700s.

Left: Proleek dolmen.

Dublin

City and County

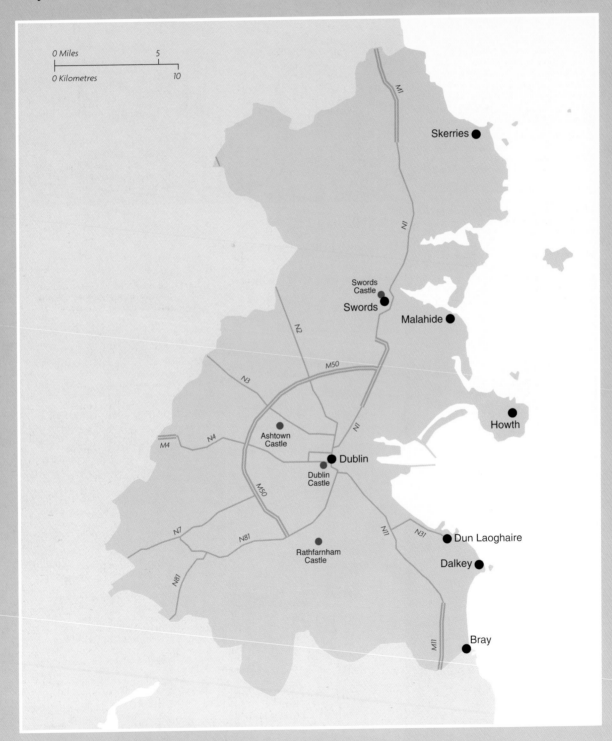

0 Miles 5
0 Kilometres 10

M1

N1

Skerries ●

Swords
Castle
Swords ●

Malahide ●

N2

M50

Howth ●

N3

M4 N4

Ashtown
Castle ●

N1

Dublin ●
Dublin
Castle

M50

N7

N81

N81

Rathfarnham
Castle ●

N11

N31

Dun Laoghaire ●

Dalkey ●

M11

Bray ●

Ashtown Castle

Dúchas • ££ • Open at weekends from November to mid-March, daily mid-March to October

In 1978 it was decided that the official residence of the Papal Nuncio, a villa built in the late 1700s called Ashtown Lodge, could not be properly repaired, so it was pulled down. It was a surprise to all concerned when the demolition revealed this tiny tower house of the late 1500s.

The tower has now been restored and can be visited by guided tour as part of a visit to the Phoenix Park Heritage Centre, which is located in the old stables nearby. Frankly, though, it's a bit dull.

In Phoenix Park.

Dublin Castle

Dúchas • £££ • Open daily, but in the afternoon only on weekends and bank holidays

The original Norman castle, a formidable medieval fortress consisting of a square of walls with massive round towers at the corners, was more or less completely destroyed by an explosion and resulting fire in 1684. Something much more like a palace was built to replace it in the 1700s, but on exactly the same plan as the castle, with four ranges around a courtyard.

Most of these buildings are now government offices, but the sumptuous rooms once used by British kings to receive visitors have been set aside as state apartments for use on important occasions, and these can be visited by guided tour. They are unquestionably worth seeing, for several reasons: partly for the lavish furnishings in places like the throne room, so opulent and so arrogant; and partly because history is still being made in these rooms, which can be closed at short notice if they are needed for government meetings. When I was here, a set of talks on the then-wavering peace agreement in Northern Ireland had been held here just four days previously. It all adds up to a unique insight into Irish and British history in the last 300 years.

Fortunately, there is an interesting bit of the original castle to see, too. Buried deep under a later building and uncovered by recent excavations is the base of one of the Norman round towers, along with part of the moat and a sally port. It's intriguing.

In the centre of Dublin, off Lord Edward Street.

Ashtown Castle is a tiny tower house built in the late 1500s on lands later incorporated into the hunting estate of Phoenix Park.

Below: The state apartments at Dublin Castle are part of a palace built in the 1700s to the same plan as the Norman castle that once occupied the site.

167

Rathfarnham Castle

Dúchas • ££ • Open daily May to October

It's now more a stately home than a castle, but Rathfarnham started life as one of the later types of fortified manor, not unlike *Portumna Castle*, Co Galway (*see page 128*) or *Raphoe Castle*, Co Donegal (*page 146*). Just like Raphoe, Rathfarnham consisted of a large rectangular block with towers of an unusual type at each corner: instead of being square, the towers were angular, in the style of the 'angle bastions' popular in military fortifications at the time.

One thing that marks Rathfarnham out is that it is very early for a fortified manor of this kind, built in about 1580 for the Archbishop of Armagh, Adam Loftus.

What makes it interesting today, however, is that it remained in use as a house for a long time, eventually ending up as a Jesuit college. It is now being restored, and the details of its construction and decoration that are being revealed by the process are fascinating. Visits are by guided tour only, but it's well worth going.

At Rathfarnham, south Dublin, just off the R114.

Below: Having had lots of later additions removed, Rathfarnham Castle is being restored to full glory.

Swords Castle

Fingal County Council • Free • Open daily

The extensive ruin of a castle belonging to the Archbishop of Dublin, now owned by the local council and undergoing a slow process of restoration. It stands right in the middle of the town of Swords, just across the road from the very hi-tech offices of Fingal County Council, and the contrast between the glass of the offices and the stone battlements of the castle makes for a rather pleasing effect.

The castle developed over a period of some 400 years, starting shortly before 1200 when John Comyn was appointed as the first Norman Bishop of Dublin. It is an enclosure-type castle, consisting of a large circuit of walls with the most important accommodation occupying several large towers in the wall, and a series of buildings built up against it.

The process of restoration is likely to be a slow one, because it's being done hand in hand with a detailed investigation using modern archeological techniques, and it's quite interesting to see that in progress. You might well bump into archeologists wandering around taking magnetometer readings or doing something equally painstaking and scientific. While the work

is under way, entry to the castle is free. Notice that you must use the entrance from the park (not go through the main gatehouse on the side facing the town) and call in at reception in the office hut by the gate to let them know you're here, so they can open up the doors if need be.

The first part of the castle to be restored, completed in 1998, is a large tower known as the Constable's Tower because it was lived in by the man in charge of the castle. It has three floors, with smaller rooms in a side-tower opening off each. The replica fixtures, such as the drawbars and the latches on the doors, are quite interesting. Also restored is a section of wall either side of the tower, with a walkway that you can walk along.

The other large buildings of the castle were all on the other side of the courtyard, facing the town. The most substantial ruin is the gatehouse, along with the buildings on either side of it: to its right (looking from inside the castle courtyard) was a range of accommodation for lay visitors, while to the left was a large chapel. Parts of its tiled floor have survived. Next to the chapel stood the archbishop's own apartments.

In Swords, Co Dublin; in the Ward River Valley Linear Park just north of the town centre.

■ See also...

Casino, Marino

*Dúchas, ££, open daily from May to October, two days
per week in February, March, April and November.
In Marino, north-east of the city centre.*

Very pretty and picturesque 'pleasure house' of 1759,
a remarkable example of neo-classical design, with
16 rooms crammed into a tiny-looking space.

Christ Church Cathedral, Dublin

*Church authorities, ££, open daily all year round.
In Christchurch Place, near Dublin Castle.*

The more enjoyable of the city's two cathedrals,
subtly restored and with an archaic feel. It has a
rather good crypt running the length of the church,
with interesting fragments of stonework on display.

Drimnagh Castle

*Privately owned, ££, open from April to September
on Wednesday, Saturday and Sunday afternoons,
rest of year Sunday afternoon only. Longmile Road,
5km (3 miles) south-west of Dublin city centre.*

Greatly modified but genuine castle, lived in as a
house continuously until the 1950s, with a notable
moat and formal gardens in the style of the 1600s.

Dunsoghly Castle

*Privately owned, no access. Just off the N2 not far
from the airport, near St Margaret's, Co Dublin.*

This enormous tower house of the 1400s can only
be viewed from a distance, but it is certainly a sight
worth seeing. It still has its original wooden roof,
used as a model in the restoration of several castles.

Joyce Tower, Sandycove

*Privately owned, £££, open April to October daily but
afternoon only on Sunday. In Sandycove, Co Dublin.*

Martello tower of the early 1800s later converted into
a house. It now contains the James Joyce Museum.

Kilmainham Gaol

*Dúchas, £££, open daily all year. In Kilmainham,
about 4km (2.5 miles) west of the city centre.*

This empty, preserved Victorian gaol has played a
part in many historic episodes. Worth seeing.

Lusk heritage centre

*Dúchas, £, open from mid-June to mid-September,
Fridays only. In Lusk, Co Dublin.*

A Victorian church incorporating a round tower of
about 1000AD now houses a series of exhibitions.

Malahide Castle

*Fingal Council, £££, open daily all year (but afternoons
only at winter weekends). In Malahide, Co Dublin.*

Oldish castle with apparently original medieval
great hall, heavily adapted in later years to a house
with a Gothic look. Tours are rather dull.

Monkstown Castle

Dúchas, no access. In Monkstown, Co Dublin.

An interesting-looking affair consisting of a greatly
modified tower house of the late 1400s connected to
a large gatehouse by a stretch of Victorian wall.
Currently derelict and inaccessible.

St Audoen's Church

*Dúchas, ££, open from June to September daily.
Cornmarket, High Street, Dublin.*

Now the only medieval parish church left in Dublin,
still in use but open to visitors in summer.

St Mary's Abbey

*Dúchas, ££, open mid-June to mid-September,
Wednesday and Sunday only. Off Capel Street, Dublin.*

Surviving chapter house of a Cistercian abbey.

St Patrick's Cathedral

*Church authorities, ££, open daily all year round.
In Patrick Street, Dublin.*

Large and very impressive cathedral, basically of
the 1200s but greatly restored.

*The Constable's Tower at Swords was one of the
first parts of the castle to be restored.*

Northern Ireland

Fermanagh, Tyrone, Londonderry, Antrim, Armagh and Down

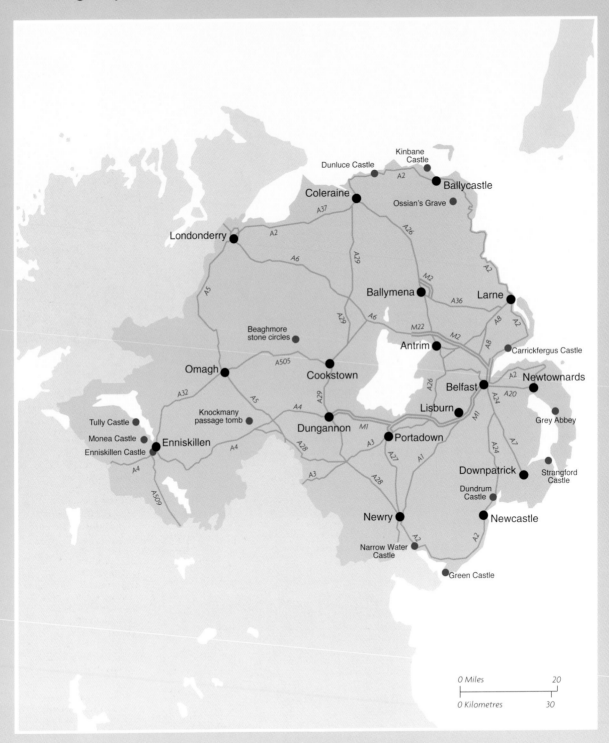

Beaghmore stone circles

Environment & Heritage Service • Free •
Open access at any reasonable time

The remarkable stone alignments at Beaghmore include this row of larger stones leading towards two circles.

This is the largest and in many ways the most impressive prehistoric site in Northern Ireland. It's an intriguing complex of stone circles, stone rows and small cairns which was uncovered only in the 1940s, when peat-digging revealed the tops of some stones. An archeological excavation followed, revealing all the monuments you see today, and it is thought that there may be many more still buried in the surrounding area.

None of the monuments is large or dramatic, but seeing a number of them set so closely together is distinctly thought-provoking. There are three pairs of stone circles, made up of fairly small stones, with stone rows meeting them, and with small round cairns nearby.

In the case of the first pair of circles you come to, for example, there are several stone rows which appear to lead to a narrow gap where the two stone circles almost meet; and the gap is filled by a small, round cairn.

As well as the three pairs of circles, there is also a separate circle, and this one is unique in that the space within the stones is filled with hundreds of smaller pointy stones all set on end, so that they stick up jaggedly. Why? Who knows.

Another distinctive feature is apparent in one of the stone circles that make up the last pair. This circle has two larger stones placed next to each other, like an entrance. It's a feature that echoes the stone circles of south-western Ireland, but those also have an 'axial' stone laid on its side opposite the entrance.

There is no mention of any burials or other traces of human activity having been found at the site, and there is no way of

knowing what purpose the monuments served or how they were used. It has been observed that two of the stone rows are aligned towards the south-west, in the direction of the setting sun at midwinter solstice, the shortest day of the year.

It's somehow satisfying that this place is a puzzle without an answer, however, and it in no way detracts from the satisfaction of visiting these interesting monuments in their remote moorland location. It's also a pleasure to be greeted by such welcoming access arrangements: alongside the small car park there's a picnic bench, and also a sand pit in which small hands can be kept happily busy building their own stone circles while the adults stroll off to muse over the real monuments.

West of Cookstown, Co Tyrone, signposted from the A505.

Left: This circle has two larger stones set close to each other, looking as if they may have been meant as an entrance.

Carrickfergus Castle

Environment & Heritage Service • £££ •
Open daily all year (afternoon only on Sunday)

There are only two 'real' Norman castles, with big, square keeps, in the whole island of Ireland: this one, and *Trim* in Co Meath (*see page 160*). Of the two, Carrickfergus is in some ways the more satisfying.

The interior of the castle is not quite as interesting as you might hope, partly because it has been modified many times over the years to keep it up to date as an artillery fortress. But the walls which look so impressive from the outside are mostly the original masonry of the early 1200s, and the layout is much as it was in 1242.

The rock on which the castle stands was originally surrounded by water most of the way round, and the first castle here, built between 1178 and 1195, stood at the far end of the rock. It consisted of most of the powerful square keep, then just three storeys high, and a small enclosure of walls, now called the Inner Ward. There was a grand hall on the east side of the courtyard.

This first castle was the work of the Anglo-Norman lord John de Courcy, who between 1178 and 1204 ruled Ulster as if it was his own kingdom. He also built the castle at *Dundrum* in Co Down (*opposite*) and his wife Affreca, daughter of the king of the Isle of Man, founded *Grey Abbey* in the same county (*see page 176*).

The keep and walls of Carrickfergus Castle have looked pretty much as they do now since as early as 1242.

In 1210, after De Courcy's death, Carrickfergus was captured by King John, but only after John's reign, in 1216, did work start on a second phase of building to improve the castle. The keep was raised to its present height by the addition of a grand upper floor, and a second set of walls (the Middle Ward) was added – only its foundations can now be seen.

A third phase of building took place between 1226 and 1242, when the castle and the region were under the lordship of Hugh de Lacy. The walls were extended to encircle the whole of the castle rock, creating the Outer Ward. A pair of large round towers made up a formidable gatehouse at the landward end.

The courtyard of the Outer Ward is now occupied by a new but unobtrusive gift shop on the right, while on the left is a fairly recent military accommodation block, with a large gun battery behind it. Throughout the castle you will find brightly painted life-size figures representing the occupants and defenders of the castle in various eras, and here on the Grand Battery there's a particularly informative group of five gunners from the early 1800s showing how one of the castle's many cannon was fired.

Elsewhere in the castle the main points of interest are the keep itself – somewhat

marred by later partitions and its modern fixtures – and the small Sea Tower, with many arrow loops on the lower level and an 'oubliette' prison cell above. Con O'Neill is said to have escaped through the cell's tiny window in 1603, using a length of rope smuggled to him in a cheese.

At the time of Edward Bruce's invasion of Ulster, Carrickfergus held out for a year against the Scots before finally falling in September 1316. It was updated for artillery in the early 1600s but had fallen into disrepair by 1689, when it was easily captured by William III's general, Schomberg. The King himself landed here the following year, at a spot on the jetty now indicated by signposts. The castle was also briefly captured by a French commander, Thurot, in 1760.

In the early 1800s, when Britain was threatened with a Napoleonic invasion, the artillery defences were considerably strengthened. The largest guns placed here to defend the sea approach to Belfast were enormous 68-pounders, firing exploding shells, set on swivelling mounts in circular granite emplacements, which were added in mid-Victorian times.

The castle remained in use as a magazine and armoury until 1928.

In Carrickfergus, Co Antrim.

Dundrum Castle

Environment & Heritage Service • £ • Open daily except winter

This is an absolutely classic site for a castle, on a long, steep-sided outcrop of rock overlooking the sea at Dundrum Bay. Initially, as you approach across the plain, you only catch a glimpse of the castle, hidden by the tall trees that now top the hill; but once you're at the car park, it becomes clear what a stylish ruin this is.

Its hilltop position enabled defenders of the castle to see for miles along the coast, and on a bright, clear day the views from the top of the keep are spectacular.

Like Carrickfergus, this is another important medieval castle. It was built by John de Courcy, the Anglo-Norman ruler of the region in the late 1100s, but the most notable feature of the castle – the massive round keep – was added a short while later, during a phase in its career when it was owned by King John.

The site has obvious defensive potential, and had previously been occupied by a ring-fort. De Courcy's first stone castle consisted of a circuit of walls around the crown of the hill, with a rock-cut ditch around the outside, and is thought to have been completed before 1200. Work must have started on the great round keep not long after, and it is mentioned in the financial records of the English exchequer, the Pipe Rolls, in 1212, at which time it was presumably complete.

The tower is a very impressive affair, of roughly the proportions of a cotton reel. Its walls are over 2m (7ft) thick. A spiral stair in the thickness of the wall takes you past doorways that once led to two upper floors, emerging at the top in a kind of gallery that runs right round to the far side of the keep. There are no floors any more, so you can look down into the interior of the keep; but you'd be far better advised to look the other way, at the superb views.

There was a well cut into the rock in the basement of the keep, and you may be able to catch a glimpse of water through a hole in the grating that now covers it. Originally the entrance to the keep was at first-floor level, leading straight into a grand hall with a high vaulted ceiling. The upper floor would probably also have been a single room, but with several small chambers opening from the gallery-like passage that ran around it.

The castle was updated in 1260 by the addition of a gatehouse, composed of two square towers, on the south-east side of the enclosure. The modern path leading to the keep ignores this gatehouse and instead uses the original entrance to the castle courtyard, now the upper ward.

The castle seems to have been in a poor state in the 1330s, when it was taken over by the Magennis family. They added a second circuit of walls to form a lower ward just below the original castle, and in the 1600s they also built a house at the bottom of this lower ward, the ruin of which still stands.

The earliest historical reference to the castle was in 1205 when, having been captured by Hugh de Lacy, it was besieged by the man who built it, John de Courcy. Five years later the castle was captured by King John, and it remained royal property until 1227, when it was granted to De Lacy in his new position as Earl of Ulster.

At Dundrum, Co Down. Signposted north of Newcastle on the A2 coast road.

Below: The big round keep at Dundrum Castle was built before 1212 inside an earlier circuit of walls.

Dunluce Castle

Dunluce Castle stands in a superb setting at the top of 100-foot cliffs, not far from the Giant's Causeway.

Environment & Heritage Service • £££ •
Open daily except Monday all year round
(afternoon only on Sundays)

There can be no doubt about it: Dunluce is the most spectacularly situated castle in the whole of the British Isles. The castle, which will be familiar to television viewers all over Britain from seeing the BBC's globe-shaped hot air balloon float past it, stands in an extraordinary clifftop location on a promontory that's practically an island, reached from the mainland only by a bridge – now of stone, formerly wooden.

Underneath the castle rock, just to make it even more dramatic, a cave cuts right through from the sea to the landward side, with a pebbly beach forming a secret landing-place for boats. There is a path down the cliff to the cave, and it is possible to get inside – though signs warn of falling rocks. The same path carries on under the castle bridge to the beach in the bay on the west side of the castle.

The exposed tunnel of a souterrain is the only surviving element of a fort that stood on the headland in the early Christian era, but the first medieval castle was built in the late 1200s or early 1300s, perhaps by Richard de Burgo, Earl of Ulster.

It is thought to have consisted of a square of walls with a round tower at each corner. The only parts of it to survive are a section of the wall on the side facing the mainland, and two of the round towers.

The rest of the ruin you see today is not so much a castle as a grand fortified manor house built in the late 1500s by the MacDonnells, owners of the castle since the early part of that century.

The MacDonnells of Antrim were direct descendants of the Scottish family of the MacDonalds, Lords of the Isles, who were exiled to Antrim in the late 1400s after falling out with James IV of Scotland. Even though Lord Alexander was pardoned and was given lands in Kintyre by James V in 1531, Antrim continued to be their main base in later years.

Dunluce came into their hands when Alexander's third son, Colla MacDonnell, married Eveleen MacQuillan, heiress of the family that had owned the castle since the 1300s. Colla's brother, Sorley Boy MacDonnell, inherited the castle in 1556, and although it was captured by an English army led by Lord Deputy Sir John Perrot in 1584, Queen Elizabeth gave it back to him two years later.

His son James inherited the castle in 1589 and rebuilt it to restore the damage inflicted by Perrot's attack. James added a new gatehouse at the far end of the bridge, with two turrets at the top corbelled out in the Scottish style. He also built an elegant loggia – a covered walk – next to the hall, traces of which can be seen to the right as you enter the castle.

The other buildings that survive are a hall-block with tall, elegant bay windows, and a whole courtyard's worth of kitchens, workrooms and living accommodation. This all dates from the 1630s, built by Randal MacDonnell for his new English wife Catherine Manners. She never liked living on the cliff-edge, and when the whole back range of the kitchen court fell into the sea during a storm in 1634, taking several servants with it, she insisted on having a new house built on the mainland.

The town which stood in the fields beside the castle was burned down in 1641. The MacDonnells moved to Glenarm Castle after 1660, and Dunluce remained habitable for a time, but gradually fell into disrepair, and its tiles and stonework were robbed.

Beside the A2 east of Portrush, Co Antrim.

Enniskillen Castle

*Environment & Heritage Service • ££ • Open all
year Tuesday to Friday; also Monday and Saturday
from May to September, Sunday in July and August*

The town of Enniskillen is in a strategic
location, on an island in the middle of the
river channels that connect Lower and
Upper Lough Erne, so it's not surprising
that the Maguires built a tower house here
in the 1400s. But there is barely any trace
left of that original medieval building, and
instead the Enniskillen Castle you see
today is basically a fort-cum-barracks of
the artillery era, constructed after 1607 to
protect an important new town.

Some of the buildings of the fort are
now used as local government offices, but
the more interesting ones are occupied by
a series of small museums.

The entrance building is greatly
modernised and houses art exhibitions and
an audio-visual show as well as a good
display covering the wildlife, archeology
and social history of Fermanagh.

The keep, built on the foundations of
the original Maguire tower, is home to the
regimental museum of the Royal
Inniskilling Fusiliers. The highlight is an
excellent 'diorama'-style model of the
town in its historic heyday.

The arches under a former barracks
block contain a useful display describing
all the ancient monuments in the area.
Finally, the Watergate, built in about 1611,
is the most distinctive of the buildings, but
you can only look at its exterior.

In Enniskillen, Co Fermanagh.

The keep and courtyard of Enniskillen Castle, which is basically an artillery fort and barracks of the 1600s.

Green Castle

*Environment & Heritage Service • £ • Open daily
from May to October*

This vast rectangular keep is a plain, blunt
sort of building, but it forms rather a
picturesque group along with the farm
built up against it in later times. The keep
is unusually long and narrow, and when it
was built in the 1230s was only two
storeys high. It was raised in height in the
mid-1400s, at which time the basement
was divided in three by cross-walls.

Very little remains of the curtain walls
that once surrounded the castle, but
visitors can climb up to the turrets in the
corners of the keep, with excellent views
over Carlingford Lough.

This was a royal castle, built to guard
the ferry crossing to Carlingford. It was
sacked by the Irish in 1270 and again by
Edward Bruce in 1316. In 1505 it was
given to Gerald, Earl of Kildare, who
probably had the large windows fitted.

*At Greencastle, Co Down. Off the A2 coast road
south-west of Kilkeel.*

*Below: The formidable-looking rectangular keep
of Green Castle provides fine views over the coast.*

Grey Abbey

Environment & Heritage Service • ££ • Open from April to September daily (Sunday afternoon only)

This is the largest and most substantial abbey ruin in Northern Ireland. The ruin was restored in the early 1900s, but has just had a fresh programme of conservation carried out to keep it from crumbling away. There's a modest visitor centre to explain its history, and a nice extra touch is a reconstruction of the monks' herb garden.

It's not a grand or impressive ruin, but it has some interesting features. Founded in 1193 by Affreca, wife of John de Courcy, the abbey was built by Cistercian monks from Cumbria. Its church was the first in Ireland to be built entirely in the Gothic style; its most striking feature is the west door, with four 'orders' of pointed arches.

Most of the cloister is ruined, but even from the foundations you can see that the chapter room would have been an especially grand one. A good part of the refectory survives: it has a high, balcony-like pulpit, reached by a stair in the wall, for readings during meals. The arch to the right was a serving-hatch through to the kitchen.

At Greyabbey, south of Newtownards, Co Down.

Below: Its spectacular setting makes Kinbane Castle well worth visiting, though the ruin is very modest.

Most of the church at Grey Abbey survives, but very little of the cloister – though the refectory is interesting.

Kinbane Castle

National Trust • Free • Open access at any reasonable time

Its spectacular coastal setting makes this a place that is not to be missed if the weather is good, even though the castle was never very big in the first place, and there's now not much of it left.

The name Kinbane means 'White Head', and refers to the small island of bright white chalk on which the castle stands.

There's a car park at the clifftop, and a footpath leads down a less steep face of the cliff towards the castle.

The castle is little more than a single ruined tower; beyond it was an enclosure that took up half the island. It was built in 1547 by Colla MacDonnell, and taken and partly destroyed by the English in 1555, but remained in use for some time afterwards. A difficult place in which to live.

Signposted from the A2 west of Ballycastle.

Knockmany passage tomb

Environment & Heritage Service • Free •
Access to exterior only at any reasonable time

This fascinating tomb is remarkable for
two reasons: its superb hilltop location,
with great views of the country all around;
and the 'passage grave art' designs which
cover three of its stones, linking it with
tombs of the 'Boyne culture', such as
Newgrange, Knowth and *Loughcrew* (*see the
'Midlands East' chapter*).

The exposed burial chamber has been
covered by a modern mound, with a funny
greenhouse-style roof on top lighting the
interior quite well. The drawback is that
an iron gate stops you from getting inside.
It seems this gate is usually locked, so all
you can do is peer from a distance at the
designs on the decorated stones at the
back of the chamber. At the very least, a
signboard outside the tomb reproducing
the designs would be helpful. They include
concentric rings, zig-zags and diamonds.

This is not quite a typical passage grave,
since the wide chamber is pear-shaped
(roughly pentagonal, to be more exact) and
has no side-niches. Rather than being
covered by a flat capstone or a corbelled
stone roof, the chamber could have had a
wooden roof, as was certainly the case at
Fourknocks in Co Meath (*see page 155*).

The slopes of the hill on which the
tomb stands are forested, with a series of
tracks open to walkers. A short circular
walk of about 1.5km (1 mile) to the tomb
leads through atmospherically gloomy
evergreens before emerging on the hillside
with open views. The walk here is steepish,
but should take you less than 15 minutes.

*Near Clogher, Co Tyrone. Signposted along a
minor road from the B83 north of Clogher.*

Monea Castle was built in 1618 by a Scotsman settling in Ulster, and its unusual design has a Scottish feel.

Monea Castle

Environment & Heritage Service • Free •
Open access at any reasonable time

As is so often the case, it's the setting that
makes the place special. The castle stands
in an out-of-the-way rural location that
lends it a wild and rugged air. Being such
a long way from civilisation has the added
advantage that the tower can be left open,
so visitors can come and look round at any
time of year (though having said that, the
castle is reached along a private drive that
runs past a cottage, so visits at peculiar
hours would not be appreciated).

The tower house is of an interesting and
unusual design, consisting of a rectangular
main block protected by two round towers
at the front, with rectangular 'cap-houses'
supported on corbels at the top of each
round tower. The cap-houses are a classic
Scottish idea, but the idea of placing them
at 45 degrees, so that defenders stationed
up here could fire in all directions, is a
unique and rather clever one.

The tower house is just a shell, so there
isn't all that much to see in its interior,
though you can pop down a stair into a
room in the basement of one of the towers.
The other tower contained a spiral stair.

The castle was built by a man called
Malcolm Hamilton at the time of the
Plantation of Ulster, when settlers from
Scotland and England were brought here
by the British authorities and given land
that had mostly been confiscated from its
native Irish owners. The idea was to
impose the rule of law, and to prove to the
local populace that civilisation brought
benefits such as greater prosperity.

Unsurprisingly, the ousted Irish lords
whose land this had been were not very
sympathetic to this way of thinking, and
so the defences of a castle like Monea
were vital. In 1619 government inspector
Captain Nichols Pynnar ordered that the
bawn here would have to be strengthened.
In 1641 Monea was captured by the
Maguires, though it was swiftly retaken by
the planters. The castle was eventually
abandoned after a fire in about 1750.

*Near the village of Monea, north of Enniskillen,
Co Fermanagh. Signposted from the A46 on the
southern shore of Lower Lough Erne.*

*Left: Its modern covering is not much to look at,
but Knockmany tomb is in a superb hilltop location.*

Narrow Water Castle

*Environment & Heritage Service • £ • Open daily
from May to October*

This is a rather charming little tower house,
details like the pointed Gothic arch of the
doorway giving it a picturesque appearance.
It gets its name from its setting on the
banks of the River Newry just before the
river joins Carlingford Lough – it would
be a pretty spot, if it weren't for the vast
dual carriageway that runs past it.

The tower is a pleasant one to visit,
with a few interesting characteristics, such
as the (relatively rare) straight stairs in the
thickness of the wall. It has three storeys
plus an attic, with a stone vault over the
ground floor. Built in about 1560 to guard
the approach to the harbour at Newry, it
passed to the Magennis family, who owned
Dundrum Castle (see page 73), in 1608.

By the A2 just north of Warrenpoint, Co Down.

Although it's badly ruined, the neolithic tomb known as Ossian's Grave is worth visiting for its fine setting.

Ossian's Grave

*Environment & Heritage Service • Free •
Open access at any reasonable time*

Although it's in a very ruinous state – so
much so that you can't immediately make
out what it was – this neolithic tomb is
nevertheless a very pleasant one to visit,
mainly because it's an excuse to stretch
your legs in a scenic location.

*Below: Narrow Water Castle is a pleasant little
tower of the 1500s, with most of its bawn wall intact.*

Cars must be left at the bottom of the
farm track, by the road, and then it's a
steepish walk of about 15 minutes, straight
past the farmhouses and on up a snaking
track to the higher slopes of the hill, where
the monument is signposted in a field to
your right. You may be joined on your
walk by a companionable little Jack
Russell terrier, who will lead the way.

The monument is in fact a type of
court-tomb, with a two-compartment
burial chamber behind a curving facade
of upright stones that faces towards the
south-east. It's also known as Lubitavish

court tomb, but it gets its more romantic
name from a local tradition that this is the
burial place of Ossian (or Oisín), the
warrior-bard son of Finn MacCumhaill.

A nearby beehive-shaped stone cairn
commemorates local poet John Hewitt
(1908–87), whose poem about the place
explains how the traditional tale is
contradicted by archeological evidence,
concluding: 'Let either story stand for true,
as heart and head shall rule'.

*Signposted from the A2 south of Cushendun;
park at the bottom of the farm track and walk up.*

Strangford Castle

Environment & Heritage Service • Free •
Access with key during usual hours only

There are several interesting tower houses in this area, but this is the most accessible and most complete of the lot. It's a very plain little tower of three storeys which had wooden floors and no stairs – there would have been ladders to the upper floors. Humble though the tower is, some care was taken to make it reasonably habitable, and there are rather nice window seats in the surprisingly sizeable windows of the upstairs rooms.

The castle was built in the late 1500s and was one of a pair that guarded the mouth of Strangford Lough and the ferry crossing; its partner on the other side, at Portaferry, is not normally open to the public.

In the middle of Strangford, Co Down. Key from house opposite as directed by a sign.

Tully Castle

Environment & Heritage Service • £ • Open daily from April to September

This pretty little tower house, standing in formal gardens in a very scenic setting not far from the shore of Lower Lough Erne, is a thoroughly pleasant spot to visit today, giving no hint of the castle's brief and rather tragic history.

It was built by Sir John Hume, a 'planter' lord from Scotland, between 1610 and 1613. On Christmas Eve of 1641, with most of the menfolk away, the castle was attacked by Rory Maguire. Next day Lady Hume agreed to surrender; but when the castle's doors were opened, the Maguires killed all its occupants bar the Hume family, a total of 15 men, and 60 women and children. Presumably many of these people were the inhabitants of the village of 24 families

Tully Castle is a very house-like variation on the tower house theme, with gardens in the style of the 1600s.

which the Humes had founded nearby. The castle was burned down, and the Humes never attempted to restore it.

It's hard to believe that such terrible scenes took place in what today is such a peaceful and quiet corner of the world. The ruin is neat and tidy and the gardens are well cared for, stocked only with plants that would have been grown here in the early 1600s.

The castle is an interesting variety of tower house, far more house than tower. Surprisingly, it even had a thatched roof. The large, south-facing windows must have made it a very comfortable home.

It has a T-plan layout, with the entrance through a tower right in the middle of the main block of the house. One of its most striking features was that, inside the entrance hall, a large staircase led up to the first floor; spiral stairs were still the norm, and just such a stair leads from the first floor to the second, and its corbelled base can be seen at the front of the house.

Most of the walls of the bawn survive, though much reduced in height, along with towers at each corner and lots of cobblestone paving around the courtyard, which inspired the design of the gardens.

On the shores of Lower Lough Erne 8km (4.8 miles) north of Derrygonnelly, Co Fermanagh.

Left: Strangford Castle is a modest tower house of the 1500s built to help guard the mouth of the lough.

See also...

Audley's Castle

Environment & Heritage Service, free, open access during daylight hours. Signposted from the A25 west of the Castle Ward estate, near Strangford, Co Down.

There are several small tower houses in this area, including those at *Strangford* (*see previous page*) and *Portaferry* (*see page 182*), and the original 'Old' Castle Ward in the grounds of the later house; but this is the largest and most impressive of them. The tall, square main tower is fronted with a pair of smaller square towers which are joined at the top by an arched machicolation; the door and stairs are in one of these smaller towers. The wooden floor of the first-floor room has been restored, and the stone vault above it remains intact. The tower is said to have been built in the late 1400s.

Bonamargy Friary

Environment & Heritage Service, free, open access at any reasonable time. On the A2 just east of Ballycastle, Co Armagh.

Attractive ruin of a tiny Franciscan friary founded in about 1500. Most of the church has survived, along with the east side of the cloister; and in fact, it seems that this was all the stonework there was, and the other two sides of the cloister would probably have had wooden buildings.

Castle Balfour

Environment & Heritage Service, free, open access to exterior only at any reasonable time. In Lisnaskea, Co Fermanagh, signposted from the main street.

Ugly to look at, but not uninteresting, this derelict T-plan tower house, built in a Scottish style between 1616 and 1625, is approached through a churchyard but looks its best from a grassy area round the back, where its full size can be appreciated. The interior is sometimes left open for visitors.

Its most unusual feature is an odd bay at the front. The gun-loops by the door are carved decoratively in the form of flowers. The hall on the first floor is intact, and the kitchen in the basement under it is quite impressive.

Above: Castle Caulfield.

Below: Bonamargy Friary.

Castle Caulfield

Environment & Heritage Service, free, open access at any reasonable time. Signposted on the south side of the village of Castlecaulfield, west of Dungannon, Co Tyrone.

Ruin of a house built in 1611 by Sir Toby Caulfield on the site of an earlier defended residence of the Donnelly family. An odd little gatehouse attached to one side is thought to be part of the earlier defences, which might explain why its gun-loops seem to face into the interior of the courtyard. There's a worn badge of arms over the gate.

In its ruinous state, Sir Toby's 'castle' looks as if it was on an L-plan, but in fact it was originally U-shaped, and one wing is now missing. It was never a particularly strong structure defensively, and was burned down by Patrick Donnelly in 1641. It must have been rebuilt not long afterwards, however, since Sir William Caulfield lived here in the 1660s and allowed Oliver Plunkett, who was later made a saint, to use the courtyard for ordinations in the 1670s. John Wesley preached here a century later.

The big fireplaces, large mullioned windows and impressive octagonal chimneystacks give a taste of the original grandeur of the building, but it's now little more than a shell, and a broken one at that.

Clough Castle

Environment & Heritage Service, free, open access at any reasonable time. By the junction of the A25 and A24 at Clough, Co Down.

This is one of the best examples you will see anywhere of an earthwork motte-and-bailey castle of the type the Normans built all over Ireland in their early years here. It's very much worth seeing. Though stone buildings were constructed on the motte at a later date, the original layout – the high, round mound of the motte, and the lower raised area of the bailey – is still clear.

The earthworks were built in the late 1100s – or possibly just after, in the reign of King John – and a stone gate-tower and hall were added later, with the former converted to a tower-house in the 1400s.

Cregganconroe court tomb

Environment & Heritage Service, on farmland, free, open access at any reasonable time. Signposted from the A505 west of Cookstown, Co Tyrone.

A decent example of a neolithic court tomb, if not terribly easy to get to, reached by a longish walk along a track. Behind its semicircular forecourt is the usual two-compartment burial chamber; and as is often the case, there are other burial chambers set into the cairn that surrounds the monument.

Devenish Island early monastic site

Environment & Heritage Service, free, open access at any reasonable time. On Lower Lough Erne just north of Enniskillen, Co Fermanagh. Accessible only by boat; ferries available from a landing stage signposted off the A32, or from Enniskillen.

A most appealing early monastic site on an island in the lake, with a splendid round tower of the 1100s, one of the last to be built, and several ruined churches, including the remains of an Augustinian priory.

Drumskinny stone circle

Environment & Heritage Service, free, open access at any reasonable time. Signposted on a minor road off the A35 north of Kesh (turn for Castlederg) or the B72 north of Ederney, Co Fermanagh.

A small but rather attractive stone circle in a very out-of-the-way location, with a recently discovered row of 24 stones running at a tangent from the circle, and a small cairn nearby. These features are very reminiscent of *Beaghmore (see page 171)*. Some of the stones in the circle are modern replacements and are marked 'MOF', for 'Ministry of Finance'.

Dunseverick Castle

National Trust, free, open access at any time. Signposted on the B146 just west of Dunseverick, off the A2 between Ballycastle and Portrush.

A small ruined tower guards the narrow approach to a small headland. It's a location very similar to *Dunluce Castle* and *Kinbane Castle (see pages 174 and 176)*, and though the castle remains don't even begin to compare with the former, and the setting is not nearly as dramatic as the latter's, this is still an impressive choice of location. There is excellent walking to be had along the coast path from here, with the Giant's Causeway not too distant.

Harry Avery's Castle

On farmland, free, open access at any time. Just to the south-west of Newtownstewart, Co Tyrone.

Looking more like a folly than anything else, two half-round towers joined by a short piece of wall stand on top of a hill overlooking the valley of the River Derg. The castle is thought to have been built by Henry Aimbreidh O'Neill, who died in 1396.

Hillsborough Fort

Environment & Heritage Service, free, open access at any reasonable time. In Hillsborough, Co Down.

This unusual site is a square artillery fort with angle bastions on its corners, built by Colonel Arthur Hill in about 1650. In the mid-1700s it was turned into a landscaped garden. The original gatehouse was rebuilt as a whimsical toy fort, and a gazebo was built on the side opposite. This last building is also open to the public, though with limited hours, and a charge is made for admission.

Inch Abbey

Environment & Heritage Service, free, open access at any reasonable time. Signposted from the A7 north of Downpatrick, Co Down.

Along with *Grey Abbey (see page 176)*, this was one of four abbeys that once stood near Strangford Lough: of the other two, at Comber and Newry, no traces have survived. There's not much more than one end wall left of the large Gothic-style church here at Inch, but it's an attractive-looking ruin in well-kept grounds beside the River Quoile, and the foundations give a good idea of the scale of both the church and the cloister buildings.

Jordan's Tower, Ardglass

Environment & Heritage Service, £, open daily during usual hours. In Ardglass, Co Down.

This little seaside town was the busiest port in Ulster in the 1400s, and as a result it had more tower houses than any other town in Ireland. The largest of these has now been restored and is used as a local museum. The three-storey tower, built in the 1400s, has two smaller towers on the front joined by an arch at the top, very like *Audley's Castle (opposite)*.

Legannany dolmen

Environment & Heritage Service, free, open access at any reasonable time. Signposted from the B7 near Finnis, south-west of Ballynahinch.

Said to be the best-known dolmen in Northern Ireland, this is a rather comical monument, but its location is superb, with fine views of the Mourne Mountains.

Below: Dunseverick Castle.

Navan 'fort'

Site: free, open access at any reasonable time. Visitor centre: ££, open daily all year round. Signposted on the A28 west of Armagh.

Often referred to by its ancient name, Emain Macha, this was one of the three great ritual enclosures of Celtic Ireland (the others were *Tara* in Co Meath and *Rathcrogan,* or Crúachain, in Co Roscommon – *see pages 159 and 134 respectively*).

In an enclosure on the top of the hill stands a large mound which on excavation revealed a fascinating sequence of ritual buildings, including a massive, round, hut-like structure, built out of timber in 94BC (the exact date is known by tree-ring dating), which was immediately filled up with stones and then burned down.

The drawback is that the monument is not much to look at, and the extremely complicated story of what the excavations uncovered is a tricky one to make sense of. That's where the visitor centre comes in. The new building is the same size and on the same pattern as the short-lived iron age structure, and its displays attempt to explain the finds.

Nendrum early monastic site

Environment & Heritage Service. Site: free, open access at any reasonable time. Visitor centre: £, open April to September. Beside Strangford Lough, signposted from the A22 at Lisbane, Co Down.

An intriguing monastic site in an attractive setting on an island reached by a causeway. There are two outer walls surrounding the stone rampart of the 'inner cashel', inside which are traces of a number of early church buildings and a round tower.

Portaferry Castle

Environment & Heritage Service, free, open access to view exterior only at any reasonable time. Near the ferry landing at Portaferry, Co Down.

Another small tower house, built in the early 1500s by the Savage family and forming a pair with *Strangford* (*see page 179*) to guard the mouth of Strangford Lough. This one is slightly different in that it has a stair-tower that guards the entrance, making it L-shaped in plan. It is in decent condition, but is not usually open to the public.

And…

Ardboe high cross *(free, open access at any reasonable time), on the shores of Lough Neagh, off the B73 at Ardboe, Co Tyrone* – This high cross of the 800s or 900s is impressively tall (almost 3m, or more than 18ft) and is said to be the only one in Northern Ireland that is all of a piece, rather than being rebuilt from parts of other crosses. However, it is pretty badly weathered.

Belfast Castle *(Belfast City Council, limited access to house during usual hours, free access to park), signposted in the middle of Belfast* – A Victorian imitation castle built in the Scots Baronial style in 1870; it now houses a local heritage centre, and the grounds are a public park with fine views.

Bellaghy Bawn *(Environment & Heritage Service, ££, open daily all year), in Bellaghy, on the A54 north of Magherafelt* – Rare example of a defended manor from the time of the Plantation of Ulster, with just one large round tower surviving from the original bawn wall and defences. The house now contains exhibitions on local history as well as being a study centre dedicated to the locality's most famous son, poet Seamus Heaney.

Boa Island Celtic carved stone *(in cemetery), on Boa island, which is crossed by the A47 at the top of Lower Lough Erne* – This most unusual Celtic statue has two faces carved on it, one on each side. It stands in Caldragh cemetery, signposted off the main road 1.6km (1 mile) west of Lusty Beg Island.

Castle Ward *(National Trust: house ££, open at weekends from April to October, daily from June to August; grounds free, open access during usual hours all year round), west of Strangford, Co Down* – Grand mansion, with the ruin of the original tower house of the 1500s, Old Castle Ward, in its grounds.

Crom Old Castle *(National Trust, £££ for access to the Crom Estate, open April to September daily), signposted off the A34 near Newtownbutler* – Ruined tower house on country estate better known for its wildlife, on shore of Upper Lough Erne.

Downhill Castle *(National Trust: grounds free, open access, from dawn to dusk all year round; Mussenden Temple ££, open in the afternoon only, at weekends from April to September and daily in July and August), off the A2 west of Coleraine* – Ruin of a bishop's palace of the 1700s in its own estate with superb coastal views, plus the unusual neo-classical round library known as Mussenden Temple.

Drumena Cashel *(Environment & Heritage Service, free, open access at any reasonable time), signposted from the A25 west of Castlewellan, Co Down* – Large stone-walled enclosure with an easily accessible T-shaped souterrain high enough to stand up in.

Giant's Ring *(National Trust, free, open access at any reasonable time), by the B23 south-west of Belfast* – This vast earthwork, a roughly circular bank of gravel and boulders some 185m (600ft) in diameter, is a very rare example in Ireland of a neolithic henge monument, with a chambered tomb in the middle.

Harryville mote *(Environment & Heritage Service, free, open access at any reasonable time), by the A26 on the south side of Ballymena, Co Antrim* – Looming over the neighbouring Sainsbury's, this is a fine high motte (usually spelt 'mote' in Ireland) with accompanying raised bailey.

Kilclief Castle *(Environment & Heritage Service, free, open access to view exterior only at any reasonable time), by the A2 in Kilclief, south of Strangford, Co Down* – Another good example of a small tower house in this area. This one was built in the 1400s as a residence of the Bishops of Down; it has two small towers joined at the top by an arch.

Old Castle Archdale *(National Trust, free, open access at any reasonable time), on the Castle Archdale estate, on the shore of Lower Lough Erne west of Irvinestown* – Very ruinous tower (just one wall remains) but with a fairly impressive gate.

White Island early monastic site *(Environment & Heritage Service, free, open access at any reasonable time), reached by boat from castle Archdale Country Park* – Island site famous for its fascinating carvings of a range of human figures.

Left: Legannany dolmen (see previous page).

Opposite page: Dunluce Castle.

Bibliography

The best **general history** of Ireland that I have yet come across is *The Oxford History of Ireland*, edited by RF Foster (Oxford University Press 1989/1992, paperback, ISBN 0 19 285271 X). It has the advantages of being relatively recent and very readable, but like many essentially academic works it does tend to give theories about the major incidents rather than tell the actual stories of those incidents, which can be frustrating for the ordinary reader.

For a general **guide to historic monuments** in Ireland, I can recommend the very useful *Guide to National and Historic Monuments of Ireland* by Peter Harbison (Gill and Macmillan 1992, paperback, ISBN 07171 1956 4), which since its last update now covers Northern Ireland as well as the Republic. It is widely available at places like the giftshops of historic sites in Ireland, and would be ideal for exploring an area in a little more detail. It is illustrated with old prints and engravings, which is good fun.

Rather less useful, but inexpensive and entertaining, is *Heritage: A Visitor's Guide*, published in the Republic by the government heritage service Dúchas in their old guise as the Office of Works, edited by Éilis Brennan (The Stationery Office, Dublin, 1990, ISBN 0 7076 0102 9). It's a guide to many (but by no means all) of the properties now cared for by Dúchas, with coverage of scenic areas and national parks too. It has a lot of colour photos, and you see it on sale quite cheaply because it is a bit out of date.

There is currently no particularly good overview of **Irish archeology** available, though there is meant to be one on the way from OUP in their *Oxford Archeological Guides* series. If it's as good as the one on Scotland, this will be invaluable. In the mean time, the best way to get a general picture of prehistory is with a book like *Archeology of the British Isles* by Andrew Hayes (Batsford 1993, paperback, ISBN 0 7134 7305 3) or the slightly more intense and detailed *Prehistoric Britain* by Timothy Darvill (Batsford 1987, paperback, ISBN 0 7134 5180 7).

There is, however, a series of small books published by Country House of Dublin under the collective title *The Irish Treasures Series*, which contains a number of interesting and very up-to-date discussions of a specific type of monument.

There's one in particular in this series that I have found most useful and informative, and that's *Stone Circles in Ireland* by Séan Ó Nualláin (Country House 1995, ISBN 0 946172 45 5).

I can also recommend *Crannogs: Lake-dwellings of Early Ireland* by Aidan O'Sullivan (Country House 2000, ISBN 1 86059 091 8).

For **Celtic** times, the most up-to-date work is for me also one of the most intriguing books ever published on the subject, and it is by the leading archeologist in this field. *The Ancient Celts* by Barry Cunliffe (Penguin 1999, paperback, ISBN 0 14025 4226) is just out in paperback and is essential reading for anyone who wants to know the truth about the Celtic history of Britain and Ireland. It's a book with a wide range both geographically and in time, establishing the Celts of Ireland, Wales and England in the full context of Atlantic trading routes in the bronze age.

For **Norman** times and in particular the Anglo-Norman 'invasion' of Ireland, a good (if slightly academic) work is *The Normans in Britain* by David Walker (Blackwell 1995, ISBN 0 631 18582 8). This book covers the ways in which the Normans took root (or otherwise) in England, Wales, Scotland and Ireland, and has the great virtue of separating out the material for each country, yet also providing a context for each. It's better on Ireland than on most of the rest of its subject matter, in fact. And again, it has the advantage of being very up-to-date.

Still the only major work on **castles** to even attempt to provide a comprehensive list of Irish castles is *Castles of Britain and Ireland* by Plantagenet Somerset Fry (David and Charles 1996, ISBN 0 7153 0242 6). It can be scholarly in its tone, but as a work of detailed research it is impressive and as a reference resource it is more or less invaluable. Perhaps the most approachable part of it is the introduction, which offers an excellent survey of how and why castles were built, and features a separate section on Irish castles.

Finally, if you are exploring **the south-west** of Ireland and you want to see some of the smaller field monuments, there is a great series of hand-drawn maps by Jack Roberts, illustrated with line drawings by the same hand and published by Bandia Publishing. These maps are widely available in the area. The ones I found useful were *Antiquities of West Cork* (ISBN 1 001 08 31 01) and *Antiquities of the Beara Peninsula* (for which there is no ISBN).

Principal castles, listed by county

Index of places

Entries in **bold type** are main entries within the regional chapters;
those in normal type are from the 'See Also...' or 'And...' sections.